8080/8085 ASSEMBLY LANGUAGE PROGRAMMING

8080/8085 ASSEMBLY LANGUAGE PROGRAMMING

by

Judi N. Fernandez

Ruth Ashley

Co-Presidents

DuoTech, Inc.

JOHN WILEY & SONS, INC.

New York • Chichester • Brisbane • Toronto • Singapore

Library of Congress Cataloging in Publication Data:

Fernandez, Judi N 1941–
8080/8085 assembly language programming.

Includes index.
1. Assembler language (Computer program language)—Programmed instruction. 2. INTEL 8080 (Computer)—Programming—Programmed instruction. 3. INTEL 8085 (Computer)—Programming—Programmed instruction.

I. Ashley, Ruth, joint author. II. Title.
QA76.73.A8F47 001.64'24 80-39650
ISBN 0-471-08009-8

Printed in the United States of America

10 9 8 7 6 5 4

ACKNOWLEDGMENTS

The authors would like to express their thanks to several people who assisted in the development of this book. P. Scot McIntosh provided technical assistance and timely, intelligent reviews. Donna and John Tabler tested the material presented in the book. Our children, Paul Ashley and Davida Fernandez, helped in innumerable ways.

We'd also like to acknowledge the designers and manufacturers of 8080 and 8085 microprocessor chips and the software and machines that depend on them.

ABOUT THE AUTHORS

Judi Fernandez and Ruth Ashley are Co-Presidents of DuoTech, Inc., a small company that specializes in the development of training materials for the computer industry. Both authors are computer programmers with many years of experience in all levels and types of language. They have developed many courses to train programmers and are the authors of several other Wiley Self-Teaching Guides.

Although much of their professional work centers around large-scale computers such as the IBM S/370, in their own offices and at home the authors use Z80-based microcomputers. 8080/8085 Assembly Language is one of the languages they use to program their own computers.

TO THE READER

We assume that you have selected this book because you want or need to program a microcomputer using 8080 or 8085 Assembly Language. We also assume that you already know something about computers and computer programming to start with—enough to be able to handle terms like input, CPU, terminal, file, and loop without having them explained to you. If not, this book is probably not the place to start. We have not tried to explain how to attack a problem and design a program to solve it. We concentrate here on Assembly Language code and how to use it. Although knowledge of another programming language is not required, it certainly would be helpful.

HOW TO USE THIS BOOK

This Self-Teaching Guide consists of 12 chapters that have been carefully sequenced to introduce you to 8080/8085 Assembly Language and to help you develop a useful set of programming skills. We have made every effort to organize the material in the best possible learning sequence, so that you can begin programming as quickly as possible. You will learn to code easy programs, then successively more complex programs until you have mastered the language.

Each chapter begins with a short introduction followed by objectives that outline what you can expect to learn from it, and ends with a Self-Test which allows you to measure your learning and practice what you have studied. Each chapter also contains a review that draws together all the material you have studied in the chapter.

The body of each chapter is divided into frames—short numbered sections in which information is presented or reviewed, followed by questions which ask you to apply the information. The correct answers to these questions follow a dashed line after the frame. As you work through the book, use a folded paper or a card to cover the correct answer until you have written yours. And be sure you actually write each response, especially when the activity is coding Assembly Language instructions. Only by actually writing out the instructions, and checking them carefully, can you get the most from this Self-Teaching Guide.

CONTENTS

CHAPTER ONE

INTRODUCTION

Before you can begin learning to understand and code instructions, you need to know some background concepts about the language. You need to know a little of how the microcomputer works and what it consists of.

In this chapter, we'll discuss 8080/8085 Assembly Language and compare it to other computer languages. You'll learn what type of programs are generally written in Assembly Language. Then we'll talk about the 8080/8085 microprocessor itself. You'll learn what makes up the microprocessor and learn how data is stored in the computer in bits and bytes. You'll learn what registers are and what they are used for in an 8080/8085 microcomputer.

When you complete this chapter, you'll be able to:

- Classify 8080/8085 Assembly Language as to its level and use.
- Identify the size and characteristics of bits and bytes.
- Name the 8080/8085 registers and their functions.
- Identify the functions of the 8080/8085 status flags.

1. 8080 and 8085 Assembly Languages are used to program computers that contain 8080 or 8085 microprocessor chips made by Intel and other companies, or any computer that has an 8080 or 8085 assembler. The two languages are very similar. The 8085 chip is more advanced and allows a few more instructions than the 8080 chip. We'll treat both languages as one in this book and refer to it as 8080/8085 Assembly Language or just Assembly Language.

Computer languages are usually categorized as *low-level* or *high-level.* A low-level language is very machine-oriented; the lowest level language is the machine's own language, which is comprised entirely of digits. A high-level language is more oriented to humans; the instructions use English words or abbreviations and English-like syntax.

Assembly Languages are always low-level languages. The language of an assembler is very close to the actual machine language, but, instead of using digits, you use alphanumeric codes. (Alphanumeric means that it is made up of letters, numbers, and symbols such as *.)

(a) Which of the following statements are true of 8080/8085 Assembly Language?

_____ low-level

_____ high-level

_____ uses only digits

_____ uses alphanumeric codes

_____ uses English-type words and phrases

(b) Which of the following types of computers can be programmed using 8080/8085 Assembly Language?

_____ any computer

_____ any computer that has an 8080/8085 microprocessor chip

_____ any microcomputer

(c) See if you can identify the following instructions as machine language, Assembly Language, or high-level language.

ADD 1 TO COUNTER. __________________________

000 000 100 011 000 110 __________________________

ADI 1 __________________________

- - - - - - - - - - - - -

(a) low-level, uses alphanumeric codes; (b) any computer that has an 8080/8085 microprocessor chip; (c) high-level, machine, Assembly

2. You've probably heard of such high-level languages as COBOL, FORTRAN, and BASIC. These languages have the advantages of being easy to learn and use. But there are disadvantages. A high-level program must be translated into machine language before it can be used. The translation is done by a program called a compiler. This compilation step is time consuming. Also, the machine-language program produced by the compiler is never the most efficient program possible. One high-level instruction, such as ADD, may be translated into ten or more machine-language instructions.

When you use Assembly Language, you have to think less like a human and more like a computer. For example, to add two numbers, the steps you follow are:

(1) move the first number to a special place (the accumulator);

(2) add the second number to it;
(3) make sure the result isn't too large for the accumulator (check for overflow);
(4) do something about overflow if it occurs;
(5) check and set the sign (positive or negative) of the result;
(6) store the result in memory.

Assembly Language programs are also translated, but it's a much simpler process called assembling. Assembling is a one-to-one translation of the alphanumeric instructions into their machine-language counterparts. So when you code in Assembly Language, you're virtually coding in machine language. The alphanumeric codes save you the bother of using the digital form of the instructions.

By coding at the machine level, you can code a much more efficient program than a compiler can produce. This is one main advantage of using Assembly Language. The other major advantage is that you have more control over the computer. Instructions exist at the Assembly Language level that have no high-level equivalents. They allow you to access and control computer functions at a very minute level. For example, only in Assembly Language can you directly address an 8080/8085 register such as the accumulator that is used for arithmetic.

Match the languages with their characteristics.

_____ (a) Assembly

_____ (b) high-level (COBOL, FORTRAN, BASIC, etc.)

1. more efficient
2. less efficient
3. compiled
4. assembled
5. more control
6. easier to learn and use

— — — — — — — — — — — —

(a) 1,4,5; (b) 2,3,6

3. When do you use Assembly Language? Some people use it all the time. But most people use it when they're writing *system* programs as opposed to *application* programs.

An application program is a program that solves some sort of problem for a user. If your computer is in a business setting, then typical applications might be payroll and inventory. If your computer is in a scientific setting, then typical applications might be statistical analysis and graph plotting.

A system program is one that solves a problem for the computer system itself. System programs are frequently used by programmers, computer operators, and by other computer programs. (An application program will call a system program to read data from a terminal, for example.)

Typical system programs are:

- input/output (I/O) routines that transfer data between peripheral devices and main storage. (A peripheral device is a device that is attached to the main part of the computer; terminals, printers, disk, and tape units are all peripheral devices. Main storage is the storage area inside the computer itself, usually on separate chips connected to the microprocessor chip.)
- compilers that translate high-level code into machine language
- librarians that organize disk files and keep up-to-date directories

An application program may be used once a week or even once a day. A system program may be used several times an hour. Some of the more important system programs, such as the I/O routines, are used several times a second. It's critical that a system program be as efficient as possible. And that's one reason we use Assembly Language to code system programs, even when we have high-level languages available to us. Another reason is to take advantage of that extra measure of control that's available with Assembly Language and not with high-level languages. System programs frequently require you to make full use of the computer's capabilities.

Match the two types of programs with their characteristics.

_____ (a) system programs

_____ (b) application programs

1. typically used by non-computer staff, such as accounting department, research staff
2. typically used by computer programmers and operators
3. frequently used by other programs
4. solves computer problems
5. solves user problem
6. typically coded in Assembly Language
7. typically coded in high-level language
8. commonly used on daily, weekly, or monthly basis
9. may be used several times per minute

(c) List two reasons that we usually use Assembly Language for system programs. ______________________________

____

(a) 2,3,4,6,9; (b) 1,5,7,8; (c) efficiency and control

Any low-level language is very involved with the physical structure (architecture) of the system it programs. Before you can begin learning to code Assembly Language instructions, you need to know more about the microprocessor itself. In the next section of this chapter, we'll explore the critical details of the 8080/8085 chip.

BITS AND BYTES

4. We've been using the term microprocessor, but let's stop and define it. A *microprocessor* is a chip or set of chips inside the microcomputer containing the logic circuits that make the rest of the computer work. The microprocessor contains some control circuits and some special storage areas called registers. Main storage (also called internal memory, main memory, internal storage, core memory) is usually located on separate chips external to the microprocessor itself. The registers and main storage are both used to store data while it's being worked on.

Data is stored in *bytes* (pronounced "bites"). A byte is the amount of space it takes to store one alphanumeric character such as the letter 'A', the number '5', or the symbol '&', or a value up to 255. The size of a storage area is usually given in terms of the number of bytes it can hold. 1K stands for 1024 bytes, or 2^{10} bytes.

(a) Which of the following are considered part of the microprocessor?

_____ main storage

_____ registers

_____ peripheral devices

_____ logic circuits

(b) If your computer has 20K bytes of main storage, how many characters can it hold? (K stands for 1024.) __________

(c) If a register holds one byte, how many characters can it hold?

____

(a) registers and logic circuits; (b) 20,480 characters; (c) one

5. To store a character in a byte, it must be encoded as a binary number. In this frame, we'll explain what binary numbers are and why we have to use them.

The binary number system has a base of two instead of ten as the decimal number system has. It has only two digits—zero and one. Figure 1.1 shows the binary equivalents for the first ten decimal numbers. You'll

Decimal	Binary
0	0
1	1
2	10
3	11
4	100
5	101
6	110
7	111
8	1000
9	1001
10	1010

FIGURE 1.1. Binary Equivalents

be learning a great deal more about the binary number system in the next chapter. For now, the important things to remember are that only two digits are involved and that binary numbers are generally longer than decimal numbers.

Because binary numbers have only two digits we can represent them electronically. For example, an electric pulse in a circuit can represent a one and no pulse can represent a zero. This is why we use binary numbers rather than decimal numbers inside the computer. The input/output devices, such as the terminal, translate data between decimal and binary.

(a) The binary number system has a base of ________________.

(b) The digits of the decimal number system are 0,1,2,3,4,5,6,7,8,9. Write the digits of the binary number system. ________________

(c) Using Figure 1.1, what is the binary equivalent of the decimal number 5? ________________

(d) Which is easier to represent electronically, a binary number or a decimal number? ________________

(e) In order to use a computer, you have to translate all your data into binary numbers before you type it on the terminal or punch it on cards. True or false? ________________

— — — — — — — — — — — —

(a) two; (b) 0,1; (c) 101; (d) a binary number; (e) false—the I/O devices do the translating.

6. One binary digit is called a *bit.* ("Bit" is an acronym for "*BI*nary digi*T*" or maybe "*B*inary dig*IT*.") A bit is either a one or a zero. There are two basic types of data: numeric and alphanumeric. Numeric data can be converted directly to binary and stored in memory.

We use a code system to translate alphanumeric data into binary numbers. It takes several bits to represent one character. The number of bits depends on the code system we use. For example, one popular system is called ASCII (American Standard Code for Information Interchange). It requires seven bits per character. The letter A is encoded as 1000001. The number 5 is encoded as 0110101. The symbol & is encoded as 0100110.

Another popular code system is EBCDIC (Extended Binary-Coded Decimal Interchange Code). It uses eight bits per character. The letter A is encoded as 11000001. The number 5 is encoded as 11110101. The symbol & is encoded as 01010000.

Remember that a byte holds one character. So a byte holds several bits. In the 8080/8085 microprocessor, one byte contains eight bits. (This is becoming the standard byte size throughout the computer industry.) So a byte in the 8080/8085 chip is large enough to use either ASCII or EBCDIC code. For numeric data, it can hold a value up to 255.

ASCII is usually pronounced ASK-ey and EBCDIC is usually pronounced EBB-see-dick.

(a) A binary digit is also called a ________________

(b) A bit can have one of two values. What are they? ________

(c) Suppose your microcomputer has 20K bytes of main storage. How many bits does it have? ________________

— — — — — — — — — — — —

(a) bit; (b) 0,1; (c) 160K or 163,840

7. Let's review what you have learned about bits and bytes. Match each term with its characteristics.

_____ (a) bit

_____ (b) byte

1. holds one character
2. holds a zero or a one
3. holds eight zeros and/or ones
4. the smaller storage area
5. the larger storage area
6. memory size is given in terms of this

— — — — — — — — — — — —

(a) 2,4; (b) 1,3,5,6

THE REGISTERS

Memory is used to store data that is not currently being worked on. When you want to work on data, you bring it into one of the registers. The following frames show you what the 8080/8085 registers are and how they are used.

8. A register is a very small storage area. Most of the registers only store one byte. A couple of them are two bytes long.

The 8080/8085 microprocessor has ten registers. They are named as follows: A, B, C, D, E, H, L, PC, SP, and flag. Some of the registers have intended purposes designed by the manufacturers.

The A register is perhaps the most important, or, at least, the one you'll use the most. It is also called the *accumulator* because you use it for arithmetic operations.

The A register is also used for input/output operations. When data is read, it comes into the A register. When data is written, it goes out from the A register. Since the A register is so heavily used, most programs immediately move input into another register.

(a) The average register is large enough to store __________ bytes.

(b) How many registers does the 8080/8085 microprocessor have? ______

(c) The A register is also called the ______________________________.

(d) Which of the following are intended uses of the A register?

_____ to hold the sum of an addition

_____ to hold characters to be output to a terminal

_____ to receive input characters

— — — — — — — — — — — — — —

(a) one or two; (b) ten; (c) accumulator; (d) all are correct

9. The B, C, D, and E registers have no special purpose. We call them general-purpose registers. You can use them for any kind of small, temporary data storage. If you need to store a value that requires two bytes, you can pair B with C or D with E. These four registers are usually referred to as the B–C pair and the D–E pair.

(a) Which of the following are legitimate register pairs?

_____ A with B

_____ B with C

_____ C with D

_____ D with E

_____ any two registers may be paired

(b) The B, C, D, and E registers are (general-purpose/special-purpose) ______________________________ registers.

— — — — — — — — — — — — — —

(a) B with C and D with E; (b) general purpose

10. The H and L registers can also be treated as a pair. They are almost always used to hold memory addresses. This is an important point and bears some explaining.

You've already learned that main memory is made up of bytes, each byte capable of holding one character or a number up to 255. Each byte in memory also has an *address*. This is simply a number that identifies where the byte is stored. The first byte is at 0000; the second byte is at 0001; the third byte is at 0002; etc. (Think of memory as a large bank of post office boxes. Each box is numbered so that the user can find it. The number is its address.)

When we want to access a byte in memory, we must use its address. We must say "store the contents of register B in memory location 100," or "add the contents of memory location 110 to the accumulator."

In Assembly Language, we reference the memory address by placing it in the H–L pair. Then we use the special letter M (for memory) to tell the computer to use the address in H–L to find the data. For example, here is an Assembly Language instruction: MOV A,M. This instruction says "move the data from the byte at the memory address given by the H–L register pair to register A."

(a) What would be the address of the fifth byte in memory? __________

(b) What would this instruction mean: ADD M?

_____ Add the value of the byte in memory that is addressed by the H–L pair to the accumulator.

_____ Add the letter "M" to the accumulator.

_____ Add register M to the accumulator.

(c) If you want to store a byte at address 1000, how would you tell the computer the right address?

_____ Put 1000 in register A.

_____ Put 1000 in the B–C pair.

_____ Put 1000 in the H–L pair.

_____ Put 1000 in register M.

— — — — — — — — — — — — — —

(a) 0004; (b) add the value of the byte in memory that is addressed by the H–L pair to the accumulator; (c) Put 1000 in the H–L pair.

11. The H–L pair are so named because of their function. "H" stands for the leftmost or "high-order byte" and "L" stands for rightmost or "low-order byte" of a memory address. By joining the two bytes, they can hold a maximum value of 65,535.

(a) In the 8080/8085 chip, how long is a memory address? ____________

(b) Suppose register H contains 01 and register L contains 53. What memory address is being pointed at? ____________

(c) What's the largest memory address in an 8080/8085 microprocessor?

____

— — — — — — — — — — — —

(a) two bytes; (b) 0153; (c) 65,535

12. The program counter (PC) register is a double (two-byte) register that tells the computer what to do next.

A computer program is made up of a series of instructions (such as MOV A,M). They are stored in main memory when the program is executed. The instructions are executed one at a time. As each instruction is picked up from memory for execution, the memory address of the first byte of the *next* instruction is stored in the PC register. When an instruction has finished executing, the computer checks the PC to find out where to pick up the next instruction.

The programmer can use certain Assembly Language instructions to change the address in the PC register. These are called jump instructions because they cause the computer to jump to another memory location instead of executing the program in sequence. You will be learning to use the jump instructions in this book.

(a) (*Review*) How long is a memory address in the 8080/8085 microcomputer? ____________

(b) Which register holds the address of the next instruction? ____________
How long is it? ____________

(c) The programmer can change the value in the PC register with a ____________ instruction.

— — — — — — — — — — — —

(a) two bytes; (b) PC; two bytes; (c) jump;

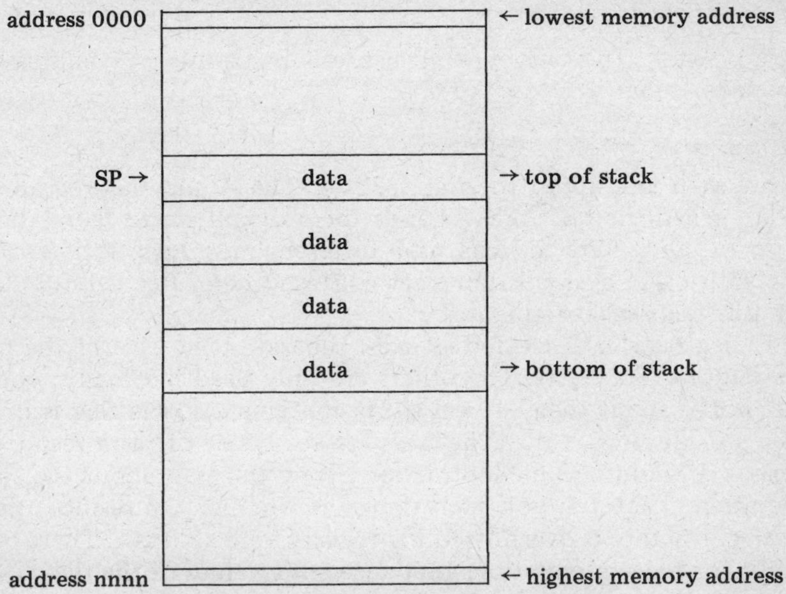

FIGURE 1.2. A Data Stack in Memory

13. The SP register is another double register. SP stands for *stack pointer.* Here again, this bears some explanation. There are some Assembler instructions that allow you to store data in a memory stack and retrieve it again. It's called a stack because of the way it behaves. Imagine a stack of plates. When you add one more, it goes on top. When you remove one, you get the top plate—that is, the one that was stacked last. This is frequently referred to as "last in, first out" or LIFO. This is how an 8080/8085 memory stack works. It is a very handy tool in Assembly Language programming as you will see when you learn how to use it in Chapter 9 of this book.

The stack pointer is a register that always keeps track of (or points to) the current top of the stack in memory. (See Figure 1.2. Notice that the "top" of the stack is the *lowest* address and the "bottom" of the stack is the *highest* address.) Whenever you add something to the stack, the stack pointer is decreased, or decremented. Then the data is stored at the new address in the stack. Whenever you remove something from the stack, it's removed from the address in the stack pointer. Then the stack pointer is increased, or incremented. So the SP is always pointing to the top of the stack.

(a) What does SP stand for? ______________________

(b) How big is the stack pointer register? ______________________

Why? ______________________

(c) Where does SP point, to the top or bottom of the stack? ____________

(d) Name the other two-byte register you have studied. ____________

(a) stack pointer; (b) two bytes; because it holds memory addresses which are two bytes long; (c) top; (d) PC

14. Now we'll talk about the flag register. The A and flag registers together are called the PSW. PSW stands for *program status word.* In different types of computers this can have different meanings; so if you're familiar with other systems don't get confused here. Pay careful attention to how this flag register operates.

The flag register is treated as eight separate bits. Five of the bits are used as flags or indicators. The others are only used internally; you don't need to worry about them. If a flag bit contains a 1, the flag is on. If it contains a 0, the flag is off. The flags are set on or off as a result of operations such as addition and subtraction. They tell you about the result of the operation. They tell you such things as whether the result is positive or negative, whether it overflowed the register, and so forth. There are many Assembly Language instructions that access the values of the flags.

Here are the five flags:

> The *carry flag:* This flag is turned on if the operation overflowed the register.
>
> The *auxiliary carry flag:* This flag is turned on if there was a carry from the fifth to the fourth bit in the register. This information is used in certain mathematical operations.
>
> The *zero flag:* This flag is turned on if the operation resulted in zero.
>
> The *sign flag:* This flag reflects the sign of the value if signed numbers are being used. If it's on, the number is negative; if it's off, the number is positive or zero.
>
> The *parity flag:* This flag reflects the number of ones in the value. If it's on, there are an even number of ones in the value (even parity). If it's off, there are an odd number of ones (odd parity). We'll be teaching you how to check parity in this book, but you won't be coding any parity handling routines.

(a) What does PSW stand for? ____________________

(b) How large is the PSW? ____________________

(c) How many flags are in the flag register? ____________________

(d) Which flag tells you if the result of an arithmetic operation overflowed the register? ____________________

(e) Which flag tells you if the result of a subtraction is negative?

____

(f) Which flag tells you if the result of an addition is zero?

____

(g) Which flag tells you if the result of an arithmetic operation has an even number of ones? ____________________

— — — — — — — — — — — — —

(a) program status word; (b) two bytes (flag and A registers); (c) five; (d) carry; (e) sign; (f) zero; (g) parity

15. The A and flag registers are sometimes paired, and sometimes act as a double register. Most of the time, however, they're treated as separate registers.

(a) Name the registers that are frequently paired. ________________

(b) Name the registers that are sometimes paired. ________________

(c) Name the double (two-byte) registers.____________________

— — — — — — — — — — — — —

(a) B–C, D–E, H–L; (b) A–flag (PSW); (c) PC and SP, also A–flag (PSW)

REVIEW

Here's what you have learned in this chapter.

- Computer languages can be classified as high level and low level. A high-level language is more "humanized"—it uses English words and syntax. It is easier to learn and use, but it is less efficient and gives the programmer less control. A low-level language is more like the machine's internal language. It uses alphanumeric codes. It gives the programmer more control and produces more efficient programs.
- 8080/8085 Assembly Language is a low-level language used to program microcomputers containing the 8080 or 8085 microprocessor chip. It is frequently used for writing system programs as opposed to application programs. An application program solves a user problem such as payroll. A system program solves a computer problem such as input/output. System programs are quite heavily used and need to be efficient; they also need to make full use of the system's capabilities.
- A microprocessor is a chip or set of chips containing control circuits and registers. A byte is the amount of storage space necessary to hold one character or a number up to 255. In the 8080/8085, a byte contains eight bits. A bit is a binary digit.

The binary number system has only two digits, zero and one. Computers use the binary number system because the two digits can be represented electrically. All data is translated into binary codes as it enters the system. Two popular coding systems are ASCII and EBCDIC.

- The 8080/8085 chip has ten registers.
  - The A register, or accumulator, is used for arithmetic and I/O operations.
  - The B–C pair and the D–E pair are available for general purposes.
  - The H–L pair is used to address memory.
  - The PC (program counter) holds the memory address of the next instruction. Assembly Language jump instructions are used to change this address.
  - The SP (stack pointer) points to the top of a memory stack. The stack is used for temporary storage of data on a LIFO (last in, first out) basis.
  - The flag register is used as five on/off flags that reflect the status of the result of certain operations such as addition and subtraction.
    - The carry flag indicates register overflow.
    - The auxiliary carry flag indicates overflow between bits five and four; it is only used internally.
    - The zero flag indicates a zero result.
    - The sign flag gives the sign of the result.
    - The parity flag indicates whether the result contains an even or odd number of ones.
  - The A and flag registers may be paired as the PSW (program status word).

Now complete the Self-Test to practice what you have learned.

CHAPTER 1 SELF-TEST

1. Is 8080/8085 Assembly Language a low-level or high-level language?

____

2. Which of the following are characteristics of system programs?

______ a. used by non-computer staff

______ b. used by programmers

______ c. used by programs

______ d. solve business or scientific problems

______ e. solve computer system problems

______ f. high usage rate

______ g. low usage rate

3. The microprocessor chip contains ______________________ and ______________________.

4. Memory size is stated in terms of ______________________.

5. In the 8080/8085, how many bits are in a byte? ______________

6. One byte can hold:

______ a. one alphanumeric character

______ b. a value up to 255

______ c. eight characters

______ d. a zero or a one only

7. One bit can hold:

______ a. one alphanumeric character

______ b. a value up to 255

______ c. eight characters

______ d. a zero or a one only

8. Name the registers described below.

______ a. General-purpose registers

______ b. Holds five status flags.

______ c. The accumulator.

______ d. The high-order byte of a memory address.

______ e. The low-order byte of a memory address.

______ f. Holds the next instruction address.

______ g. Points to the stack.

______ h. Refers to the flags and accumulator.

9. Name the register pairs. ______________________

10. Name the two-byte registers. ______________________________

11. Match the flag names with their descriptions.

_____ carry flag	a. shows register overflow
_____ auxiliary carry flag	b. shows whether the number of one bit is even or odd
_____ parity flag	c. shows whether a value is zero
_____ sign flag	d. shows overflow between fifth and fourth bits
_____ zero flag	e. shows the sign of a value

Check your answers below.

Self-Test Answer Key

1. low-level
2. b, c, e, f
3. registers and control circuits
4. bytes
5. eight
6. a and b
7. d
8. a. B, C, D, E
   b. flag
   c. A
   d. H
   e. L
   f. PC
   g. SP
   h. PSW
9. B–C, D–E, H–L, and A–flag
10. PSW, PC, and SP
11. carry flag—a
    auxiliary carry flag—d
    parity flag—b
    sign flag—e
    zero flag—c

If you missed any of these, you may want to review the appropriate frames before going on to Chapter 2.

CHAPTER TWO

NUMBER SYSTEMS AND DATA REPRESENTATION

The binary number system was briefly introduced in Chapter 1. In the study of Assembly Language programming, number systems are so important that they warrant a chapter to themselves. You must become comfortable not only with binary but also hexadecimal (base 16) numbers.

Of the two major code systems, ASCII and EBCDIC, your microcomputer probably uses ASCII. EBCDIC is used mainly by larger IBM computers. Therefore, we'll also introduce you to ASCII code in this chapter.

By the time you have finished this chapter, you will be able to:

- add and subtract binary numbers;
- add and subtract hexadecimal numbers;
- convert numbers among binary, decimal, and hexadecimal;
- using a chart, interpret ASCII codes.

THE DECIMAL NUMBER SYSTEM

We need to start by reviewing some basic facts about the system you've used every day since the first grade—the decimal number system. This review will give you the concepts and terminology you need to learn about other number systems.

1. The decimal number system has a base of ten. What does that mean? Essentially, it means that we count in groups of ten.

oooo oooo o	This many objects we call 9.
If we add one more, we make one group, which we call 10.	ooooo ooooo

The number 10 means:

1 0

one group of ten — *no singles*

When we get ten groups of ten, we make a larger group.

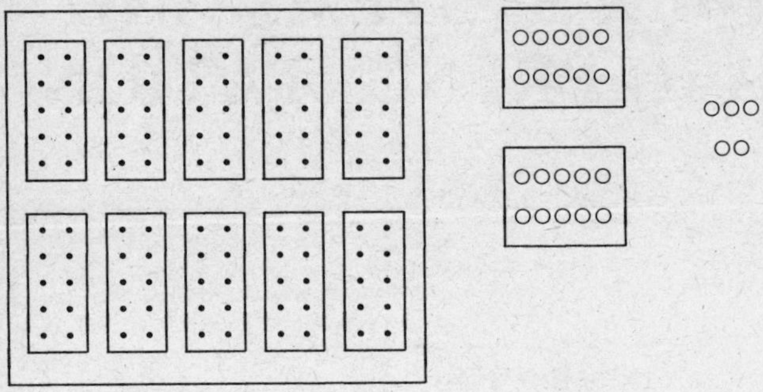

is written 125.

1 2 5

one group of ten tens — *two groups of ten* — *five singles*

The same principle holds true for all number systems.

(a) What is the base of the decimal system? __________________

(b) The binary number system has a base of two. Draw the number of objects represented by 101B. (We use B to indicate binary.)

(c) The hexadecimal number system has a base of 16. Draw the number of objects represented by the number 11H. (We use H to indicate hexadecimal.)

(a) ten

(b) 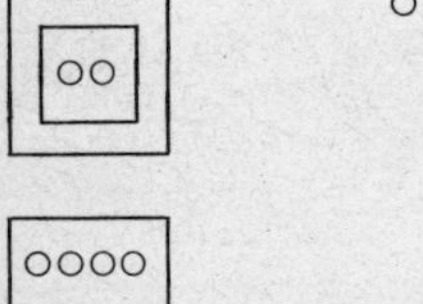

(one group of two-twos; no group of two; one single—five objects altogether)

(c) 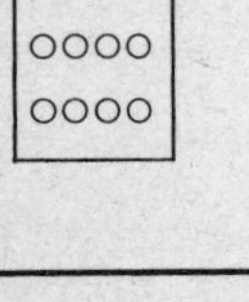

(one group of sixteen; one single; seventeen objects altogether)

2. Because the decimal system has a base of ten, each column represents a power of ten. The singles, or units, column represents 10^0.

1 2 5

1×10^2 $\quad$ 2×10^1 $\quad$ 5×10^0

Any number to the zero power equals 1. $10^0 = 1$. $5^0 = 1$. $45^0 = 1$. $154387269416333.61527^0 = 1$. $X^0 = 1$.

The second column from the right, the group-of-ten column, represents 10^1. Any number to the first power equals itself. $10^1 = 10$. $5^1 = 5$. $45^1 = 45$. $154387269416333.61527^1 = 154387269416333.61527$. $X^1 = X$.

The third column from the right represents 10^2. The fourth column 10^3, etc. Here is how we break down a decimal number:

$$\begin{aligned} 10523 = {} & 1 \times 10^4 = 1 \times 10000 = 10000 \\ & 0 \times 10^3 = 0 \times 1000 = 0 \\ & 5 \times 10^2 = 5 \times 100 = 500 \\ & 2 \times 10^1 = 2 \times 10 = 20 \\ & 3 \times 10^0 = 3 \times 1 = \underline{3} \\ & \qquad 10523 \end{aligned}$$

Use the framework below to break down the decimal value 1984.

1984 = _____ $\times 10^3$ = _____ x _____ = _____

_____ $\times 10^2$ = _____ x _____ = _____

_____ $\times 10^1$ = _____ x _____ = _____

_____ $\times 10^0$ = _____ x _____ = _____

1984

— — — — — — — — — — — — — —

$$\begin{aligned} & 1 \times 10^3 = 1 \times 1000 = 1000 \\ & 9 \times 10^2 = 9 \times 100 = 900 \\ & 8 \times 10^1 = 8 \times 10 = 80 \\ & 4 \times 10^0 = 4 \times 1 = \underline{4} \\ & \qquad 1984 \end{aligned}$$

3. The above shows how you would convert a decimal number to the decimal number system. The result is the same as the original because we didn't change number systems. In other number systems, you use the same method.

The binary value 101 is converted to decimal like this:

$$\begin{aligned} 101B & = 1 \times 2^2 = 1 \times 4 = 4 \\ & = 0 \times 2^1 = 0 \times 2 = 0 \\ & = 1 \times 2^0 = 1 \times 1 = \underline{1} \\ & \qquad 5 \end{aligned}$$

The hexadecimal value 11H is converted to decimal like this:

$$\begin{aligned} 11H = 1 \times 16^1 &= 1 \times 16 = 16 \\ 1 \times 16^0 &= 1 \times 1 = \underline{\ 1} \\ & \qquad\qquad 17 \end{aligned}$$

(a) Convert the number 106H to decimal.

(b) Convert the number 1101B to decimal.

(a)
$$\begin{aligned} 106H = 1 \times 16^2 &= 1 \times 256 = 256 \\ 0 \times 16^1 &= 0 \times 16 = 0 \\ 6 \times 16^0 &= 6 \times 1 = \underline{\ 6} \\ & \qquad\qquad 262 \end{aligned}$$

(b)
$$\begin{aligned} 1101B = 1 \times 2^3 &= 1 \times 8 = 8 \\ 1 \times 2^2 &= 1 \times 4 = 4 \\ 0 \times 2^1 &= 0 \times 1 = 0 \\ 1 \times 2^0 &= 1 \times 1 = \underline{\ 1} \\ & \qquad\qquad 13 \end{aligned}$$

4. Now let's talk about the individual digits in the decimal number system. Decimal is based on ten and so there are ten digits: 0,1,2,3,4,5,6,7,8,9. When you add 1 to 9, you get a group of ten so you move to the left one column.

9 + 1 = 10

0 is the lowest-valued digit and 9 is the highest-valued digit.

(a) The binary number system has a base of two. How many digits does it need? ________________ What are they? ________________

What's the lowest-valued digit? ____________ What's the highest-valued digit? ________________________________

(b) The hexadecimal number system has a base of sixteen. How many digits does it need? ________________________________

Hexadecimal uses letters when it runs out of decimal digits. What do you think the hexadecimal digits are? ________________

____

What's the lowest-valued digit? ________________________________

From the digits you used, what's the highest-valued digit? ________

— — — — — — — — — — — — —

(a) two; 0,1; 0; 1; (b) sixteen; the standard hexadecimal digits are 0,1,2,3,4,5,6,7,8,9,A,B,C,D,E,F; 0; F

5. Now you've reviewed the decimal number system and you've learned quite a bit about binary and hexadecimal, too. These questions will let you practice what you've learned.

(a) What is the decimal base? ________

(b) What is the binary base? ________

(c) What is the hexadecimal base? ________

Convert the following numbers to decimal.

(d) 110B =

(e) 21H =

Give the digits for these number systems.

(f) Decimal ________

(g) Binary ________

(h) Hexadecimal ________

(i) What is the highest digit in decimal? ________

(j) What is the highest digit in binary? ________

(k) What is the highest digit in hexadecimal? ________

— — — — — — — — — — — — —

(a) ten; (b) two; (c) sixteen;

(d) 110B = $1 \times 2^2 = 1 \times 4 = 4$
$1 \times 2^1 = 1 \times 2 = 2$
$0 \times 2^0 = 0 \times 1 = \underline{0}$
6

(e) 21H = $2 \times 16^1 = 2 \times 16 = 32$
$1 \times 16^0 = 1 \times 1 = \underline{1}$
33

(f) 0,1,2,3,4,5,6,7,8,9; (g) 0,1; (h) 0,1,2,3,4,5,6,7,8,9,A,B,C,D,E,F;
(i) 9; (j) 1; (k) F

THE HEXADECIMAL NUMBER SYSTEM

You may be saying to yourself, "I see why I might need to understand binary since the computer uses it. But why do I have to learn the hexadecimal number system?" We'll explain how hexadecimal is used in the following frames.

6. Sometimes we want to communicate with the computer in binary numbers instead of decimal. For example, memory addresses are usually not translated into decimal. But binary numbers are long and awkward and it's easy to make mistakes when reading, writing, and typing them. So instead of using binary directly, we use hexadecimal as a go-between.

Hexadecimal and binary numbers are directly related. Four binary digits equal one hexadecimal digit. So each byte can be expressed in two digits rather than eight. This saves a lot of bother when you are coding instructions to the computer. The computer can easily convert hex to binary; all work is actually done in binary.

The computer also prints some data in hexadecimal. For an example, look at Figure 2.1. This is a portion of an assembler listing—the report we get when a program has been assembled. We have circled the data that has been printed in hexadecimal. It includes memory address information and the machine language instructions. The computer prints them out as hex, but internally only binary is used.

(a) What number system is used inside the computer? ________________

(b) What number system is used as a shorthand for binary numbers?

____

— — — — — — — — — — — — — —

(a) binary; (b) hexadecimal

7. The binary system is based on two and the hexadecimal system is based on sixteen. $2^4 = 16$. Therefore, there is a direct relationship between a group of four binary digits and a hexadecimal digit.

Figure 2.2 is a table showing the binary values for all the hexadecimal digits. Use the table to answer the questions below.

Give the binary equivalents of these numbers.

(a) 3H = ________________

(b) 9H = ________________

(c) AH = ________________

(d) CH = ________________

instruction addresses
hex numbers
machine language

```
0100                          org   100H
0100 CD2B01                   call  input
0103 78                       mov   a,b
0104 FE35                     cpi   '5'
0106 C20F01                   jnz   notfiv
0109 212101         five      lxi   h,fivmsg
010C C31201                   jmp   outmsg
010F 212601         notfiv    lxi   h,notmsg
0112 3E05           outmsg    mvi   a,5
0114 46             looper    mov   b,m
0115 CD3901                   call  output
0118 23                       inx   h
0119 D601                     sui   1
011B C21401                   jnz   looper
011E C30000                   jmp   0
0121 5249474854fivmsg db     'right'
0126 57524F4E47notmsg db     'wrong'
012B F5            input push a
012C CD4C01        status call test
012F CA2C01                  jz    status
0132 DB1C                    in    1ch
0134 E67F                    ani   7fh
0136 47                      mov   b,a
0137 F1                      pop   a
0138 C9                      ret
0139 F5            output push a
013A 3E10          statout mvi  a,10h
013C D31D                    out   1dh
013E DB1D                    in    1dh
0140 E60C                    ani   00001100b
0142 FE0C                    cpi   00001100b
0144 C23A01                  jnz   statout
0147 78                      mov   a,b
0148 D31C                    out   1ch
014A F1                      pop   a
014B C9                      ret
014C AF            test      xra   a
014D D31D                    out   1dh
014F DB1D                    in    1dh
0151 E601                    ani   1
0153 C8                      rz
0154 3EFF                    mvi   a,0ffh
0156 C9                      ret
0157                         end
```

FIGURE 2.1. Sample Assembler Listing

Give the hexadecimal equivalents of these numbers.

(e) 1010B = ________________

(f) 1000B = ________________

(g) 0101B = ________________

(h) 1111B = ________________

(i) 0110B = ________________

— — — — — — — — — — — —

(a) 0011B; (b) 1001B; (c) 1010B; (d) 1100B; (e) AH; (f) 8H; (g) 5H; (h) FH; (i) 6H

8. Converting between larger binary and hexadecimal values is also easy.

decimal	hexadecimal	binary
0	0	0000
1	1	0001
2	2	0010
3	3	0011
4	4	0100
5	5	0101
6	6	0110
7	7	0111
8	8	1000
9	9	1001
10	A	1010
11	B	1011
12	C	1100
13	D	1101
14	E	1110
15	F	1111

FIGURE 2.2. Decimal-Hexadecimal-Binary Equivalence

If a binary number has more than four digits, divide it into groups of four starting from the right.

1,0010,0101

Fill in leading zeros as necessary to make groups of four digits.

0001,0010,0101

Then translate each group into hex. ("Hex" is short for hexadecimal.)

0001,0010,0101B = 125H

Give the hexadecimal equivalents for each of the following numbers.

(a) 101110B = ________________

(b) 1111000B = ________________

(c) 10000B = ________________

— — — — — — — — — — — —

(a) 2EH; (b) 78H; (c) 10H

9. You can convert hex into binary one digit at a time. For example, 52BH is equivalent to 0101 0010 1011B. Many programmers like to write binary numbers with a space every four digits to simplify conversion.

Give the binary equivalents for each of the following numbers.

(a) 23H = ________________

(b) FBH = ________________

– – – – – – – – – – – – – –

(a) 0010 0011B or 10 0011B; (b) 1111 1011B

10. Recall that an 8080/8085 memory address is two bytes, or sixteen bits. So it takes four hex digits to write a memory address. The first memory address is 0000H.

(a) What is the second memory address? ________________

(b) What is the eleventh memory address? ________________

(c) What is the highest possible memory address (the largest hex value that will fit in two bytes)? ________________

(d) In decimal, how many memory addresses are possible? ________________

– – – – – – – – – – – – – –

(a) 0001H; (b) 000AH; (c) FFFFH; (d) 65,535

$$
\begin{aligned}
15 \times 16^3 &= 15 \times 4096 = 61440\\
15 \times 16^2 &= 15 \times 256 = 3840\\
15 \times 16^1 &= 15 \times 16 = 240\\
15 \times 16^0 &= 15 \times 1 = \underline{15}\\
& \qquad\qquad\qquad 65,535
\end{aligned}
$$

(The value 65,535 is the same as $16^4 - 1$.)

11. Here are some more binary-hexadecimal conversion problems for you.

(a) Suppose the A register contains the value F0H. In binary, what is the value? ________________

In decimal? ________________

(b) Suppose the H–L pair contain 0010H. In binary, what is the value?

____

In decimal? ________________

(c) In the PSW, the least significant (right hand) bit is the carry flag. For each of the following values, convert to binary to find out whether the carry flag is on or off.

23H: ________________

0AH: ________________

F1H: ______________

FFH: ______________

(a) 1111 0000B; 240; (b) 0000 0000 0001 0000B; 16; (c) on; off; on; on (Remember the spaces we show aren't really there. We've separated the binary digits into groups of four to make it easier for *you* to read them.)

DECIMAL CONVERSIONS

Now you've been introduced to the binary and hexadecimal number systems and you can make these conversions: binary ---→ decimal, binary ---→ hexadecimal, hexadecimal ---→ binary, and hexadecimal ---→ decimal. In the following frames, we'll show you how to convert decimal ---→ binary and decimal ---→ hexadecimal.

12. Figures 2.3 and 2.4 show the value of some powers of two and sixteen, respectively. You'll need them to convert from decimal. To show you how it's done, we'll convert 437 to hexadecimal.

A. First, we find the largest power of 16 that will divide into 437. It's 16^2, or 256. [16^3 (4096) is too big.]

From this, we know that our answer is going to have three digits, since we'll have some number times 16^2.

```
___    ___    ___
16²    16¹    16⁰

     256)437
```

```
 1
___    ___    ___
16²    16¹    16⁰

        1
   256)437
       256
       ---
       181
to next step
```

B. We divide 256 into 437. The quotient is our first digit because it tells us how many 16^2s there are in 437. We save the remainder for the next step.

C. We divide the remainder by 16^1. The quotient becomes the second digit of the answer. Note that we convert the decimal 11 to a single hexadecimal digit, B.

```
 1      B     ___
16²    16¹    16⁰

       (11)
    16)181
       16
       --
        21
        16
        --
         5
```

n	2^n
0	1
1	2
2	4
3	8
4	16
5	32
6	64
7	128
8	256
9	512
10	1024
11	2048
12	4096
13	8192
14	16,384
15	32,768
16	65,536

FIGURE 2.3. Powers of Two

n	16^n
0	1
1	16
2	256
3	4096
4	65,536
5	1,048,576
6	16,777,216
7	268,435,456
8	4,294,967,296

FIGURE 2.4. Powers of 16

$\frac{1}{16^2}$ $\frac{B}{16^1}$ $\frac{5}{16^0}$

```
    11
16)181
   16
    21
    16
    (5)
```

D. Since we're down to the units column ($16^0 = 1$), the remainder becomes the last digit.

If any quotient or the final remainder comes out greater than 15, a mistake has been made somewhere, so you need to recalculate it.

Now convert the following decimal numbers to hexadecimal.

(a) 25 = __________

(b) 100 = __________

(c) 241 = __________

(d) 716 = __________

(e) 4291 = __________

(a) 25 = 19H

```
      1
16)  25
     16
      9
```

(b) 100 = 64H

```
      6
16)100
     96
      4
```

(c) 241 = F1H

```
     15
16)241
   16
    81
    80
     1
```

(d) 716 = 2CCH

```
        2                12
256)716             16)204
    512                16
    204                 44
                        32
                        12
```

(e) 4291 = 10C3H

```
         1          0          12
4096)4291    256)195     16)195
     4096                   16
      195                    35
                             32
                              3
```

13. Decimal ---→ binary conversions are done just the same as decimal ---→ hex except that you use powers of two instead of powers of sixteen. For our example, we'll convert 21 to binary.

A. The largest power of two that will divide into 21 is 2^4 = 16. This tells us that the answer has five digits.

```
 1
2^4   2^3   2^2   2^1   2^0
          1
      16)21
         16
          5
```

B. The next lower power of two, 2^3 = 8, produces a zero quotient.

```
 1     0
2^4   2^3   2^2   2^1   2^0
        0
      8)5
        0
        5
```

C. The next lower power of two, 2^2 = 4, will divide into 5.

```
 1     0     1
2^4   2^3   2^2   2^1   2^0
            1
          4)5
            4
            1
```

D. The next lower power of two, 2^1 = 2, produces a zero quotient. And the final remainder is 1.

```
 1     0     1     0     1
2^4   2^3   2^2   2^1   2^0
            0
          2)1
            0
           (1)
```

When converting to binary, each quotient will either be 1 or 0. If you get a quotient (or final remainder) larger than 1, you've made a mistake somewhere.

Convert the following decimal numbers to binary.

(a) 10 = __________

(b) 16 = __________

(c) 25 = __________

(d) 33 = __________

— — — — — — — — — — — — — —

(a) 1010B; (b) 10000B; (c) 11001B; (d) 100001B

14. Now you can convert a number from any one system to any other. Practice by filling in the chart below.

decimal	hexadecimal	binary
210	(a)	(b)
(c)	96H	(d)
(e)	(f)	1011 0111B
(g)	22AH	(h)
49	(i)	(j)

(k) What is the largest number (in decimal) that the accumulator can hold? __________

— — — — — — — — — — — — — —

(a) D2H; (b) 1101 0010B; (c) 150; (d) 1001 0110B; (e) 183; (f) B7H; (g) 554; (h) 0010 0010 1010B; (i) 31H; (j) 0011 0001B; (k) 255 (FF or 1111 1111; this is equivalent to $16^2 - 1$, or $2^8 - 1$.)

ADDITION

In order to read assembler listings, you need to be able to do simple addition and subtraction in binary and hexadecimal. We'll cover addition first.

15. Do you remember learning how to add? If you had the usual education, you memorized the addition facts from 1 + 0 through 9 + 9. Then you learned to handle larger numbers in columns.

No, you don't have to memorize math facts in hexadecimal and binary. We'll give you some tables to use. But you should be able to figure out simple addition problems without using the tables.

Here's the hex count from 1H to 20H:

0 1 2 3 4 5 6 7 8 9 A B C D E F 10 11 12 13 14 15 16 17 18 19 1A 1B 1C 1D 1E 1F 20

Here are some sample problems that you can work out using the hex count line above.

2H + 3H = 5H
1H + 6H = 7H
AH + 0H = AH
9H + 1H = AH (A critical fact! 10D = AH)
2H + BH = DH
7H + 5H = CH (Count on your fingers if you have to: 7,8,9,A,B,C.)
FH + 1H = 10H (Another critical fact! 16D = 10H)

Now you solve the problems below.

(a) 10H + BH = __________

(b) 5H + FH = __________

(c) 9H + 2H = __________

(d) 5H + 5H = __________

(e) 19H + 1H = __________

(f) 1FH + 1H = __________

(g) 15H + BH = __________

– – – – – – – – – – – – – –

(a) 1BH; (b) 14H; (c) BH; (d) AH; (e) 1AH; (f) 20H; (g) 20H

16. The hexadecimal addition and subtraction table is located in Appendix A. To use it for addition, find the row for one addend and the column for the other addend. The intersection gives the sum.

Use the table to solve these problems.

(a) 5H + 9H = __________

(b) AH + BH = __________

(c) 3H + 9H = __________

(d) DH + DH = __________

– – – – – – – – – – – – – –

(a) EH; (b) 15H; (c) CH; (d) 1AH

17. Binary addition is very simple. There are only three math facts.

```
   0B         0B         1B
 + 0B       + 1B       + 1B
 ----       ----       ----
   0B         1B        10B
```

See if you can solve the problems below.

```
(a) 101B       (b) 1000B       (c) 10B
     10B                1B          11B
    ----            -----          ----

    ____            _____          ____
```

--- ----------

(a) 111B; (b) 1001B; (c) 101B

18. Now let's do some problems with carrying.
Decimal examples:

```
     /            //
    257          3265
  +  28        + 2149
  -----        ------
    285          5414
```

Hexadecimal examples:

```
     /            ///
    2AH          39FFH
  + 1BH        +  B25H
  -----        -------
    45H          4524H
```

When you carry a 1 to the second column from the right, you are actually carrying 10H or 16.
Binary examples:

```
     //             /////
    10110B         111101B
  +    10B       +   1111B
  --------       ---------
    11000B        1001100B
```

Solve the problems below.

```
(a)    2BH       (b)    11011B       (c)    FFFH
     + 2BH            +  1100B            +    1H
     -----            -------             ------

     _____            _______             ______

(d)    111B      (e)    1110B        (f)    DEFH
     +   1B           +  111B             + 927H
     ------           ------              ------

     ______           ______              ______
```

(a) 56H; (b) 100111B; (c) 1000H; (d) 1000B; (e) 10101B; (f) 1716H

SUBTRACTION

19. To use the hex tables for subtraction, find the minuend (the smaller number) across the top. Then go down that column until you find the subtrahend (the larger number). Go across to the left column to find the answer.
Examples:

```
  1DH       10H       15H
-  EH     -  8H     -  7H
  ---       ---       ---
   FH        8H        EH
```

Problems:

```
(a)  BH        (b)  10H        (c)  13H
   - 5H           -  AH           -  7H
   ----           -----           -----

   ____           _____           _____

(d)  17H
   -  BH
   -----

   _____
```

(a) 6H; (b) 6H; (c) CH; (d) CH

20. Now let's try some subtraction with borrowing.
Decimal examples:

```
   8           20
  495          316
-   9        -  28
  ---          ---
  486          288
```

Hexadecimal examples:

```
   91           1
  4A20H        21H
-   B7H      - 1FH
  -----        ---
  4969H         2H
```

Now try to work these problems.

```
(a)  325H      (b)  116H      (c)  10AH
   -  BH          -  2FH         -  BBH
   -----          ------         ------
   _____          ______         ______
```

```
(d)    3211H
     -  BCDH
     --------
```

```
         1                  0                    F
(a)   325H         (b)   116H         (c)     10AH
    -   BH             -  2FH              -   BBH
    ------             ------              -------
      31AH               E7H                   4FH

       210
(d)   3211H
    -  BCDH
    -------
      2644H
```

21. Binary subtraction is simpler than hex subtraction. Here are the binary subtraction facts:

```
   0B        1B        1B        10B        10B
 - 0B      - 0B      - 1B      -  1B      -  0B
 ----      ----      ----      -----      -----
   0B        1B        0B         1B        10B
```

You can see that the addition facts still hold. The important thing to remember in binary subtraction is that 10B – 1B = 1B. Now solve these problems.

```
(a)   1100B       (b)   10111B       (c)   11111111B
    -  100B           -   101B           - 10101010B
    -------           --------           -----------
```

(a) 1000B; (b) 10010B; (c) 01010101B

22. Binary subtraction often requires borrowing. Here are some examples.

```
    00 0                  0
   1110110B            10101B
 -    1101B          -    10B
 ----------          --------
    101101B            10011B
```

Find the answers to these problems.

```
(a)   11110B        (b)   101010B
    -  1101B            -   0101B
    --------            ---------
```

```
         0                 0 0
(a)   11110B        (b)   101010B
    -  1101B            -   0101B
    --------            ---------
      10001B              100101B
```

23. Sometimes you have to borrow through zero. This is the trickiest part of subtraction. Let's look at how it works in decimal. We'll use the problem 50001 – 16.

A. We borrow from the first non-zero digit. ALL THE INTERVENING ZEROS CHANGE TO HIGHEST-VALUED DIGITS. (Don't think of them as 9's; think of them as highest digits.) The borrowing column receives 10, so it becomes 11.

```
   4999
   50001
-     16
```

B. The units column is then completed.

```
   4999
   50001
-     16
       5
```

C. The remainder of the problem is subtracted in normal fashion.

```
   4999
   50001
-     16
   49985
```

Here are some hex examples:

```
   9FF1              0FFFF               5F
   A0071H          3100000BH           1601H
-     49H      -          FH      -     107H
   9FFD8H          30FFFFCH            14FAH
```

Here are some binary examples:

```
   01              01110               011
   100010B         100000101B          1000B
-     100B     -         111B     -       1B
    1110B          111110B              111B
```

Now work these problems. Remember to use highest-valued digits for the appropriate number system.

```
(a)   C0001H      (b)   2A00BH      (c)   1000B
    -    5H           -    FFH          -   11B
```

- - - - - - - - - - - - - -

```
      BFFF              9FF               011
(a)   C0001H      (b)   2A00BH      (c)   1000B
    -    5H           -    FFH          -   11B
      BFFFCH            29F0CH             101B
```

24. For practice, find the sums and differences below.

```
(a) 1001 1111B               (b) 1110 0000 1111B
  +   10 0011B                          +  1010B
```

(c)
```
  1001 1111B
-   10 0011B
```

(d)
```
  1110 0000 1111B
-           1010B
```

(e)
```
  426AH
+   B9H
```

(f)
```
  60D0H
+ 51E2H
```

(g)
```
  426AH
-   B9H
```

(h)
```
  60D0H
- 51E2H
```

— — — — — — — — — — — —

(a) 1100 0010B; (b) 1110 0001 1001B; (c) 0111 1100B; (d) 1110 0000 0101B; (e) 4323H; (f) B2B2H; (g) 41B1H; (h) 0EEEH

ASCII CODE

So far, you have learned how to handle hexadecimal and binary numbers. You'll use this information frequently as you develop programs. But when a number is entered into the system from the outside, it's not translated directly into binary; it's always treated as alphanumeric data and encoded by a code system such as ASCII or EBCDIC. In this book, we'll use ASCII and assume that the first bit (the leftmost or high-order bit) is zero since ASCII only uses seven bits out of the eight available bits.

25. Appendix B shows ASCII code. Each character shown in the grid is represented by two hex digits. These are shown on the top and left of the grid. For example, 50H is the ASCII code for the letter P. Use Appendix B to answer the questions below.

Write the ASCII code (in hex) for the following characters.

(a) * : __________

(b) 3 : __________

(c) A : __________

(d) c : __________

Give the character indicated by each of the following ASCII codes.

(e) 35H : __________

(f) 4DH : __________

(g) 77H : __________

(h) 25H : __________

— — — — — — — — — — — —

(a) 2AH; (b) 33H; (c) 41H; (d) 63H; (e) 5; (f) M; (g) w; (h) %

26. Notice particularly how the ten decimal digits are coded in ASCII. The code always starts with 3H. The second half of the byte is equal to the decimal digit. Thus, 0 is coded as 30H, 1 is coded as 31H, etc.

(a) If you type and enter the character '5', what will be received in the A register? (Choose one.)

_____ 0000 0101B (binary for decimal 5)

_____ 05H (hex for decimal 5)

_____ 0011 0101B (35H)

(b) Suppose you write a program to add together registers A and B.

Register A contains the ASCII code for 2. What is it? __________

Register B contains the ASCII code for 3. What is it? __________

What will the sum be? (Give the answer in ASCII code.) __________

What is the character form of that code? __________

— — — — — — — — — — — —

(a) 00110101B (35H); (b) 32H, 33H, 65H, e

Later in this book you'll learn how to handle numeric values so your programs don't produce erroneous arithmetic results.

27. The codes from 00H through 1FH and 7F are special codes that control the action of the output device. These are recommended codes used by most systems. A terminal or other device may interpret them differently. You use them by sending (or *writing*) the appropriate byte to the device. For example, if you write the code 07H, the bell on the output device will ring. (Nothing will be printed.) If the terminal does not have a bell, it won't recognize 07H as a special code. All unrecognized codes are ignored or printed as blanks. Refer to the explanations in Appendix B to answer these questions.

(a) What code will cause one character to be deleted (DEL)? __________

(b) What code will cause the output device (printer or video screen) to start a new page (FF)? __________

(c) If you want to start a new line on a printer or a video terminal, you need to write a carriage return (CR) followed by a line feed (LF). What are the ASCII codes for these two characters?

____

(d) What if your program sends 0BM, for vertical tab, to a terminal that does not have a vertical tabbing capability? What will happen?

____

— — — — — — — — — — — — — —

(a) 7FH; (b) 0CH; (c) 0DH and 0AH; (d) it will be ignored or a space will be printed. Don't be frightened by all those special characters. Most of them are only for special equipment and special applications. Remember, too, that your equipment may use different codes. Check your manuals if you want to use these codes.

REVIEW

In this chapter, you have studied data representation in the computer.

- The binary number system is based on two. Each column represents a power of two. The least significant digit represents 2^0, the next left column represents 2^1, and so forth. Zero is the lowest digit and one is the highest digit.
- Binary numbers are converted to decimal by multiplying each column by the appropriate power of two and summing the results.
- Decimal numbers are converted to binary by dividing by successive powers of two, starting with the largest power that will fit into the decimal number.
- The binary math facts are:

  0 + 0 = 0; 0 + 1, or 1 + 0 = 1; 1 + 1 = 10.
- The hexadecimal (or hex) number system is based on 16. Hex numbers are used merely as shorthand for binary numbers. The computer will report numbers to you in hex, and you can give it hex numbers, too.

  Each column represents a power of 16. The least significant column is 16^0, the next column is 16^1, etc. The digits are 0,1,2,3,4,5,6,7,8,9,A,B,C,D,E,F. F is the highest digit.
- Hex numbers are converted to decimal numbers by multiplying each column by the appropriate power of 16 and summing the results.
- Decimal numbers are converted to hexadecimal by dividing by successive powers of 16, starting with the largest power that will fit into the decimal number.
- The hex math facts are shown in Appendix A.
- Binary and hex numbers are directly related. Four binary digits equal one hex digit. Numbers can be converted between the two systems on sight if you memorize the table of equivalents, from 0B = 0H through 1111B = FH. (See Figure 2.2.)
- Data entering the system through a terminal is always treated as alphanumeric data and is encoded in a code system such as ASCII.

Appendix B shows ASCII code. Assume that the leftmost (high order or most significant) bit is always zero.

Now take the Self-Test for this chapter.

CHAPTER 2 SELF-TEST

You may use Figures 2.2 through 2.4 and Appendices A and B for this Self-Test.

1. Convert to decimal.

   a. 21H = __________D　　d. 10H = __________D

   b. 16H = __________D　　e. 100H = __________D

   c. 7H = __________D　　f. 255H = __________D

2. Convert to decimal.

   a. 101B = __________D　　d. 1001B = __________D

   b. 10100B = __________D　　e. 1111B = __________D

   c. 1100B = __________D　　f. 11011B = __________D

3. Convert to hex.

   a. 101B = __________H　　d. 1110B = __________H

   b. 11011011B = __________H　　e. 100000B = __________H

   c. 10001B = __________H　　f. 11011B = __________H

4. Convert to binary.

   a. 16H = __________B　　d. 2H = __________B

   b. 7H = __________B　　e. 10H = __________B

   c. 21H = __________B　　f. AH = __________B

5. Convert to hex.

   a. 21D = __________H　　d. 16D = __________H

   b. 4D = __________H　　e. 100D = __________H

   c. 10D = __________H　　f. 255D = __________H

6. Convert to binary.

   a. 8D = __________B　　d. 85D = __________B

   b. 25D = __________B　　e. 52D = __________B

   c. 38D = __________B　　f. 18D = __________B

7. Add.

```
a.   101101B       b.   11111B       c.   1000110B
   +    101B          +   110B          +   11010B
```

8. Add.

```
a.   64H           b.   FF1H         c.   21B3H
   + ABH              +  A9H            +  C15H
```

9. Subtract.

```
a.   100101B       b.   110000B      c.   100000B
   -   1110B          -     11B         -  11111B
```

10. Subtract.

```
a.   100AH         b.   A0007H       c.   3D09H
   -   2BH            -    BFH          -  1AAH
```

11. Write the alphanumeric character for each of these ASCII codes.

a. 23H = ______ d. 62H = ______

b. 37H = ______ e. 7DH = ______

c. 4AH = ______ f. 3FH = ______

12. Write the ASCII code for each of these characters or control functions.

a. '5' = ______ d. line feed = ______

b. '[' = ______ e. space = ______

c. carriage return = ______ f. 'H' = ______

Now check your answers.

Selt-Test Answer Key

1. a. 33D d. 16D
   b. 22D e. 256D
   c. 7D f. 597D

2. a. 5D d. 9D
   b. 20D e. 15D
   c. 12D f. 27D

3. a. 5H d. EH
   b. DBH e. 20H
   c. 11H f. 1BH

4. a. 10110B d. 10B
   b. 111B e. 10000B
   c. 100001B f. 1010B

5. a. 15H d. 10H
   b. 4H e. 64H
   c. AH f. FFH

6. a. 1000B d. 1010101B
   b. 11001B e. 110100B
   c. 100110B f. 10010B

7. a. 110010B b. 100101B c. 1100000B

8. a. 10FH b. 109AH c. 2DC8H

9. a. 10111B b. 101101B c. 1B

10. a. FDFH b. 9FF48H c. 3B5FH

11. a. # d. b
    b. 7 e. }
    c. J f. ?

12. a. 35H d. 0AH
    b. 5BH e. 20H
    c. 0DH f. 48H

If you missed any of these, restudy the appropriate frames before going on to Chapter 3.

This has been a very brief look at number systems and data representation. If you would like to learn more, try the Wiley Self-Teaching Guide, *Background Math for a Computer World*, by Ruth Ashley.

CHAPTER THREE

INSTRUCTION FORMAT

In the preceding two chapters you have been studying necessary background information. Now you're ready to begin attacking the subject of Assembly Language itself. In this chapter, we'll look at the format of an Assembly Language instruction. You'll learn how to code all the various parts of an instruction. You'll also be exposed to a lot of instructions that you'll be using later in this book.

When you have finished this chapter, you will be able to:

- Given the format for an Assembly Language instruction —
  - — identify the required and optional parts;
  - — identify parts that must be filled in and parts that are used as is.
- Given Assembly Language code in incorrect format, recode it in correct format.
- Create a label for an instruction or a data area.
- Identify the types of instructions that need labels.
- Code the following types of operands:
  - — register names;
  - — memory addresses;
  - — immediate data.

1. Figure 3.1 shows part of a sample program that we'll use throughout this chapter to demonstrate the format of Assembly Language instructions. The INPUT and OUTPUT details aren't shown.

The first six lines are descriptive comments. They are printed whenever the program is printed but otherwise they are ignored by the computer. They are intended for human beings who are reading the program. In lines 8, 10, and 11, the words following the semicolons are also comments.

The first instruction, CALL, arranges to read a byte from the terminal and store it in register B. The second CALL instruction arranges to write the same byte to the same terminal, thus allowing the typist to see

```
; THIS PROGRAM READS AND STORES
; CHARACTERS FROM THE TERMINAL
; UNTIL A CARRIAGE RETURN IS
; RECEIVED.  THEN THE PROGRAM IS
; TERMINATED.
;
GETST     CALL   INPUT
          CALL   OUTPUT   ; ECHO BYTE
          MOV    A,B
          CPI    0DH      ; COMPARE TO <CR>
          JZ     STOP     ; JUMP IF <CR>
          MOV    M,B
          INX    H
          JMP    GETST
STOP      HLT
INPUT     ...
          ...
OUTPUT    ...
          ....
```

FIGURE 3.1. Sample Program

what was typed. Because of the way INPUT and OUTPUT are coded, register A is the same after the CALL as it was before.

The third instruction (MOV) moves the byte from the B to the A register. The fourth instruction (CPI) compares the byte (in register A) to 0DH, the ASCII code for a carriage return. The fifth instruction (JZ) causes a jump to the instruction labeled STOP if, and only if, the byte equals 0DH.

The sixth instruction (MOV) stores the byte in memory. The seventh instruction (INX) increments the memory address in the H–L register pair. The eighth instruction (JMP) returns control to the instruction labeled GETST (the first instruction). And the final instruction you see halts the program.

(a) What happens if the user types '3'?

_____ It is displayed, then stored in memory and the computer waits for the next character to be typed.

_____ It is stored in memory and the program halts.

_____ It is displayed, then the program halts without storing it.

(b) What happens if the user types a carriage return?

_____ It is stored in memory and the computer waits for the next character to be typed.

_____ It is stored in memory and the program halts.

_____ The program halts without storing it.

- - - - - - - - - - - - - -

(a) It is stored in memory and the computer waits for the next character to be typed; (b) The program halts without storing it.

GENERAL INSTRUCTION FORMAT

The format of an Assembly Language instruction is dictated by the program that will translate it—the assembler. Different assemblers have different requirements for instruction formats, but we can find some common points. We'll discuss the common points, show you what our assembler requires, and try to help you figure out what your assembler needs.

2. Here is a common Assembly Language instruction format:

[*label*] *operation* [*operands*] [;*comments*]

In this format definition, we have used brackets [] to indicate an optional field. Any individual instruction may or may not include this field.

"Optional" may not mean that you, the programmer, can choose to include the field or not. For example, the use of operands is dictated by the instruction. A MOV instruction must have two operands; a JMP instruction must have one operand; and a HLT instruction must have no operands. (See examples in Figure 3.1.)

On the other hand, the comments field is always used at your own option. No instruction requires comments; no instruction forbids them.

(a) Which of the following fields are optional?

_____ label

_____ operation

_____ operands

_____ comments

(b) Which is required in every Assembly Language instruction?

_____ label

_____ operation

_____ operands

_____ comments

(c) What does "optional" mean?

_____ You can choose whether or not to use it.

_____ Not every Assembly Language instruction will require it.

- - - - - - - - - - - - - -

(a) label; operands; comments; (b) operation; (c) Not every Assembly Language instruction will require it.

3. Here's the general format again:

[*label*] *operation* [*operands*] [;*comments*]

Words in italics indicate the type of data you insert in the instruction. For example, to code a MOV instruction, you insert the code MOV for *operation*. The square brackets surround data that is optional, depending on the instruction. You never code the brackets.

Words, codes, and symbols we show in regular type must be coded "as is" in the instruction. In the general format that we are using, *comments* must be preceded by a semicolon. If comments are not coded (they're always optional), the semicolon is not coded either. For example, here's a specific instruction format:

[*label*] MOV *r1*,*r2* [;*comments*]

This tells us that the label is optional, the operation MOV must be coded as it appears, and there are two required operands to be inserted, separated by a comma. Comments are optional, but if you use them, they must be preceded by a space and a semicolon.

Don't forget that your assembler program may require a general format somewhat different than this. For example, many assemblers require labels to be terminated with colons. Others allow the colon but do not require it. Still others do not permit a colon in a label.

(a) Which of the following are coded as is in any Assembly Language instruction that uses comments?

______ *label*

______ *operation*

______ *operands*

______ ;

______ *comments*

(b) Which only indicate the type of data to be inserted in the instruction?

______ *label*

______ *operation*

______ *operands*

______ ;

______ *comments*

(c) All 8080/8085 assemblers require *comments* to be preceded by a semicolon. True or false? ______________

— — — — — — — — — — — — —

(a) ; (b) *label; operation; operands; comments;*
(c) false—many do but some don't

Now that we've looked at the general format, let's take a close look at the individual parts.

THE *LABEL* FIELD

4. A label gives a name to an instruction. You then use that name as an operand in other instructions. There are two major ways we use labels.

- Jump instructions: When we want to jump to an instruction, we give it a label. Then we jump to that label. In Figure 3.1, there are two labels: GETST and STOP. The JZ instruction ("jump if zero") jumps to STOP. The JMP instruction ("jump") jumps to GETST.
- Data names: We assign names to data storage areas in our programs. Then our instructions refer to the data areas by name rather than numeric address. The names serve as labels for the storage areas.

Which of the following would you label?

_____ (a) Every instruction in the program.

_____ (b) Every fifth instruction in the program.

_____ (c) Instructions that have to be jumped to.

_____ (d) Jump instructions.

_____ (e) Data storage areas.

_____ (f) The last instruction in the program.

_____ (g) The first instruction in the program.

— — — — — — — — — — — — —

(c) and (e) are the best answers. Many programmers also label (g) to give the program a name.

5. Your assembler will have a set of rules for proper labels. In this book, we'll use the rules shown below. They're fairly common.

- A label must be 1 to 6 characters long.
- It can contain letters (A–Z) or digits (0–9). No special characters such as $, —, /.

- It must start with a letter.
- It must start in column 1.
- The following cannot be used as labels:
  - register names (A–E, H, L, PSW, SP)
  - M (This acts like a register in programs.)
  - 8080/8085 operation codes (such as MOV and ADD)

According to *our* rules, which of the following are legal labels?

_____ (a) START
_____ (b) MOV
_____ (c) 3RDONE
_____ (d) THIRD
_____ (e) B100
_____ (f) TRY#5
_____ (g) EXCEPTION
_____ (h) A
_____ (i) 1
_____ (j) K

— — — — — — — — — — — — — —

(a), (d), (e), and (j) are correct
((b) is an operation code; (c) starts with a digit; (f) contains an illegal character; (g) is too long; (h) is a register name; and (i) starts with a digit)

6. Most programmers prefer to use meaningful names as labels. For example, suppose you want to give a name to the first instruction of a routine that adds two numbers. ADDER is a better name than B1 or X.

Meaningful labels will help other people read your programs with understanding and will also help you when you return to a program you haven't worked on for a couple of months.

Which of the following labels are better:

(a) For a data storage area that will hold a social security number—SSN, SOCSEC, or N9? ______________________________

(b) For the first instruction of a routine that reads and stores the social security number—GETNUM, RANDS, or X2T1? ______________

Now try writing some labels of your own:

(c) For the first instruction of a routine that prints a page number on a new page. ______________________________

(d) For the first instruction of a routine that counts the time in tenths of seconds until the user pushes any key. ______________

— — — — — — — — — — — — — —

(a) SOCSEC is best, SSN is second best; (b) GETNUM is best; (c) we would use NUMPAG or PAGE; (d) we would use TIMER or DELAY (You could use any meaningful name that meets the name-forming rules. It's easier if your names are pronounceable.)

7. According to *our* rules, which of the following labels are legal?

_____ (a)	STOPPER	_____ (h)	RUN-IT
_____ (b)	GATER	_____ (i)	SP
_____ (c)	ENDER	_____ (j)	*
_____ (d)	END#1	_____ (k)	3010
_____ (e)	ENDTWO	_____ (l)	RUN10
_____ (f)	JMP	_____ (m)	FORCE
_____ (g)	JONES	_____ (n)	T/N

Write good labels for each of the following:

(o) The first instruction of a routine that handles input errors.

____

(p) A data storage area that holds the old balance. _______________

— — — — — — — — — — — — —

(b), (c), (e), (g), (l), and (m) are correct
((a) is too long; (d) contains an illegal character; (f) is an operation code; (h) contains an illegal character; (i) is a register name; (j) contains an illegal character; (k) doesn't start with a letter; and (n) contains an illegal character);
(o) we would use INERR or ERRIN; (p) we would use OLDBAL

THE *OPERATION* FIELD

8. Here's the general format again.

[*label*] *operation* [*operands*] [;*comments*]

You've learned how to code labels. Now let's look at the operation.

The operation is like the verb of a sentence; it tells the computer what to do. Some typical operation codes are:

MOV	for move data
ADD	for add
SUB	for subtract
IN	for read input

OUT for write output

HLT for halt

You don't make up your own operation codes. There is a standard set of 8080/8085 codes. (Your assembler may have added some special ones to the set.)

Every operation code contains from two to four letters. The operation is not optional; every instruction must have an operation. If you use only a comment, as in Figure 3.1, it is considered a comment, not an instruction. If it's an instruction, it must have an operation.

(a) In the sentence SET THE TABLE, which word is most like the operation?

_____ SET

_____ THE

_____ TABLE

(b) Can you make up your own operation codes? ________________

(c) Two of the following are not operation codes. Can you tell which two?

_____ X

_____ SUI

_____ EQU

_____ ERASE

(d) Which instructions in Figure 3.1 require an operation?

____

- - - - - - - - - - - - - -

(a) SET; (b) no; (c) X is too short and ERASE is too long; (d) all instructions; the comments aren't instructions.

9. Your assembler may have some rules for coding the operation. A fairly common rule is that the operation must be preceded by at least one space. If the instruction contains a label, the space or spaces separate the label from the operation. If there is no label, the space or spaces tell the assembler that there is no label.

Most programmers code their programs so that the operation codes and the operands are lined up in columns. (See Figure 3.1 again.) This makes programs much easier to read. It also allows us to add labels later on if we need to. We always start the operation code in column eight (to leave room for a six-character label plus one space). We always start the operands in column 13 (to leave room for a four-character operation code followed by a space).

A section of Assembly Language code is shown below. Some of the instructions are coded correctly and some incorrectly. Recode the entire section correctly and legibly. Use the coding form provided.

```
START   IN   010

ADD   B

OUT   010

STOP   HLT
```

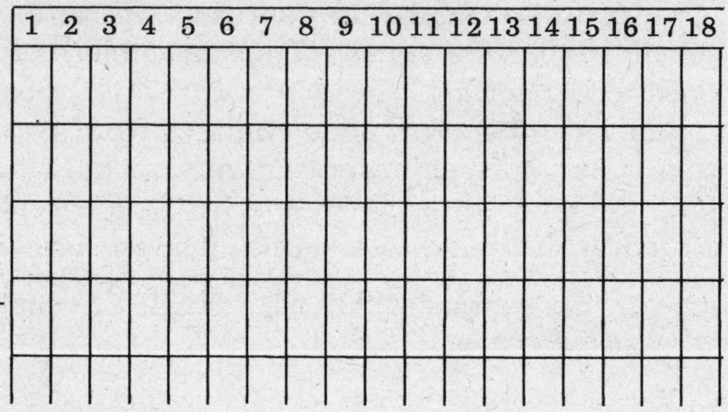

— — — — — — — — — — — — —

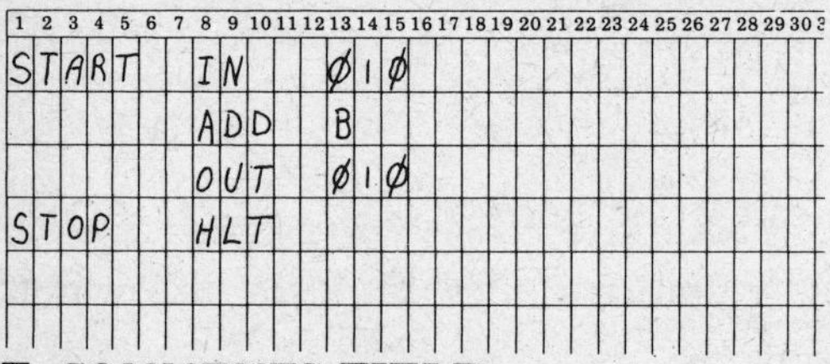

THE *COMMENTS* FIELD

10. Here's the general format again.

[*label*] *operation* [*operands*] [;*comments*]

You've learned how to code labels and operations. We're going to skip over operands for now and discuss comments first. Then we'll finish up the chapter with operands, which is a very large topic.

Comments are used to document the program. They're ignored by the assembler. They're used by human beings who are reading the program. Our assembler lets us code comments through column 71.

Why do we add comments to a program? To help others understand what the program is doing. The effect or intent of a program or segment is not always clear from reading the labels, operations, and operands.

We also write comments for ourselves. Sometimes we can forget the intention of a routine by the next day. Reading an Assembly Language program written a month ago can be like reading hieroglyphics.

(a) Are comments required or optional? ______________________

(b) Which is better, to limit comments or to use them freely?

____

(c) Suppose you're writing a program for your own purposes and it will never be seen by anyone else. Should you add comments or not?

____

— — — — — — — — — — — — —

(a) optional; (b) use comments freely; (c) yes, you should

11. Most assemblers allow you to code separate comment lines. These are lines that do not contain any label, operation, or operands—just narrative comments. For our assembler, we indicate a separate comment line by coding a semicolon in column 1. Then we can use the rest of the line (through column 71) to code our comments. (Leaving the rest of the line blank provides some spacing which makes the program easier to read.)

Figure 3.1 is an example of a well-commented program. Use it to answer the questions below.

(a) How many separate comment lines are there? ________________

(b) How many instructions contain comments? ________________

(c) Why did we include a line that contains only a semicolon in column 1? ________________

— — — — — — — — — — — —

(a) 6; (b) 3; (c) for spacing

12. Below is the sample code you formatted before. Add the following comments to the coding form:

(a) On separate lines at the beginning, say: THIS ROUTINE ADDS 1 TO AN INPUT BYTE AND WRITES THE RESULT. Break the line anywhere convenient.

(b) On the second instruction, add the comment: REG B CONTAINS 01H.

```
1 2 3 4 5 6 7 8 9 10 11 12 13 14 15 16 17 18 19 20 21 22 23 24 25 26 27 28 29 30 31 32 33 34 35 36 37 38 39 40 41 42 43 44


START  IN   Ø1Ø
       ADD  B
       OUT  Ø1Ø
STOP   HLT

```

— — — — — — — — — — —

```
1 2 3 4 5 6 7 8 9 10 11 12 13 14 15 16 17 18 19 20 21 22 23 24 25 26 27 28 29 30 31 32 33 34 35 36 37 38 39 40 41 42 43 44
; THIS  ROUTINE ADDS 1 TO AN INPUT BYTE
;  AND  WRITES THE RESULT.
START  IN   Ø1Ø
       ADD  B         ; REG B CONTAINS  Ø1H
       OUT  Ø1Ø
STOP   HLT

```

THE *OPERANDS* FIELD

13. Here's the general format again.

[*label*] *operation* [*operands*] [;*comments*]

Now we'll talk about the operands.

An operand is like the object of a sentence; it describes the receiver of the action. In the instruction JMP GETST, GETST is the operand. Control is transferred to GETST. In the instruction ADD B, B is the operand. The value in register B is added to the value in the accumulator (register A).

In each of the following instructions, what is the operand?

(a) `ADD C` : __________

(b) `SUB A` : __________

(c) `STA SOCSEC`: __________

(d) `ADI 21H` : __________

— — — — — — — — — — — —

(a) C; (b) A; (c) SOCSEC; (d) 21H

14. You must code whatever operands an instruction calls for. For example, the ADD instruction requires one operand and it must be the name of a register. The MOV instruction requires two operands, both registers. The STA instruction requires one operand and it must be a memory address—we used a data name above. The HLT instruction requires no operands. No instruction requires more than two operands.

How many operands do each of the following instructions have?

(a) `CPI 05H` : __________

(b) `STC` : __________

(c) `MVI B,0AAH`: __________

(d) `DCX B` : __________

(e) `RM` : __________

— — — — — — — — — — — —

(a) one; (b) none; (c) two; (d) one; (e) none

15. Your assembler will have coding rules for operands. Here are some fairly common rules:

- Operands must be separated from the operation code by at least one space.
- No spaces are permitted within the operands, except inside quotation marks.
- If an instruction requires two operands, they are separated by a comma.

(a) If your assembler uses the format rules as presented in this chapter and you want all your instructions to line up in columns (as in Figure 3.1), in what column will you start the label? ______________

The operation? ______________ The operands? ______________

(b) Code A and B as operands in this instruction: MOV ______________

(c) Code PSW as the operand of this instruction: PUSH ______________

– – – – – – – – – – – – – –

(a) 1, 8, 13; (b) MOV A,B; (c) PUSH PSW

There are three basic types of operands—register names, memory addresses, and immediate data. In the following frames, we'll show you how to use all three types.

REGISTER NAMES

16. You've already learned about the registers: flag, A, B, C, D, E, H, L, PC, and SP.

Many instructions require register names as operands. In the instruction format, we'll use *r1* and *r2* to indicate that a register name should be used. Here are some examples:

[*label*] ADD *r1* [;*comments*]

The ADD instruction adds the value in the specified register to the value in the A register.

[*label*] MOV *r1*,*r2* [;*comments*]

The MOV instruction moves a byte from *r2* to *r1*.

(a) Write an instruction to add the contents of register C to the accumulator. ______________

(b) Write an instruction to move the value of register D into register H.

____

– – – – – – – – – – – – – –

(a) ADD C; (b) MOV H,D

17. The letter M can also be used as a register name in an instruction. M refers to the data at a particular location in memory. As you may recall, the H–L register pair is often used to hold the address of a byte in memory. M refers to the contents of the address stored in the H–L register pair. Thus, if the H–L pair contains memory address 0134, and the byte at that address contains the letter X, then any reference to M as a register refers to the letter X, the data in the address stored in H–L.

(a) Write an instruction to add the data addressed by H–L to the value in the A register. ______________________

(b) Write an instruction to move the data stored at the location addressed by H–L to register B. ______________________

— — — — — — — — — — — — — —

(a) ADD M; (b) MOV B,M

18. When an instruction format calls for a register, you must use a single register. You can use either register H or register L in an ADD instruction. And you can use either in the MOV instruction as *r1* or *r2*. But you can't use a register pair or a double register. You can't use PC or flag directly where an instruction calls for a register. Which of the following would be valid ADD instructions?

_____ (a) ADD PSW
_____ (b) ADD A
_____ (c) ADD B
_____ (d) ADD C
_____ (e) ADD D
_____ (f) ADD E
_____ (g) ADD DE
_____ (h) ADD H
_____ (i) ADD HL
_____ (j) ADD PC
_____ (k) ADD SP
_____ (l) ADD M
_____ (m) ADD N

— — — — — — — — — — — — — —

b, c, d, e, f, h, l

19. Some instructions require register pairs as operands. In that case, you use the first name of the pair as the operand: B for the B–C pair, D for the D–E pair, H for the H–L pair, and PSW for the flag–A pair.

Here's the format of the INX instruction:

[*label*] INX *rp* [;*comments*]

This instruction increases the value of a register pair by 1. The *rp* means that a register pair is required. The instruction INX E would be rejected by the assembler because E is not the name of a register pair.

Write an instruction to increment the D-E pair. ("Increment" means to increase by 1.) ______________

— — — — — — — — — — — — — —

INX D

MEMORY ADDRESSES

20. Many instructions require memory addresses as operands. You can code a numeric address or a label of another instruction.

In the formats for these instructions, we'll use *addr* to show that a memory address is required.

Here are some examples:

[*label*] JMP *addr* [;*comments*]

This instruction causes control to be transferred to the specified memory address. Make sure the address is the first byte of a valid instruction.

[*label*] STA *addr* [;*comments*]

This instruction stores the value in register A at the specified memory address.

(a) Write an instruction to store the value in register A at address 0215H.

____

(b) Write an instruction to jump to address 0100H. ______________

(c) Write an instruction to store the contents of register A at a memory location named NEWNUM. ______________

(d) Write an instruction to jump to an instruction labeled NEXBYT.

____

— — — — — — — — — — — — — —

(a) STA 0215H; (b) JMP 0100H; (c) STA NEWNUM;
(d) JMP NEXBYT

21. If you're coding a numeric address, you'll probably have to follow rules similar to these:

- You can use the decimal, binary, hexadecimal, and octal number systems. (We're not covering octal in this book; its base is eight.) We usually use hexadecimal to code memory addresses.
- Some method must be used to differentiate between the number systems. Most assemblers use suffixes: B for binary D or nothing for decimal, H for hexadecimal. We have already been using these

suffixes in this book. (Some assemblers use prefixes rather than suffixes.)

- To differentiate between a hexadecimal number and a label, most assemblers require that all hex numbers start with numeric digits. Leading zeros are used for this purpose as in 0FFH.

(a) Write an instruction to jump to address 100H. ____________

(b) Write an instruction to jump to address C5D3H. ____________

(c) Show how to code the binary number 01100110 following our format rules. ____________

(d) Show another way to code the decimal number 255. ____________

(e) What's wrong with this instruction: JMP 0000100011111010?

____

____

(f) What's wrong with this instruction: JMP CA5FH?

____

____

(a) JMP 100H; (b) JMP 0C5D3H (don't forget the leading zero); (c) 01100110B; (d) 255D; (e) the operand will be interpreted as a decimal address because it doesn't end in B; it's way too big as decimal, since the maximum is 65,535D; (f) nothing if there's an instruction in the program labeled CA5FH, but, if it's meant as a hex address, it must start with a digit.

IMMEDIATE DATA

22. Some instructions require that the operands actually contain the data to be used. This is known as *immediate* data because the data immediately follows the operation code in the instruction. The computer doesn't have to go through an extra step of getting the data from memory or a register.

An immediate operand must represent one or two bytes of data. You can use immediate data in any form. For example, you could use 12, 12D, 0CH, or 1100B to represent the decimal value 12. One byte can hold a value up to FFH—that's 255 decimal. Immediate data that represents an address is two bytes long. Some instructions require one byte, others two bytes of immediate data.

Which of the following are valid immediate data?

_____ (a) M _____ (c) 100H

_____ (b) 0110B _____ (d) 48

_____ (e) 2456H _____ (g) E

_____ (f) 65,535H _____ (h) 24H

---

b, c, d, e, h (M and E are valid as registers but not as immediate data. 65,535H is too large, even for a two byte immediate operand.)

23. In instruction formats, we show immediate data as *i*.

[*label*] ADI *i* [;*comments*]

This instruction adds the immediate byte to the accumulator.

[*label*] MVI *r1*,*i* [;*comments*]

This instruction moves the immediate byte into the indicated register.

To code a numeric value, follow the same coding rules as for numeric addresses except that immediate data can be either one or two bytes. Most assemblers also allow you to code an ASCII value in its character form by enclosing it in single quotes. For example, you could code the letter A as 41H or as 'A'. But don't do this until you've made sure that your assembler can handle it.

(a) Code an instruction to add 1 to the accumulator. _____

(b) Code instructions to add the ASCII code for * to the accumulator. Show two ways to do this. _____

(c) Code an instruction to move FFH into register H. _____

(d) Code an instruction to move the ASCII value for B into the accumulator. _____

(a) ADI 1 (the value 1 is the same in binary, hex, and decimal, so you could have used 1D, 1H, or 1B); (b) ADI '*' or ADI 2AH (either will work, but the former is much clearer to another reader if your assembler can handle it); (c) MVI H,0FFH; (d) MVI A,'B', or MVI A,42H

USING EXPRESSIONS

24. Many assemblers allow you to use expressions as operands. An expression is like the right side of an equation, as in X = Y + 5. In instructions that require addresses as operands, the expression must work out to be a legitimate address. Thus, 3 + 5 would be okay because it works out to 8, or 0008H. But 5 — 9 would not be valid because it yields a negative

number. FFF5H + CH would not be valid because it yields a value above FFFFH. Some programmers like to use address expressions such as START + 5 where START is a label in the program. The result would be an address 5 bytes beyond the first byte of the instruction or data labeled START.

In instructions where the operand must be a one-byte immediate value, the expression must work out to fit in one byte. Your assembler may permit negative values here.

If your assembler allows expressions, it will have its own rules for how they are coded. Usually, + is used for addition and – for subtraction. Multiplication, division, and exponentiation may or may not be allowed. Compound expressions (more than two factors) may or may not be allowed.

You need to be especially careful when you use an expression as an operand. They are prone to error. For example, DATA+2 as an address refers to a location two bytes beyond the first byte of the area labelled DATA. If new lines are inserted, the value at that location may change. So you need to use caution. Expressions as operands make programs harder for someone else to read. You can solve many programming problems without using an expression as an operand. You'll see later in this book how you can use expressions as "relative addresses" to refer to any byte in memory.

Which of the expressions below would be valid in a program that uses 0FFFH bytes of storage? (You can assume the labels all refer to legitimate addresses.)

_____ (a) CONTRL+24	_____ (d) END–14H
_____ (b) 12–18	_____ (e) 1000H–4H
_____ (c) 18–12	_____ (f) END+0FFFH

— — — — — — — — — — — — — —

a, c, d, e (*b* would result in a negative value; *f* would be beyond the end of the program.)

REVIEW

Let's review what you've learned in this chapter.

- The general format of an Assembly Language instruction for the majority of assemblers is:

  [*label*] *operation* [*operands*] [;*comments*]

  Brackets indicate optional items. Italics indicate items that must be inserted. Regular type indicates items that are used as is.

- A label gives a name to the instruction. The label is then used as an operand in place of an address. Every assembler will have rules for the formation of labels. Here are some common rules:

— one to six characters
— numbers or letters, no special symbols
— start with a letter
— start in column 1
— don't use register names or operation codes

Most programmers prefer to use meaningful names as labels.

- The operation code is a two- to four-character code that is standard for 8080/8085 Assembly Language. It tells the computer what to do. Most assemblers require that it be preceded and followed by at least one space.
- Comments are used to document the intention of routines and individual instructions that might not otherwise be clear. We document for ourselves as well as others. Comments are ignored by the assembler and do not appear in the machine language version of the program. In many assemblers, they are separated from the operands by at least one space and are preceded with a semicolon or other special character.
- Most assemblers allow separate comment lines by coding a semicolon or other special symbol in column 1.
- The operands describe the object of the instruction. An instruction may have zero, one, or two operands. No spaces may appear in the operands section except within quotation marks. Two operands are usually separated by a comma.
- Some instructions require register names as operands. We use *r1* and *r2* to indicate that register names are to be used. A register pair is indicated by *rp*. Use the name of the first register of the pair, or PSW in the case of the flag–H pair.
- Some instructions require memory addresses as operands. With most assemblers, you can code the address in binary, decimal, hex, or octal. We recommend always using hex for addresses. A memory address is two bytes long and must be in the range of 0 to 65,535 (FFFFH). There must be some way of differentiating among the number systems. Many assemblers use suffixes: B for binary, H for hex, D, or nothing, for decimal. They may also require that a hex address start with a number.
- Some instructions require immediate data as operands. This is indicated by *i* in our format statements. Immediate data is data that is used directly from the instruction. The rules for formation of a two-byte immediate value are the same as the rules for the formation of numeric addresses. Some immediate values are limited to one byte; these can be negative. Many assemblers allow ASCII values to be used by enclosing the desired character in quotes thus, '#'.

- Many assemblers allow you to use expressions as operands. The expression must evaluate to a value that is in the proper range for an address or an immediate byte, whichever is called for.

CHAPTER 3 SELF-TEST

1. Here is the format for the LDAX instruction:

   [*label*] LDAX *rp* [;*comments*]

   Label each part 'O' for optional or 'R' for required.

   _____ a. label

   _____ b. LDAX

   _____ c. rp

   _____ d. comments

2. Use the format for the LDAX instruction in question 1. Label each part 'R' for 'replace with indicated data' or 'U' for use "as is."

   _____ a. label

   _____ b. LDAX

   _____ c. rp

   _____ d. ;

   _____ e. comments

3. Below is some Assembly Language code in incorrect format. Use the coding form to recode it correctly.

```
THIS ROUTINE STORES
REGISTERS A AND B IN MEMORY.

LXI   H,STORE     POINT H-L AT MEMORY
MOV   M,A
INX   H
MOV   M,B
      HLT
STORE DS 2
```

1	2	3	4	5	6	7	8	9	10	11	12	13	14	15	16	17	18	19	20	21	22	23	24	25	26	27	28	29	30	31	32	33	34	35	36	37	38	39	40	41	42	43	44	45	46	47	48	49	50	51	52	53	54	55

4. Create meaningful labels for the following.

   a. A routine that reads and stores an incoming message from the user. ______________________

   b. A memory area used to store the incoming message from question a. ______________________

   c. A routine that sorts records in a disk file in numeric order.

   ____

   d. A tax table stored in memory.

   ____

5. Which of the following need labels?

   _____ a. All instructions.

   _____ b. Instructions that are jumped to.

   _____ c. The first and last instruction of a program.

   _____ d. All data areas in memory.

   _____ e. Data areas in memory that we want to reference by name.

6. Here's the format of a LDA (load A) instruction:

   [*label*] LDA *addr* [;*comments*]

   Code an instruction to load A from address 2514H. ______________

7. Here's the format of the ADI (add immediate) instruction.

   [*label*] ADI *i* [;*comments*]

   Code an instruction to add the value 20H to the accumulator. ______

8. Here's the format of the ADD instruction:

   [*label*] ADD *r1* [;*comments*]

Code an instruction to add the contents of register C to the accumulator. ______________________

9. Here's the format of the LXI (load extended immediate) instruction:

[*label*] LXI *rp,i* [;*comments*]

Code an instruction to load 0 into the H–L pair. ______________

Check your answers below.

Self-Test Answer Key

1. a. 0
   b. R
   c. R
   d. 0

2. a. R
   b. U
   c. R
   d. U
   e. R

3.

```
; THIS ROUTINE STORES
; REGISTERS A AND B IN MEMORY.
;
       LXI   H,STORE    ; POINT H-L AT MEMORY
       MOV   M,A
       INX   H
       MOV   M,B
       HLT
STORE  DS    2
       END
```

4. Your answers are correct if they contain 1 to 6 letters and numbers with an initial letter. They're good if they are meaningful. Here are some sample correct answers.

   a. READIN
   b. INTEXT
   c. SORTER
   d. TAXTAB

5. b and e

6. LDA 2514H

7. ADI 20H

8. ADD C

9. LXI H,0

If you missed any, restudy the appropriate frames before going on to the Manual Exercise.

MANUAL EXERCISE

Now it's time to get out your assembler manual and find out the exact instruction format for your system. If you don't have an assembler yet, you'll have to skip this exercise and go on to Chapter Four.

If you do have an assembler, use the manual to find the answers to the questions below.

1. What is the general instruction format? ____________

2. What are the rules for forming a label?
   (a) Maximum number of characters? ____________
   (b) What characters can be used? ____________
   (c) Any punctuation allowed or required? ____________
   (d) Any restrictions on the first character? ____________
   (e) Any other rules? ____________

   ____

3. How are labels separated from operation codes? ____________

4. Are there any rules on the coding of operation codes? (For example, are they restricted to any particular columns?) ____________

   ____

5. What are the rules for coding operands?
   (a) What symbol is used to separate two operands? ____________
   (b) Are spaces allowed in the operands? ____________
   (c) Any other coding rules? ____________

   ____

6. What are the rules for coding comments?
   (a) How are comments separated from operands? ____________

(b) Any limitations on size? ______________________

(c) Any other rules? ______________________

____

7. How can you code a separate comment line? ______________________

____

8. How do you differentiate between binary, hex, and decimal numbers?

____

9. How do you differentiate between a label and a hex number?

____

10. Can you code addresses in binary, hex, or decimal? ______________

11. Can you code immediate data in binary, hex, or decimal? ______________

12. Can you use expressions as operands? ______________________

When you have answered all these questions, go on to Chapter Four.

CHAPTER FOUR

ELEMENTARY INSTRUCTION SET

Now you're ready to actually begin learning to use some Assembly Language instructions. In this chapter, we're going to introduce a very basic set of instructions, the ones you'll need most of the time no matter what program you're writing. You'll learn enough instructions to be able to read data from the terminal, move data around from place to place inside the microprocessor, add and subtract, write data out to the terminal, specify which instruction to process next, and stop processing.

When you have finished this chapter, you will be able to:

- Code the following instructions:
  - MOV (move)
  - MVI (move immediate)
  - LXI (load extended immediate)
  - ADD (add)
  - ADI (add immediate)
  - INX (increment extended)
  - SUB (subtract)
  - SUI (subtract immediate)
  - DCX (decrement extended)
  - JMP (jump)
  - HLT (halt)
  - CALL (call)
- Solve the following types of programming problems:
  - read data from a terminal
  - store data in memory
  - write data to a terminal
  - add and subtract single bytes
  - create closed loops
  - stop a program

DATA MOVEMENT

We'll start with a couple of data movement instructions; they move data from one place to another. There are many instructions that move data, but in this chapter you'll study the two most basic ones: MOV and MVI.

1. MOV stands for "move." The MOV instruction copies one byte of data from one register to another. It does not *remove* the data from the first location. After the move has been completed, both registers contain the same data.

The format of the instruction is:

[*label*] MOV *r1*,*r2* [;*comments*]

The first operand, *r1*, is the receiving register. The former value of this register is destroyed and the value in *r2* replaces it. The second operand, *r2*, is the sending register. Its value is not affected by the move. Both the MOV operands must be single registers; you can't use register pairs, addresses, or immediate data.

Take the time to memorize the direction of the move. It goes from *r2* to *r1*. Most people have difficulty remembering this at first. They tend to think the move goes in the other direction. (Perhaps because they read the instruction as "move *r1* to *r2*," which is wrong. It should be read "move r1 *from* r2.") It's worthwhile to get this right immediately because all the Assembly Language instructions that involve data movement work from the second operand to the first operand.

Use this example to answer the questions below:

MOV A,C

(a) Name the sending register. ______________________

(b) Name the receiving register. ______________________

(c) What is wrong with this instruction: MOV ART,'*'?

____

— — — — — — — — — — — — —

(a) C; (b) A; (c) the operands aren't registers

2. Let's see how the MOV instruction works. In this example the instruction says to move to C from A. The A register contains 15 (hex 0F) in binary form, and the C register contains 2 (hex 02). After the move, the A Register still contains 15 because it is the sending register. The C register also contains 15. The previous value of the C register, 2, has been lost.

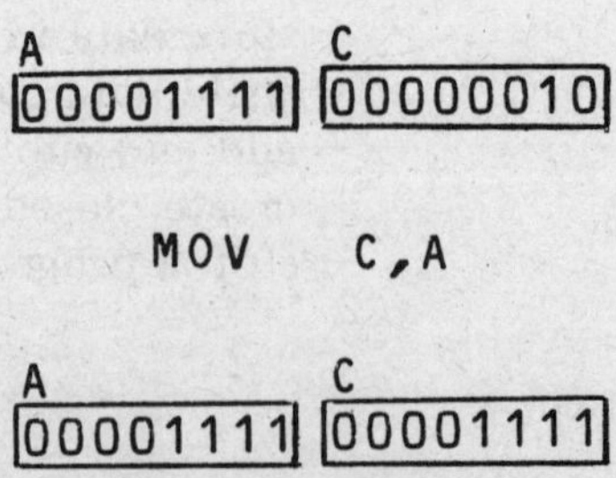

```
A                      L
|00001111|             |00000000|

          MOV   L,A

A                      L
|00001111|             |00001111|
```

In this example, the A register contains 15 and the L register contains 0. The instruction says to move to L from A. After the move, both registers contain 15. The former value of the L register has been lost.

(a) Write an instruction to move the value in register A into register C.

____

(b) Write an instruction to move the value in register E to register L.

____

(c) In the diagram below, show the values of the registers after the move.

```
A              B
|00000000|     |01010101|

     MOV   B,A

A              B
|        |     |        |
```

- - - - - - - - - - - - - -

(a) `MOV  C,A`; (b) `MOV  L,E`; (c) A `00000000` B `00000000`

3. The MOV instruction can reference a memory address as M. Remember that M refers to the byte at the memory address contained in the H–L register pair.

```
A            H-L                  byte 51
|00010101|   |0000000000110011|   |00010000|

             MOV   M,A

A            H-L                  byte 51
|00010101|   |0000000000110011|   |00010101|
```

In this example, the A register contains 21. The H–L pair contain the memory address 51. The byte at address 51 contains the value 16. The instruction says to move data to memory from A. After the move, the A register and the H–L pair are unchanged. But the byte at address 51 has been changed to contain the same value as the A register, 21.

(a) Write an instruction to move the value in memory to register A.

____

(b) Write an instruction to move the value in register D to memory.

____

(c) Write an instruction to move the value in register A to memory.

____

(d) In the diagram below, show the values in the registers and in memory after the move.

C	H-L	byte 10
01111110	0000000000001010	11110000

```
MOV   C,M
```

C	H-L	byte 10

\- - - - - - - - - - - - -

(a) `MOV   A,M;`   (b) `MOV   M,D;`   (c) `MOV   M,A;`

(d) C `11110000` H-L `0000000000001010` byte 10 `11110000`

4. The MOV instruction moves one byte at a time. If you want to move more than one byte, you have to write more than one instruction. For example, suppose you want to move the values in registers A and B to registers H and L. You would need two instructions:

```
MOV   H,A

MOV   L,B
```

The MOV instruction treats the paired registers as single registers. The instruction MOV B,D moves the value of register D to register B but has no effect on registers C or E.

(a) Write a set of instructions to move the values of the D–E pair to the H–L pair.

____

____

(b) Write a set of instructions to move the value in the A register to the B, C, and D registers.

(c) In the diagram below, indicate the values in the registers after the MOV instruction has been processed.

B [01010101]   H-L [00000000 | 11111111]

MOV H,B

B [   ]   H-L [|]

(d) Extra Thought Question: See if you can write a set of instructions to swap the values in registers H and L. (You may use any other registers in the process.)

- - - - - - - - - - - - - -

(a) MOV H,D

MOV L,E

(b) MOV B,A

MOV C,A (or MOV C,B)

MOV D,A (or MOV D,C or MOV D,B)

(c) B [0101010]   H-L [01010101 | 11111111]

(d) MOV E,H

MOV H,L

MOV L,E

(This is not the only solution, but it demonstrates the *nature* of the correct answer. You need to preserve the value in one register by moving it to a third register (we've used E in our solution); then move the value from the other register into the saved one; and finally, move the saved value into the other register. Later on, we'll show you a way to swap the values in two registers using only two instructions—without using a third register.)

5. Now that you've seen how to use the MOV instruction, let's turn our attention to the MVI instruction. MVI stands for "move immediate." It moves one byte of immediate data into a register. Here's the format:

MVI *r1*,*i*

The first operand, *r1*, is the receiving register just as with the MOV instruction. The second operand, *i*, is a byte of immediate data. When the instruction is executed, the immediate data is moved into the receiving register.

(a) Show three ways to represent the decimal value ten as an immediate byte. ____________________

(b) Show two ways to represent the ASCII character Z as an immediate byte. ____________________

(c) What value will the instruction MVI B,4 place in register B? (show the binary digits) ____________________

— — — — — — — — — — — — —

(a) 0AH, 10D, 10, 1010B (any three); (b) 5AH or 'Z'; (c) 0000 0100B

6. As you've seen, the instruction MVI A,25 would move the decimal value 25 (converted to binary) into register A. (Up to decimal 255 fits in one byte.) There are many ways to express an immediate value. You can use whichever suits you best.

(a) Write an instruction to move the ASCII code for the letter A into the B register. ____________________

(b) Write an instruction to move decimal eleven into the A register.

____

(c) Write instructions to move binary '00000010 00001111' into the D–E pair. (Feel free to use hex equivalents.)

____

____

(d) Write instructions to move high values (all ones) into the H–L pair.

____

____

— — — — — — — — — — — — —

(a) MVI B,'A'; (b) MVI A,11 (You could have used many different means to express the decimal eleven. For example, you could have used 0BH or 00001011B.); (c) MVI D,2H; MVI E,0FH; (d) MVI H,0FFH; MVI L,0FFH (Remember that hex operands can't start with a letter.)

7. Another instruction that moves data is LXI (load extended immediate). It loads a two-byte immediate value into a register pair. In the 8080/8085 mnemonic codes, "X" (extended) usually means that a register pair is involved. "I" usually means an immediate value is involved.

The format of LXI is:

[*label*] LXI *rp*,*i* [;*comments*]

The allowable values for *rp* are B, D, H, or SP. You cannot use LXI to load a value into the PSW. On the other hand, you can load a value into the stack pointer even though it's a double register rather than a paired one.

The value for *i* can be in the range of 0 to 65,535 since a two-byte value is allowed.

Which of the following are legitimate LXI instructions?

_____ (a)	`LXI A,255`	_____ (e)	`LXI H,10000H`
_____ (b)	`LXI B,4096H`	_____ (f)	`LXI PSW,23AAH`
_____ (c)	`LXI C,0`	_____ (g)	`LXI SP,0FFFH`
_____ (d)	`LXI D,0`	_____ (h)	`LXI PC,231H`

– – – – – – – – – – – – – –

(b), (d), and (g) are correct ((a), (c), (f), and (h) do not refer to legitimate register pairs and (e) has a value too large for two bytes). Notice that none of the hex values starts with a letter.

8. The LXI instruction is often used to load an address into a register pair. For example, suppose you want to move the data at address 432CH into register D. You can't move it directly with MOV or MVI, since neither uses an address as an operand. What you can do is load the address into the H–L pair with LXI H,432CH. Then you can use MOV D,M to copy the data at the address into register D.

Write instructions to solve the following problems.

(a) Move zero into the H–L pair. ______________________________

(b) Move 2100H into the B–C pair. ____________________________

(c) Move 3000H into the stack pointer. _________________________

(d) Store the contents of register B at memory address 500H.

____

____

- - - - - - - - - - - - -

(a) LXI H,0; (b) LXI B,2100H; (c) LXI SP,3000H;
(d)
```
LXI   H,500H
MOV   M,B
```

You have now learned three very useful instructions. You can move data from one register to another (MOV) and you can move immediate data to any register (MVI) or register pair (LXI).

In the next part of this chapter, we'll look at some of the addition instructions. You'll learn how to add two registers and how to add immediate data to a value in a register.

THE ADDITION INSTRUCTIONS

9. The basic addition instruction is ADD. It adds the value contained in a specified register to the value in register A. The result is stored in register A. (The former value of A is destroyed.)

You don't get any choice about the receiving field in this instruction; it is always register A. Remember that register A is also called the accumulator because it is used for arithmetic operations.

The format of the ADD instruction is:

ADD *r1*

The only operand, *r1*, defines the sending field. If you say ADD B, the value in register B will be added to the value in register A. The result is stored in A. The value in register B is not affected by the operation.

Consider the instruction ADD H.

(a) What is the receiving register? ______________________

(b) What is the sending register? ______________________

(c) Where is the result of the addition stored? ______________________

(d) What is wrong with this instruction: ADD OLDBAL

____

(e) What do you think would be the effect of this instruction: ADD A

____

- - - - - - - - - - - - -

(a) A; (b) H; (c) in register A; (d) it doesn't name a register; (e) add A to A, or double the value in register A

10. Here are some examples of how the ADD instruction works.

```
A              C
00000000       00000111

      ADD   C

A              C
00000111       00000111
```

In this example, register A contains 0 and register C contains 7. The command says to add register C to register A. After the instruction is executed, register C still contains 7 and register A contains the sum of 0 and 7.

```
A              E
00000101       00011100

      ADD   E

A              E
00100001       00011100
```

In this example, register A contains 5 and register E contains 1CH. The instruction says to add the value in register E to the value in register A. After the command has been executed, register E still contains 1CH and register A contains the sum of 5H + 1CH, which is 21H.

(a) Write an instruction to add the value in register B to the value in register A. ____________

(b) Write an instruction to add the value in register H to the value in register A. ____________

(c) Suppose you want to add the values of registers B and C. Write a set of instructions to accomplish this. (Remember to work in the A register.)

____

____

- - - - - - - - - - - - -

(a) ADD B; (b) ADD H; (c) MOV A,B; ADD C; or MOV A,C; ADD B

11. The ADD instruction can also reference a memory address from the H–L pair.

```
A              H-L                      byte 7
|00001100|     |0000000000000111|       |00110000|

                    ADD  M

A              H-L                      byte 7
|00111100|     |0000000000000111|       |00110000|
```

In this example, register A contains 0CH. The H–L pair contain the address 0007H. At address 7, the byte contains the value 30H. After the instruction has been completed, the H–L pair contain the same value they did before; the value at address 7 is the same. Register A contains the sum of 0CH + 30H, which is 3CH.

(a) Write an instruction to add the value in memory to the value in register A. ______________________

(b) Suppose you want to add the contents of registers B and A and store the results in memory. Write a set of instructions to accomplish this.

____

____

____

— — — — — — — — — — — — —

(a) ADD M; (b) ADD B; MOV M,A

12. Suppose you want to increment the value in register L by 1. The arithmetic will have to take place in the A register. Then you'll have to get the result back into the L register. Using MVI, MOV, and ADD, write a set of instructions to accomplish this.

____

____

____

— — — — — — — — — — — — —

```
MVI  A,1
ADD  L
MOV  L,A
```

(This is one possible solution to the problem. The arithmetic must take place in the A register so either the 1 or the value in the L register must be moved into A and then the other value added in. The result must be moved back to the L register. You'll learn an easier way to increment the L register later on.)

13. Arithmetic instructions affect the status flags in the PSW register. You have already studied these flags, but let's review them briefly.

C: The carry flag is turned on if the arithmetic operation resulted in a carry outside the accumulator. Otherwise, it is turned off. That is, this flag is a 1 if the result is too large for the A register and overflows it.

Z: The zero flag is turned on if the arithmetic operation resulted in zero. Otherwise, it is turned off.

S: The sign flag is set to match the most significant (leftmost) bit in the result in the A register. The system lets you use this bit as a sign indicator. We'll treat negative values later in the book.

Other flags are also set, but these are the most important ones affected.

Below are before-and-after diagrams for an ADD instruction. Examine the diagrams, then answer the questions.

before			*after*	
C: 0	A: 01001100		C: ?	A: 11000100
Z: 1		ADD B	Z: ?	
S: 0	B: 01111000		S: ?	B: 01111000

(a) What is the value of the carry flag after the operation? ________

(b) The zero flag? ________

(c) The sign flag? ________

(d) Is the result correct? ________

– – – – – – – – – – – – – –

(a) 0; (b) 0; (c) 1; (d) yes—no carry has been lost

14. The ADI instruction (add immediate) is very similar to the ADD instruction except that the operand is one byte of immediate data. The format is:

ADI *i*

The immediate value is added to the accumulator. The status flags are set as with the ADD instruction.

(a) Write an instruction to add decimal 15 to the accumulator.

____

(b) Write an instruction to add 12H to the accumulator.

____

(c) Write an instruction to add the letter 'A' to the accumulator. (This is perfectly legal. All the processor sees is a binary value; it doesn't care what it means to humans.)

____

(d) Earlier, you wrote a set of instructions to add 1 to the L register. Rewrite that set of instructions to use MOV and ADI only.

____

____

____

- - - - - - - - - - - - - -

(a) ADI 15; (b) ADI 12H; (c) ADI 'A';
(d)
```
MOV  A,L

ADI  1

MOV  L,A
```

Now you've learned the two main addition instructions and it's time to learn the comparable subtraction instructions.

15. The two main subtraction instructions are SUB (subtract) and SUI (subtract immediate). They work similarly to the comparable addition instructions. The value in the named register is subtracted from the value in the A register, and the result is stored in the A register.

Write the correct instructions for each of the following operations.

(a) Subtract the B register from the A register. ____________________

(b) Subtract the E register from the A register. ____________________

(c) Subtract 2 from the A register. ____________________

(d) Subtract 1 from the L register.

____

____

____

(e) Subtract the B register from the memory location whose address is stored in H–L.

____

____

____

\- - - - - - - - - - - - -

(a) SUB B; (b) SUB E; (c) SUI 2; (d) MOV A,L; SUI 1; MOV L,A;
(e) MOV A,M; SUB B; MOV M,A

ADJUSTING THE H-L REGISTER

16. Because the H–L pair points to a memory address, we frequently want to increase or decrease it by one so that it points to the next or previous byte. You could use ADI or SUI to add or subtract 1. But there are special instructions to do this, as well.

INX *rp*
DCX *rp*

In these instructions, *rp* stands for a register pair. Use B for the B–C pair, D for the D–E pair, or H for the H–L pair. You cannot use these instructions with the PSW.

The INX (increment extended) instruction adds one to the value in the pair. The DCX (decrement extended) instruction subtracts one from the value in the pair. Neither INX nor DCX operations affect the status flags. (Many programmers feel that this is a serious defect in 8080/8085 Assembly Language. You have to code several extra instructions to make sure your value is still in the proper range. Other programmers feel that it is an advantage.)

(a) Code an instruction to add one to the H–L pair. ________________

(b) Code an instruction to subtract one from the H–L pair. ____________

(c) Code a set of instructions to set memory addresses 0200H, 0201H, and 0202H to zeros.

____

____

____

____

(d) INX and DCX (do/do not) __________ affect the status flags.

\- - - - - - - - - - - - -

(a) INX H;
(b) DCX H;

(c)
```
LXI  H,0200H    set H-L register to address 0200H
MVI  M,0        move 0 to 0200H
INX  H          set H-L register to address 0201H
MVI  M,0        move 0 to 0201H
INX  H          set H-L register to address 0202H
MVI  M,0        move 0 to 0202H
```

(In Chapter 6, we'll show you how to code this same routine as a loop; it's much easier.)

(d) do not

INPUT AND OUTPUT

Almost every program requires input and output (I/O) operations. Unfortunately, these are just about the hardest operations to handle. In Chapter 10 you'll see how to write an I/O routine. In this chapter, we'll call routines for the I/O operations. In an actual program, called routines are included at the end of the program. We aren't showing them here because then the examples would get too long to be useful. You'll learn later in this book how to code called routines.

17. A *routine* is a block of code that accomplishes a function. An input routine would read data from a terminal or other device. An output routine would send data to a terminal or other device. (We call this "writing" data.) Once you have written such a routine, you can use it over and over again by *calling* it.

Figure 4.1 illustrates how calling works. The bold numbers indicate the order in which the instructions are executed. When the CALL instruction is executed, control is transferred to the routine named INPUT. ("Control" refers to the instruction currently controlling the computer.) All the instructions in that routine are executed. Then control returns to the instruction immediately following the CALL instruction.

There are many advantages to calling, but we're not going to explore them now. Chapter 10 is devoted to the subject. For now, we're going to use CALLs to accomplish input and output without having to code the I/O routines. To assemble a program that uses CALLs, you need to include the called routines in your source code.

(a) A block of code that accomplishes a function can be called a

____

(b) To where does a CALL instruction transfer control?

____

(c) When a called routine finishes, where does control go? ____________

____

```
                .
                .
                .
          1   INX    H
          2   MOV    M,B
          3   CALL   INPUT
         12   MOV    A,B
         13   CPI    40H
                .
                .
                .
                .
                .
INPUT     4   XRA    A
          5   OUT    1DH
          6   IN     1DH
          7   ANI    1
          8   JZ     INPUT
          9   IN     1CH
         10   ANI    7FH
         11   RET
```

FIGURE 4.1. Effect of CALL

– – – – – – – – – – – – –

(a) routine; (b) to the beginning of a routine; (c) back to the instruction after the CALL instruction

18. In our programs, we'll use these two instructions:

CALL INPUT
CALL OUTPUT

The routine named INPUT will read one byte from a console device (such as a video terminal) and move the byte into B register. The OUTPUT routine will write one byte from B register to the same console device. ("Write" means that the byte is sent to the terminal to be displayed.) The routines will take care of moving bytes back and forth between A and B registers. The value in A will be the same after the CALL is executed as it was before.

Suppose we want to write the message "HI" on the console. Here's the program we would use.

```
MVI  B,'H'
CALL OUTPUT
MVI  B,'I'
CALL OUTPUT
```

Notice that we have to load the B register before calling OUTPUT and that we have to write one byte at a time.

(a) Code a routine to write an asterisk (*) on the console.

(b) Code a routine to read one character from the console and store it in memory.

(c) Code a routine to write whatever is in the H–L pair on the console.

— — — — — — — — — — — —

(a)
```
MVI  B,'*'
CALL OUTPUT
```

(b)
```
CALL INPUT
MOV  M,B
```

(c)
```
MOV  B,H
CALL OUTPUT
MOV  B,L
CALL OUTPUT
```

19. Here is a short Assembly Language routine.

```
MIXER  CALL INPUT
       MOV  A,B
       ADI  1
       MOV  B,A
       CALL OUTPUT
```

Which of the following best describes the function of this routine? (Choose one.)

_____ (a) It reads characters from the console and keeps a count of the number of characters read in the A register. The count is displayed on the console after each character.

_____ (b) It reads a character from the console and displays that same character on the console. Thus, the console user sees the character that was typed. (This is known as echoing.)

_____ (c) It reads a character from the console, adds one to the character value, and displays the new character on the console. If a '3' was typed, a '4' would be displayed.

— — — — — — — — — — — — —

(c) is the correct answer

20. In the last frame, we mentioned a very important function—echoing. Echoing is the process of displaying on the console whatever is typed. Write an echo routine as described in (b) in the last frame.

— — — — — — — — — — — — —

Here is our echo routine:

```
ECHO    CALL INPUT
        CALL OUTPUT
```

The first instruction reads the character from the console keyboard. The second writes it on the console display. You could have omitted the label.

21. Revise the ECHO routine you wrote so that the character is stored at memory location 200H as well as being displayed. (Remember the LXI instruction to load an address into the H–L pair.)

— — — — — — — — — — — — —

Here is our solution:

```
CALL INPUT
CALL OUTPUT
LXI  H,200H
MOV  M,B
```

We have added an instruction to set the H–L pair to 0200H, then store the character in B at that address. Your CALL OUTPUT instruction could follow the MOV instruction.

22. Write a routine to read two characters from the console and store them in memory location 0100H and 0101H.

— — — — — — — — — — — — —

There are many possible solutions to this problem. We can't show them all to you, but here's our routine:

```
LXI  H,0100H
CALL INPUT
MOV  M,B
INX  H
CALL INPUT
MOV  M,B
```

First we point H–L at address 0100H. Then we read and store one character. Then we use INX to increment H–L by one so that it's pointing at 0101H. Then we read and store the next character.

23. Code a routine to start a new line. To do this, you need to write a carriage return character and a line feed character, in either order.

A note about the ASCII control codes: You'll have to use the hex values as operands. You can't code 'LF' for line feed or 'CR' for carriage return. The system would interpret 'LF' as a two-byte value of the letter 'L' (4CH) followed by the letter 'F' (46H). Now code the new-line routine.

```
MVI    B,0DH              ;CARRIAGE RETURN
CALL   OUTPUT
MVI    B,0AH              ;LINE FEED
CALL   OUTPUT
```

TRANSFERRING CONTROL

24. The CALL instruction transfers control to a routine. When the routine has been executed, control returns to the statement following CALL. Another instruction, JMP, also transfers control to a named routine. But control doesn't return automatically from a JMP. If we say JMP INPUT, control would transfer to the INPUT routine and processing would continue from there. The address named in the JMP instruction must be the first byte of a valid instruction. JMP 100H would cause a branch to address 100H, which must be the beginning of an instruction. Here's how you might use JMP.

```
HILINE MVI  B,'H'
       CALL OUTPUT
       MVI  B,'I'
       CALL OUTPUT
       JMP  HILINE
```

This would create a *closed loop*. The computer would continue to display HI until you restarted the machine.

You can use JMP to transfer control to any instruction that has a label. You can create loops or branch as needed.

(a) Write an instruction to transfer control to a routine named LABL and then return control. ____________________

(b) Write an instruction to transfer control to a routine named LABL and leave it there. ____________________

(c) Rewrite your ECHO routine (from frame 17) as a closed loop.

____

____

____

– – – – – – – – – – – – –

(a) CALL LABL; (b) JMP LABL;

(c)
```
ECHO    CALL  INPUT
        CALL  OUTPUT
        JMP   ECHO
```

ENDING INSTRUCTIONS

So far, you have learned how to code several critical functions. You can move data, add and subtract it, and read and write it. The final set of instructions you will learn in this chapter are used to end your program.

25. The microprocessor will continue executing instructions until it is *told* to stop. If your program does not stop itself, then the microprocessor will keep on going. It will pick up the next instruction, execute that, then pick up the next instruction, and so forth. Eventually, it will pick up data that is not meant to be an instruction. When it tries to execute that, it may not be able to do so and it will stop. You usually have to restart the system manually before you can do any more processing.

There are many names for the condition where the processor has stopped because it can't figure out what to do next. Some people say "abend" for "*ab*normal *end*ing." You might also hear "abort," "crash," and "bomb." We'll use the term "bomb."

Bombs can be caused by a lot of things. A missing stop instruction is just one way to bomb. To avoid this bomb, always intentionally stop your program when the processing is finished.

(a) If your program does not stop itself intentionally, what may happen?

____

(b) A missing stop instruction is the only thing that will cause a bomb.

True or false? ______________________________________

– – – – – – – – – – – – –

(a) the program may bomb; (b) false—there are lots of causes

26. There are several ways you can stop processing. One way is to use the HLT (halt) instruction. HLT causes the microprocessor to just stop dead;

it will execute no more instructions until you manually restart it. Here's an example:

```
MIXER   CALL   INPUT
        MOV    A,B
        ADI    1
        MOV    B,A
        CALL   OUTPUT
        HLT
```

We have added the HLT statement to the MIXER routine you first saw in frame 16. Now the routine reads a character, adds 1 to it, writes the new character, and stops processing.

(a) In a previous frame, you wrote an echo routine. Add an instruction to the basic routine so it stops processing after echoing one character.

(b) After a HLT instruction has been processed, how can you restart the computer? ______________________

— — — — — — — — — — — —

(a) Here's our echo routine now:

```
ECHO   CALL INPUT
       CALL OUTPUT
       HLT
```

(b) You have to restart it manually.

27. Another way to stop processing is to intentionally put the computer in a *closed loop.* As you saw earlier, a *loop* is a routine that is repeated one or more times. We create loops using jump statements. Here's an example:

```
MIXER   CALL  INPUT
        MOV   A,B
        ADI   1
        MOV   B,A
        CALL  OUTPUT
        JMP   MIXER
```

JMP MIXER tells the computer to execute the line labeled MIXER as the next instruction. Thus, control is returned to the top of the routine. The routine is executed a second time, then a third time, and so on.

A closed loop is a loop that has no natural exit. That is, once control has entered the loop, there's no way for it to get out again. The computer user has to physically stop the program, usually by restarting the system. The MIXER routine above is probably a closed loop; it's closed if there are no exits in any of the called routines that we can't see.

(a) Which routine below is a loop? ______________________

```
STORE    CALL   INPUT              WRITE    INX    H
         INX    H                           MOV    B,M
         MOV    M,B                         CALL   OUTPUT
         JMP    STORE                       HLT
```

(b) Is it an open loop or a closed loop? ______________________

(c) How do you get out of a closed loop? ______________________

Extra Thought Questions:

(d) What does the STORE routine (above) do? ______________________

____

(e) What does the WRITE routine (above) do? ______________________

____

(a) STORE; (b) closed; (c) by restarting the system;
(d) It reads a character from the terminal, increments the memory address in H–L by 1, stores the character in memory, and cycles back to the top of the routine again for the next character, which will be stored in the next memory location.
(e) It increments H–L by 1 and writes one character from memory.

28. If you want to use a closed loop as a way of terminating processing, here's what you do:

```
MIXER    CALL  INPUT
         MOV   A,B
         ADI   1
         MOV   B,A
         CALL  OUTPUT
STOPPR   JMP   STOPPR
```

Notice that the JMP instruction refers to itself. When control reaches this instruction, a very tight closed loop is entered. This one command will be repeated endlessly until the program is interrupted externally. Many systems prefer this method of ending a program to the HLT instruction.

Rewrite your ECHO routine so that it is executed once and terminated by a closed loop.

```
ECHO    CALL INPUT
        CALL OUTPUT
STOP    JMP  STOP
```

(You could use any legal label on the JMP instruction.)

29. You have learned two ways to terminate processing in Assembly Language—the HLT instruction and a closed loop. Whichever way you choose to use is up to you. We've noticed most programmers prefer the closed loop.

If you use an operating system with your microprocessor, there may be a better way to stop. For example, we use CP/M®. We terminate our programs with the instruction JMP 0 which returns control to the operating system. Therefore, we don't have to restart the system when our programs stop. You may have a similar instruction available to you. Check your system manuals to find out.

Which instruction is the *best* way for you to terminate your programs?

_____ (a) `HLT`

_____ (b) `STOP   JMP   STOP`

_____ (c) `JMP 0`

_____ (d) Either a or b above

_____ (e) None of the above

The correct answer depends on your system. If you use CP/M®, then (c) might be the correct answer. If not, then (d) might be the correct answer. If you use another operating system, then (e) might be the correct answer.

REVIEW

In this chapter, you have learned a very basic set of instructions that you will need for almost every program. You can move data including immediate data. You can add and subtract data including immediate data. You can load, increment, and decrement a register pair. You can read and write data by using the CALL instruction. You can transfer control within the program, and you can halt processing.

In the self-test for this chapter, you'll get a chance to write routines that use these instructions.

Appendix C contains a reference summary of all the instructions in 8080/8085 Assembly Language. The instructions you have learned in this chapter are summarized there. You may refer to that summary at any time while taking the Self-Test or while studying later chapters. Caution: Don't experiment with instructions you haven't studied yet. All the exercises in this book are designed to let you practice instructions you have already studied.

CHAPTER 4 SELF-TEST

Part I. Write the correct instruction or routine for each of the following functions.

1. Move the value from register C to register L. ____________

2. Move the value from register B to memory. ____________

3. Move the value from memory to register D. ____________

4. Add 5 to the value in register A. ____________

5. Add the value in register C to the value in register A. ____________

6. Subtract 1 from the value in register A. ____________

7. Increment the H–L pair. ____________

8. Decrement the D–E pair. ____________

9. Subtract the value in register D from the value in register A. ____________

10. Add the values in registers B and C. Store the sum in register C.

    ____

    ____

    ____

11. Subtract the value in register D from the value in register E. Leave the remainder in register E.

____

____

____

12. Subtract 2 from the value in register B.

____

____

____

13. Read a character from the console and store it at memory address 225H.

____

____

____

14. Write the letter A.

____

____

____

15. Send a line feed character (see your ASCII chart) to the console.

____

____

____

16. Show two ways to stop processing.

____

____

Check your answers to Part I before going on to Part II.

Self-Test Answer Key, Part I

1. `MOV L,C`

2. `MOV M,B`

3.
```
MOV  D,M
```

4.
```
ADI  5
```

5.
```
ADD  C
```

6.
```
SUI  1
```

7.
```
INX  H
```

8.
```
DCX  D
```

9.
```
SUB  D
```

10.
```
MOV  A,B
ADD  C
MOV  C,A
```

11.
```
MOV  A,E
SUB  D
MOV  E,A
```

12.
```
MOV  A,B
SUI  2
MOV  B,A
```

13.
```
CALL INPUT
LXI  H,225H
MOV  M,B
```

14.
```
MVI  B,'A'
CALL OUTPUT
```

15.
```
MVI  B,0AH
CALL OUTPUT
```

16.
```
HLT
STOP  JMP  STOP
```

Now go on to part II of the Self-Test.

Part II. Write a complete Assembler program to read two digits from the terminal, add them, and write the answer. Assume that the two digits will be between 0 and 4, so that the sum will be a single digit. (Don't worry about negative numbers, two digit numbers, and so forth.)

Programming notes: Notice in your ASCII chart that if you add the values for 2 and 3 (32H and 33H) the sum is 65H, or the ASCII letter 'e'. To keep the answer numeric, you have to subtract 30H from it. 32H + 33H – 30H = 35H, which will print as 5.

Start a new line after each input digit.

1. Read the first character from the terminal.
2. Echo the character so the user can see what was typed. (This is always good practice unless secret codes are being typed.)
3. Store the character in register A.
4. Start a new line on the terminal. (Write a carriage return and a line feed.)
5. Read the second character.
6. Echo the character.
7. Add the two characters.
8. Subtract 30H from the sum.
9. Start a new line.
10. Write the sum on the terminal.
11. Stop processing.

FIGURE 4.2. *Logic for Self-Test Problem*

The key to a good program is in the logic design. Figure 4.2 itemizes the steps in our logic for this program. If you're not sure how to attack this problem, examine Figure 4.2 *before* trying to code your program. If you want to try solving the problem yourself, sketch out your logic first, then check our logic before writing any code.

Make your program as complete as possible, but assume the INPUT and OUTPUT routines will follow your coding; don't try to code them.

Self-Test Answer Key, Part II

Here is our program. We have numbered the lines so we can discuss them below.

```
 1.  ADDER  CALL INPUT
 2.         CALL OUTPUT ; ECHO
 3.         MOV  A,B
 4.         MVI  B,0AH  ; CARRIAGE RETURN
 5.         CALL OUTPUT
 6.         MVI  B,0DH  ; LINE FEED
 7.         CALL OUTPUT
 8.         CALL INPUT
 9.         CALL OUTPUT ; ECHO
10.         ADD  B
11.         SUI  30H    ; FIX ASCII CODE
12.         MVI  B,0AH  ; CARRIAGE RETURN
13.         CALL OUTPUT
14.         MVI  B,0DH  ; LINE FEED
15.         CALL OUTPUT
16.         MOV  B,A
17.         CALL OUTPUT
18.         HLT
19.  INPUT  routine would go here.
       .
       .
       .
20.  OUTPUT routine would go here.
       .
       .
       .
```

Lines 1 to 3 read and echo the first character and store it in register C.

Lines 4 to 7 start a new line by writing a carriage return character (0AH) followed by a line feed character (0DH).

Lines 8 to 9 read and echo the second character and store it in register A.

Lines 10 and 11 add the two characters and subtract 30H.

Lines 12 to 15 start a new line.

Lines 16 and 17 write the answer on the terminal.

Line 18 halts processing.

Lines 19 and 20 indicate where the INPUT and OUTPUT routines would be placed.

Your program does not need to match our answer exactly in order to be correct. For example, you may have chosen to store the first character someplace other than register B. You may not have started new terminal lines at the same time that we did. There are two important factors to evaluating your program when you compare it to ours:

1. Is it syntactically correct; that is, will the assembler accept it?
2. Will it accomplish the function described in the problem?

It would be beneficial to actually try out your program on your system before moving on to Chapter 5. But you'll need to be able to do the following things:

1. Code (or CALL) INPUT and OUTPUT routines that will reach your terminal.
2. Enter your program on your system.
3. Assemble and load your program. Interpret error messages and correct your program accordingly.

Since there are so many different systems, we can't tell you how to accomplish the above functions. For item 1, you may be able to borrow a routine from some other program that runs in your system. For items 2 and 3, your assembler manual should provide the necessary information. Appendix D also discusses these procedures.

If you can get it going, please test your program. Start it up, then type two digits between 0 and 4. The computer should provide the answer. A correct interchange looks like this:

```
3
4
7
```

CHAPTER FIVE

ASSEMBLER DIRECTIVES

Your system will have a set of instructions that control not the computer but the assembler program. We call these the assembler directives, because they direct the assembler itself, rather than your programs. (Another common term for them is pseudo-operations.)

The assembler directives are not standardized; different assemblers will have different directives. The set that we present in this chapter is fairly common, however.

When you have completed your study of this chapter, you will be able to:

- answer questions about the assembly process;
- identify the difference between an assembler directive and a machine instruction;
- code the following assembler directives: DS, DB, EQU, ORG, and END.

In order to understand the assembler directives you have to understand what the assembler does. And in order to understand what the assembler does, you have to understand a little bit about 8080/8085 machine language.

1. Figure 5.1 is a printout from an 8080 system that shows both the Assembly Language code (on the right) and the matching machine language code (in the middle). On the left shows the beginning memory address of each instruction.

In this instruction:

```
0000   CD0D00   MIXER   CALL INPUT
```

(a) What's the memory address? ____________________

(b) What's the machine code? ____________________

(c) What's the Assembly Language code? ____________________

```
0000 CD0D00    MIXER  CALL INPUT
0003 78               MOV  A,B
0004 C601             ADI  1
0006 47               MOV  B,A
0007 CD1B00           CALL OUTPUT
000A C30000           JMP  MIXER
000D F5        INPUT  PUSH A
000E CD2E00    STATUS CALL TEST
0011 CA0E00           JZ   STATUS
0014 DB1C             IN   1CH
0016 E67F             ANI  7FH
0018 47               MOV  B,A
0019 F1               POP  A
001A C9               RET
001B F5        OUTPUT PUSH A
001C 3E10      STATOT MVI  A,10H
001E D31D             OUT  1DH
0020 DB1D             IN   1DH
0022 E60C             ANI  00001100B
0024 FE0C             CPI  00001100B
0026 C21C00           JNZ  STATOT
0029 78               MOV  A,B
002A D31C             OUT  1CH
002C F1               POP  A
002D C9               RET
002E AF        TEST   XRA  A
002F D31D             OUT  1DH
0031 DB1D             IN   1DH
0033 E601             ANI  1
0035 C8               RZ
0036 3EFF             MVI  A,0FFH
0038 C9               RET
0039                  END
```

FIGURE 5.1. Assembler Listing

(a) 0000; (b) CD0D00; (c) MIXER CALL INPUT

2. A machine language instruction can be composed of one, two, or three bytes. The first byte is always the operation code. This one-byte code tells the 8080 or 8085 processor exactly what to do. For example, to an 8080 or 8085 chip, 76H always means 'halt'. The Assembly Language instruction HLT is always translated as 76H.

In the listing, you can see all the operation codes:

```
       ↓
0000  [CD]0D00  MIXER  CALL INPUT
0003  [78]             MOV  A,B
etc.
```

(a) How long is a machine language instruction? ______________________

(b) Which part of the machine language instruction is the operation code?

____

(c) In this instruction:

```
0005   C601   ADI   1
```

What is the operation code for ADI? ______________________

— — — — — — — — — — — —

(a) 1-3 bytes; (b) the first byte; (c) C6H

3. Many machine instructions are only one-byte long. They have only an operation code and no operands. Assembly Language instructions that have no operands, such as HLT, get translated into one-byte machine instructions.

Also, Assembly Language instructions that have register operands are translated into one-byte machine instructions. The register operand is built right into the machine language operation code. For example, ADD instructions all start with 8. ADD B is 80H, ADD C is 81H, ADD D is 82H, etc. SUB instructions all start with 9. SUB B is 90H, SUB C is 91H, etc.

Even the MOV instructions have one-byte translations. There are 63 MOV instructions. (MOV M,M is not allowed.) MOV B,B translates as 40H. MOV B,C translates as 41H. At the upper end of the scale, MOV A,M translates as 7EH and MOV A,A translates as 7FH. If MOV M,M were allowed, it would translate as 76H. Instead, 76H means halt.

(a) Which of the following types of instructions translate as one-byte machine-language instructions?

_____ instructions with no operands

_____ instructions with address operands

_____ instructions with register operands

_____ instructions with immediate operands

(b) Which of the following instructions would translate into one byte?

```
_____ LXI   H,005H
_____ HLT
_____ MOV   M,B
_____ INX   H
_____ SUI   33H
```

(c) Use Figure 5.1 to give the machine-language translation of the following instructions.

```
_____ MOV  A,B
_____ MOV  B,A
_____ PUSH PSW
_____ POP  A
_____ RET
```

- - - - - - - - - - - - - -

(a) instructions with no operands; instructions with register operands; (b) HLT; MOV M,B; INX H; (c) 78, 47, F5, F1, C9

4. Instructions with one byte immediate operands get translated into two-byte machine instructions. The first byte contains the operation code. The second byte contains the immediate data. Of course, the immediate data is converted to binary. On the assembler listing, it will be reported in hex. It is always reported as two digits; leading zeros are filled in. The H suffix is not used. You're supposed to know it's hex. For example, SUI 1 becomes D601. D6 is the operation code and 01 is the immediate data. ADI 255 becomes C6FF, where FF stands for 0FFH.

(a) Which of the following instructions would translate into two-byte machine-language instructions?

```
_____ ADI  3DH
_____ MOV  B,H
_____ MVI  B,0AH
_____ HLT
```

Using Figure 5.1, give the machine code for each of the following instructions.

(b) ADI 1 ____________________

(c) IN 1CH ____________________

(d) ANI 7FH ____________________

- - - - - - - - - - - - - -

(a) ADI 3DH; MVI B,0AH; (b) C601; (c) DB1C; (d) E67F

5. Assembly Language instructions with address operands translate into three-byte instructions. The first byte is the machine-operation code. The second and third bytes contain the numeric address. Remember that an 8080/8085 address is two bytes long.

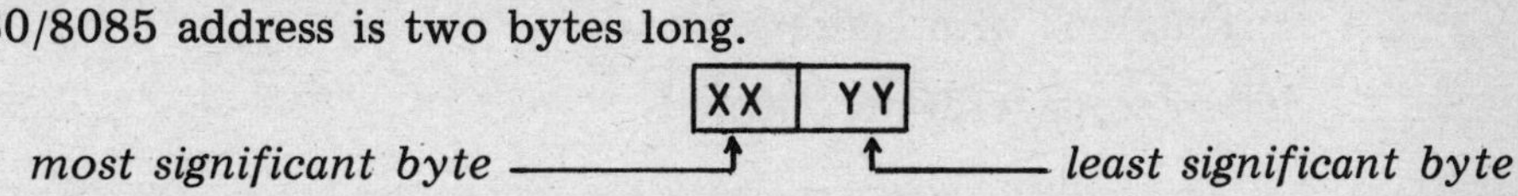

In the machine language instruction, the least significant part of the address goes into the second instruction byte and the most significant part of the address goes into the third instruction byte. In other words, the two address bytes are reversed. The processor straightens them out when it goes to use that address.

For example, JMP 0055 is translated as C35500. C3 is the machine operation code for JMP and 5500 is the address operand with the bytes reversed.

(a) Which one of the following types of Assembly Language instructions has a three-byte machine-language counterpart?

_____ instructions with no operands

_____ instructions with address operands

_____ instructions with register operands

_____ instructions with immediate operands

(b) Which one of the following instructions would translate into three-byte machine-language instructions?

_____ `HLT`

_____ `JMP 2135H`

_____ `JMP START`

_____ `SUI 23`

(c) In the machine-language instruction C32100, what memory address is referenced? _______________

— — — — — — — — — — — — —

(a) instructions with address operands; (b) JMP 2135H and JMP START; (c) 0021H

6. The LXI (load extended immediate) instruction takes a two-byte immediate operand and so yields a three-byte machine-language instruction. The second and third bytes hold the immediate data with bytes reversed. Thus, LXI H,3100H translates as 210031.

(a) Which two types of instructions take three bytes in machine language?

_____ instructions with one-byte immediate operands

_____ instructions with two-byte immediate operands (LXI)

_____ instructions with register operands

_____ instructions with address operands

_____ instructions with no operands

(b) LXI B translates as 01. Give the correct translation of LXI B,14H.

____

(a) instructions with two-byte immediate operands and instructions with address operands; (b) 011400

7. Match.

(a) one byte __________

(b) two byte __________

(c) three byte __________

1. instructions with register operands
2. instructions with address operands
3. instructions with immediate operands except LXI
4. LXI
5. instructions with no operands

(a) 1, 5; (b) 3; (c) 2, 4

Now you know how Assembly Language instructions get translated into machine-language instructions. But where do the memory addresses come from and what are they for? We'll explore that next.

8. Your program must be stored in main storage, or memory, in order to be executed. Only the machine code is stored. It's stored as a sequential series of bytes.

Imagine that the following diagram depicts the very beginning of main storage.

these are	0	0	0	0	0	0	0	0	0	0	0
the ⇨	0	0	0	0	0	0	0	0	0	0	0
addresses	0	0	0	0	0	0	0	0	0	0	0
	0	1	2	3	4	5	6	7	8	9	A

Each box represents the memory space to hold one byte. The numbers beneath represent the memory addresses in hex.

A program is loaded into main storage in straight succession. For example, if we loaded the machine code from Figure 5.1, it would look like this:

CD	0D	00	78	C6	01	47	CD	1B	00	C3	00
0	0	0	0	0	0	0	0	0	0	0	0
0	0	0	0	0	0	0	0	0	0	0	0
0	0	0	0	0	0	0	0	0	0	0	0
0	1	2	3	4	5	6	7	8	9	A	B

The first machine instruction, CD0D00, goes into bytes 0000–0002. The second machine instruction, 78, is only one byte long. It goes into the next byte, 0003.

(a) In Figure 5.1, the third machine instruction is ______________.

Where will it be stored in memory? ______________________

(b) Suppose the program shown below was loaded into memory.

```
0000   212500        LXI   H,0025
0003   46            MOV   B,M
0004   CD1600        CALL  OUTPUT
0007   23            INX   H
...    ...           ...
```

Show the memory contents in the diagram below.

0000	0001	0002	0003	0004	0005	0006	0007

(a) C601; in bytes 0004H and 0005H;

(b)

21	25	00	46	CD	16	00	23

9. Here is the memory diagram for Figure 5.1 again.

CD	0D	00	78	C6	01	47	CD	1B	00	C3	00
0000	0001	0002	0003	0004	0005	0006	0007	0008	0009	000A	000B

Compare it to the figure. The left-hand column of the listing gives the memory address for each instruction. It is the address of the *first byte*—the byte that contains the operation code. We call this the instruction address.

(a) Use the left-hand column in Figure 5.1 to locate the addresses of these instructions.

```
ADI   1       ______________________
JMP   MIXER   ______________________
IN    1CH     ______________________
```

(b) What does the instruction address tell you? ________________________

____

- - - - - - - - - - - - - -

(a) 0004H, 000AH, 0014H; (b) the memory address of the first byte—the operation code—when the program is stored in memory

10. When a program is executed, the microprocessor begins by examining location 0000H. From the operation code there, the microprocessor knows whether the first instruction is one, two, or three bytes. It picks up the instruction and advances the PC to point to the next instruction address. If the first instruction is two bytes long, for example, the PC is set to 0002. Then the first instruction, whatever it is, is executed.

Assuming that the first instruction was not a jump or a call, the PC is pointing at the first byte of the second instruction so that's the next instruction to receive control. The operation code is examined, the PC reset, and the instruction is executed. And so instructions are executed one after another straight through memory until a jump, call, or halt is encountered.

Suppose your program looks like this:

```
0000   3E05      MVI   A,5
0002   C604      ADI   4
0004   210A00    LXI   H,0AH
0007   77        MOV   M,A
```

(a) What's the first instruction to be executed? (Write your answer in Assembly Language.) ________________________

(b) Before it is executed, what will the PC be set to? ________________

(c) What instruction will be executed second? ____________________

(d) Which diagram below best depicts the way in which instructions are executed as long as there are no jumps or calls?

____ 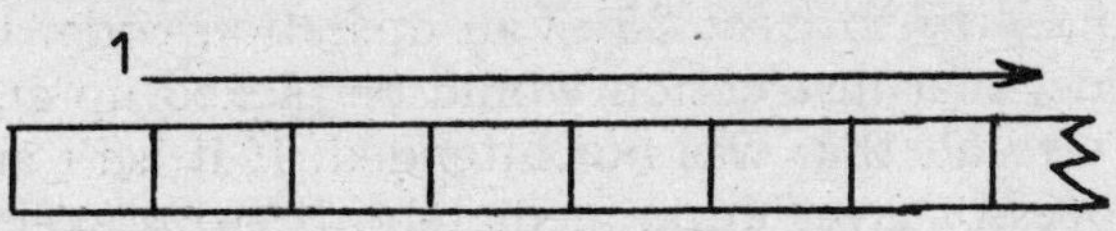

____ 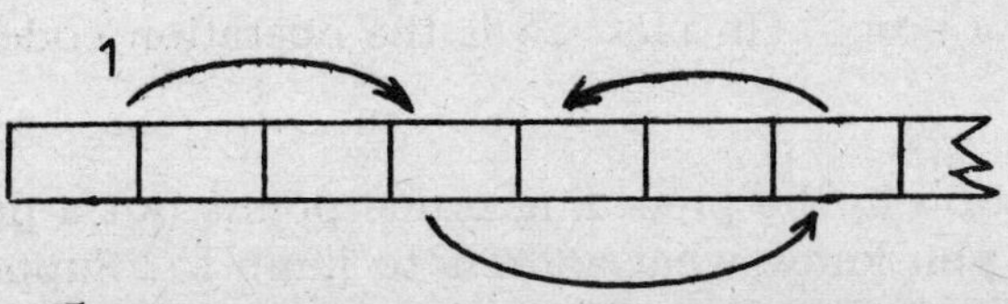

____ 

(a) MVI A,5; (b) 0002H; (c) ADI 4; (d) 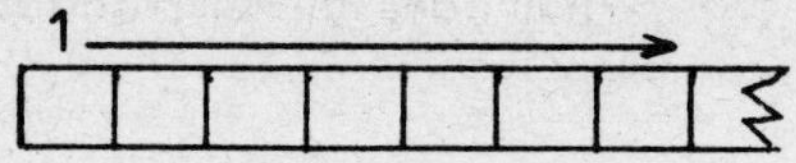

11. A jump or a call causes the address in the PC to be replaced, thus changing the straightforward sequence of instructions.

Examine the program listing below.

```
0000  3E00    MVI  A,0
0002  C30800  JMP  8
0005  212300  LXI  H,23H
0008  77      MOV  M,A
0009  76      HLT
```

(a) When the program is loaded into memory, what is the first instruction to be executed? (Give your answer in Assembly Language.)

____

(b) What is the second instruction to be executed? ______________

(c) What is the third instruction to be executed? ______________

(d) What is the fourth instruction to be executed? ______________

(e) When does the LXI instruction get executed? ______________

(f) Extra Thought Question: What do you think would happen if the second instruction said JMP 6 instead of JMP 8? ______________

____

____

____

(a) MVI A,0; (b) JMP 8; (c) MOV M,A; (d) HLT; (e) never; (f) the microprocessor would try to treat 23 as an operation code. If it is a legitimate operation code, that instruction would be picked up and executed, probably yielding a result that was not intended. If it isn't an operation code, the microprocessor gives up immediately. It stops executing the program. We call this a bomb. (In fact, 23 is the operation code for INX H.)

12. The last question in the preceding frame points out a programming problem: How do you know what address to jump to? Suppose you're writing the program shown on the next page.

```
        LXI   H,MESAGE
        MOV   B,M
        CALL  OUTPUT
        INX   H
        JMP   ????
```

You want to jump back to the MOV instruction. But how can you know its address? Do you have to count bytes from the beginning of the program? You might as well code in machine language. No, you use a symbolic address. You give the MOV instruction a label.

```
        LXI   H,MESAGE
LOOP    MOV   B,M
        CALL  OUTPUT
        INX   H
        JMP   LOOP
```

And you use the label as your JMP operand.

The assembler translates the label into an address.

Use Figure 5.1 to answer the questions below.

(a) What value did the assembler assign to the label INPUT? __________

(b) What is the machine code for the instruction CALL INPUT? ________

(c) What is the relationship between that instruction and the label?

____

(d) Labels are known as *symbolic addresses.* Explain this term.

____

____

(a) 000D; (b) CD0D00; (c) it used the address of the label as the operand, with bytes reversed; (d) a label represents an address but it uses alphanumeric symbols instead of digits.

13. Let's look at how the assembler handles labels. It actually processes your Assembly Language instructions in two passes. The first time through, it determines the address of each instruction and builds a table of labels. At that point, your program would look something like this:

```
0000        MIXER   CALL  INPUT
0003                MOV   A,B
0004                ADI   1
0006                MOV   B,A
```

(continued on next page)

```
0007                    CALL  OUTPUT
000A                    JMP   MIXER
000D            INPUT   PUSH  PSW
...             ...     ...   ...

                SYMBOL  TABLE
           MIXER = 0000
           INPUT = 000D
           ...     ...
```

The second time through, it translates the instructions. Whenever it encounters a label as an operand, it substitutes the appropriate address from its table. The final product looks like Figure 5.1.

There's no way on earth that you should ever have to translate Assembly Language code into machine code yourself. But you must understand how the assembler operates. So, just this once, pretend you're the assembler and translate the following code. Begin at address 0000H.

```
______________________  READER CALL  INPUT
______________________  JMP    READER
______________________  INPUT  PUSH  PSW

                        ...    ...   ...
```

```
0000   CD0600 (make sure you reversed the address bytes)
0003   C30000
0006   F5
...    ...
```

(Your system may also require that each program be processed by a loader before it is ready to run. The loader finalizes the addresses.)

ADDRESSING DATA

You've seen how instructions are addressed. But data bytes also need addresses. Now let's talk about how we address data in memory.

14. Your program may store data in memory. You've already seen how to use the H–L register and the M operand to move data into and out of memory. There are other instructions you'll learn later that access memory data directly.

Memory data is stored at any address you specify. For example:

```
LXI   H,00A0H
MOV   M,A
```

This set of instructions stores the contents of register A at 00A0H. You would want to be very careful not to overlay a program instruction with data. The byte at 00A0H should be reserved for data only. We usually avoid potential conflicts by putting all our data storage after our last instruction. (We'll show you how in a minute!)

Suppose your program instructions use memory addresses 0000H through 0050H. Your program also needs five bytes of memory for data. What memory addresses would you use?

____

\- - - - - - - - - - - - - -

We would use 0051H – 0055H.

We will show you three major ways to address memory—directly, symbolically, and relatively.

15. Direct addressing means that your Assembly Language instruction specifies a numeric address as an operand. You are giving the address directly.

An example of direct addressing is JMP 0310H. This set of instructions also represents direct addressing.

```
LXI  H,00A0H
MOV  M,A
```

When you use this type of addressing, the assembler and loader don't translate the addresses (other than conversion into binary). They follow your directions. (A loader program may protect your operating system by refusing to allow you to overlay it.)

When you use direct addressing, the results are not always smooth. For example, you may create gaps of unused memory. This won't cause

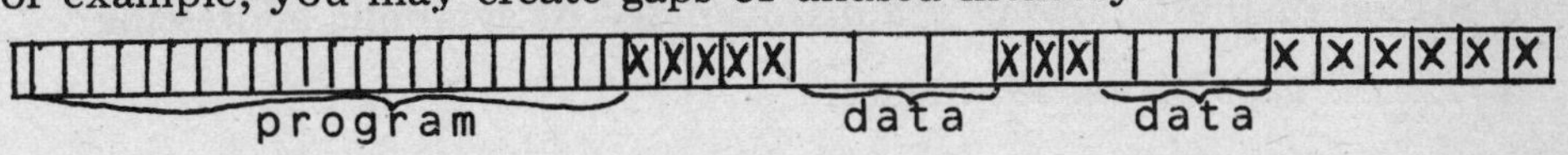

any harm unless your program is so large that it needs to conserve space or it won't fit.

What's much worse is the possibility of overlaying an instruction or other data. If you overlay an instruction with data and then try to execute that instruction, your program will bomb—unless you coincidentally overlay it with data that can be interpreted as an instruction. If you overlay other data unintentionally, the integrity of the output of your program is threatened.

Suppose your program has been laid out very smoothly:

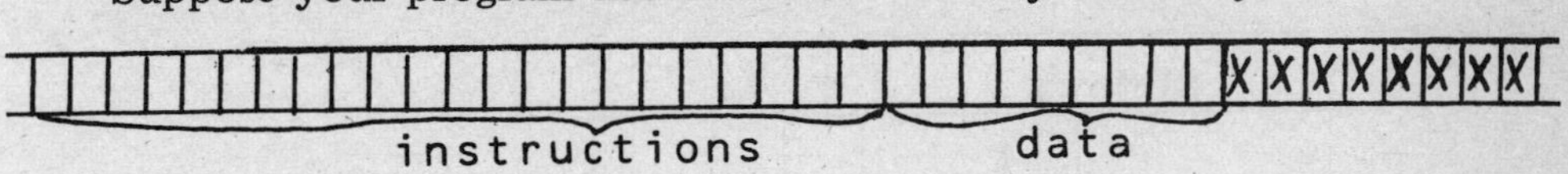

But you find that you need to insert an instruction. You will have to very carefully change every direct data address to make room for the new instruction. (And what if you miss one?)

Altogether, the disadvantages of direct addressing outweigh the advantages. Most programmers do not use it except in special cases.

(a) Which of the following is an example of direct addressing?

_____ JMP MIXER _____ JMP 0100H

(b) Which of the following can result from direct addressing?

_____ gaps of unused memory

_____ overlaid instructions and data

_____ difficulty in revising a program

— — — — — — — — — — — — — —

(a) JMP 0100H; (b) all of them

16. Symbolic addressing is done by assigning names to instructions and data areas. We do this by using labels on our Assembly Language instructions. Then we use the labels as operands. The assembler and loader determine the correct address for each label.

It's easier to avoid creating gaps or overlaying data when you use symbolic addressing. Also, it's very easy to insert an instruction, because the assembler calculates the new addresses when you reassemble the program. You don't have to worry about finding every place where you referred (for example) to address 123H so you can change it to 125H.

(a) Which of the following is an example of symbolic addressing?

_____ JMP MIXER _____ JMP 2134H

(b) Which of the following is a disadvantage of symbolic addressing?

_____ gaps of unused memory

_____ overlaid instructions and data

_____ difficulty in revising a program

— — — — — — — — — — — — — —

(a) JMP MIXER; (b) none of them

17. Relative addressing takes the form *label + n*. It's used to reach data bytes that have no names. For example, suppose we want to address this byte

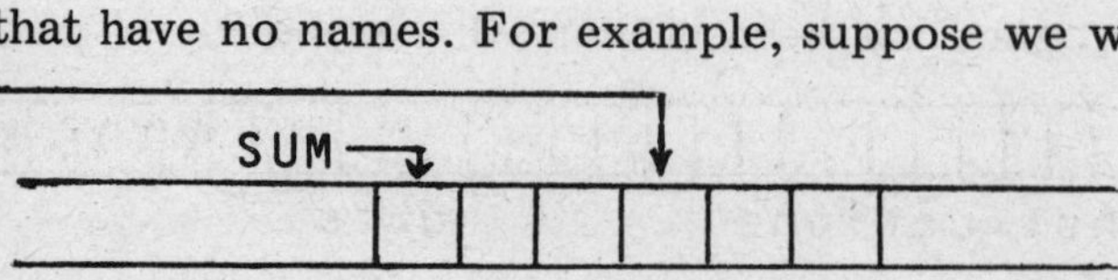

We could call it SUM+3.

When using relative addressing, watch what factor you add. In the diagram above, the first byte can be called SUM or SUM+0. The *second* byte of SUM is SUM+1. What is the third byte? ____________

— — — — — — — — — — — — — —

SUM+2

18. In summary, use this diagram to answer the questions below.

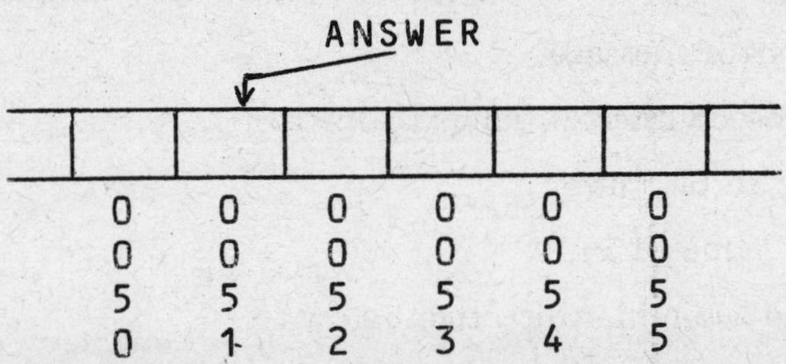

(a) Write the direct address of the byte named ANSWER. ____________

(b) Write the symbolic address for the same byte. ____________

(c) Write a relative address for the same byte. ____________

(d) Write a relative address for a byte at location 0055. ____________

— — — — — — — — — — — — — —

(a) 0051H; (b) ANSWER; (c) ANSWER+0; (d) ANSWER+4

Most of the assembler directives are used to control addressing, as you will learn in the following frames.

DEFINING DATA AREAS

We use assembler directives to assign names to data storage areas. There are two major types of data storage: initialized and uninitialized. In this book, we'll use a DB (define bytes) directive to create initialized data storage and DS (define storage) to define uninitialized storage. Your assembler may have different operation codes for these functions.

19. The DB directive defines initialized data storage. DB stands for "define bytes."

Initialized storage has values in it when the program is loaded and begun. We define the values we want to place there. The values might be used as *constants* (that is, values that don't change throughout the life of the program) or initial values of *variables* (that is, values that will change during one run of the program). An example of a constant might be a message that is written to the user, such as PLEASE ENTER YOUR USER NUMBER. An example of an initial variable might be a page number initialized to 1.

The format of the DB directive is:

[*label*] DB *value*[,*value...*] [;*comments*]

The label can be used as the symbolic address for the first byte being defined. Each value represents one byte and only one byte.

(a) Which of the following are probably examples of constants and which are probably examples of variables? Mark each example C or V.

_____ An error message.

_____ A line counter initialized to zero.

_____ A state tax rate.

_____ The value of PI.

(b) Examine the assembler directive below:

```
YEAR    DB    80
```

What will be the initial value of the memory location named YEAR?

____

(c) By what addressing methods could you refer to a byte defined like this: `DB    0`

— — — — — — — — — — — — —

(a) C, V, C, C; (b) the binary equivalent of decimal 80; (c) direct or relative (You couldn't use symbolic addressing because the byte has no name.)

20. You can specify one or more values in a DB directive, separated by commas with no embedded spaces. A byte is reserved and initialized for every value you specify. Values may be specified in any of the normal ways: binary, decimal, hex, or ASCII. Here are some examples:

```
BRACKT DB   40         ; reserves 1 byte
BRACKT DB   40,50,60   ; reserves 3 bytes
BRACKT DB   40H,50H    ; reserves 2 bytes
```

Which of the following are correctly formatted? Write OK next to those that are correct. For the incorrect ones, briefly describe the error.

(a) `TAXRAT    DB    15D ;` _______________________

(b) `DEDUCT    DB    10,20,30,40,50 ;` _______________

(c) `ABCS      DB    0AH, 0BH, 0CH ;` _______________

(d) `START DB 0100H ;` ____________

Define the following initialized storage areas.

(e) A one-byte area with no name containing the value 0.

____

(f) A two-byte area named NEWLIN containing an ASCII carriage return and line feed. ____________

(g) A three-byte area named MULTIP containing the values 10H, 20H, and 30H. ____________

(a) OK; (b) OK; (c) there should not be any spaces in the operands; (d) the value is too large, it should be 01H,00H; (e) DB 0; (f) NEWLIN DB 0DH,0AH; (g) MULTIP DB 10H,20H,30H

21. There are some special rules involving ASCII values. The easiest way to use an ASCII letter, number, or symbol as an operand is to put the character you want in quotes. You can do that in a DB like this:

```
POINT  DB  '!'
```

As a convenience, you can specify multibyte ASCII values as one value. For example,

```
BADMSG DB   'W','R','O','N','G','!'
```

is the same as

```
BADMSG DB   'WRONG!'
```

In both cases, six bytes are defined.

Only quoted characters can be defined in groups. All other values must be defined using separate operands.

Quoted operands may contain spaces inside the quotes. This is the only place where a space may appear in an operand.

If you need a single quote within a quoted operand, use two single quotes. One single quote would be interpreted as the end of the operand. Thus, to initialize an area to contain I'M TIRED, you would code:

```
TIREDM DB   'I''M TIRED'
```

Which of the following are correctly formatted? Write OK next to those that are correct. For the incorrect ones, briefly describe the error.

(a) `ABCS   DB   'A', 'B', 'C' ;` ____________

(b) `MESAGE DB   'PLEASE PRESS ENTER' ;` ____________

(c) `NAME   DB   'O'HARA' ;` ____________

(a) there should not be any spaces outside the quotes; (b) OK;
(c) the single quote inside should be two quotes

22. Let's look at what happens in memory when you use DB directives. Here's part of a sample program:

```
              MVI    A,5
               ...
              HLT
       MESAG  DB     'NAME?'
       FACTOR DB     1
```

Here's the layout in memory:

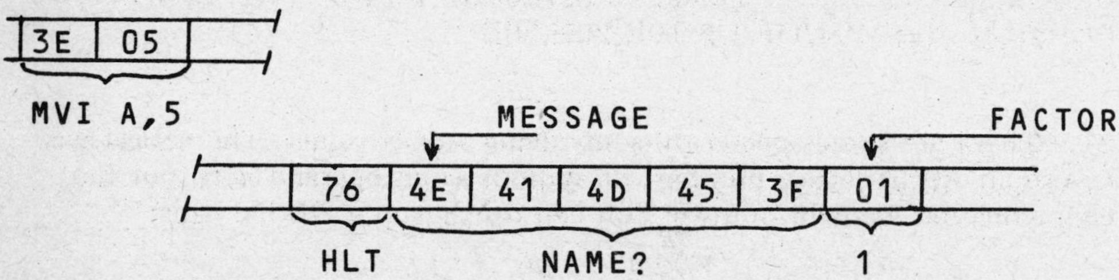

Notice that we put our data area in a location (after HLT) where control won't fall through to it.

Show the memory layout for the following program portion.

```
              LXI    H,FIRST
               ...
              HLT
       FLAG   DB     0
       FIRST  DB     'A','B','C'
```

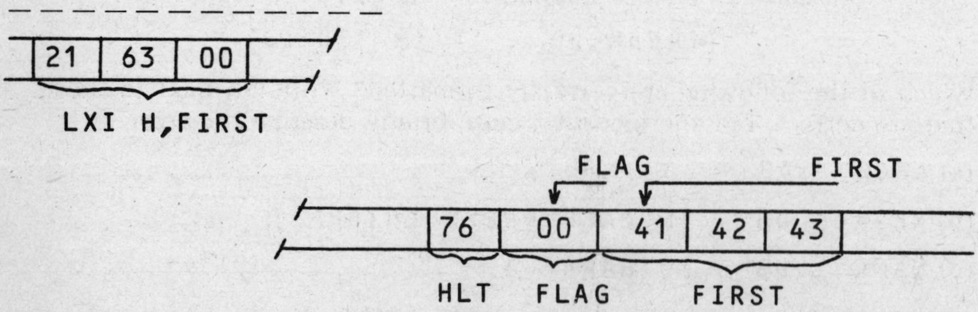

23. The DS directive defines uninitialized storage. That is, it reserves a number of bytes of storage space but doesn't set any initial values. The bytes will contain whatever values were there before; memory is not automatically cleared when a new program is started. We refer to these accidental values as "garbage."

Uninitialized space is usually used to store input values or calculated values. Such space doesn't need to be initialized because the new values overlay the garbage values anyway.

The format of the directive is:

[*label*] DS *size* [;*comments*]

The operand gives the number of bytes to be reserved. We usually state it in decimal. Here's an example:

```
        HLT
NAME    DS     10
MESAGE  DB     'HI'
```

The result in memory would be:

(a) What does uninitialized storage contain? ________________

(b) Which of the following is correct?

______ `CHECK    DS    3`

______ `CHECK    DS    'ABC'`

______ `CHECK    DS    N`

(c) Code a directive to save two bytes of uninitialized space called SPACE.

____

(d) Code a directive to save 20 bytes of uninitialized space called STORAG. ________________

(e) Fill in the result of the storage definitions below.

```
        HLT
NEWVAL  DS    4
OLDVAL  DB    0,0
FLAG1   DS    1
```

\- - - - - - - - - - - - - -

(a) garbage; (b) CHECK DS 3; (c) SPACE DS 2; (d) STORAG DS 20;

(e) 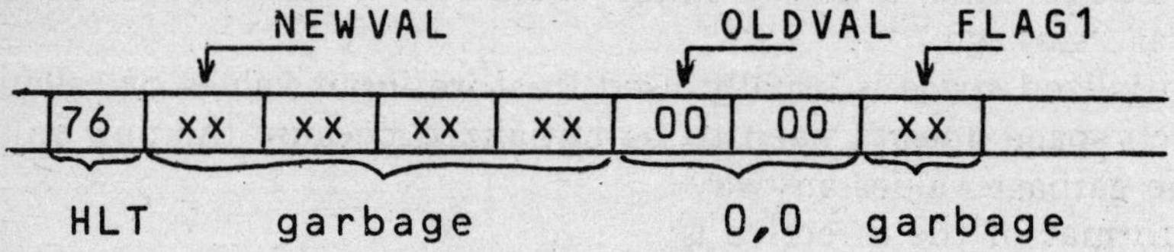

We have used x's to show garbage. You could have filled in *any* data there.

24. A label defined by DB or DS has a memory address value. It can be used as a two-byte operand in Assembly Language instructions.

It can be used in place of any *addr* operand, as in JMP *addr*. However, you should not jump to a data area because the computer can't interpret ordinary data as an instruction except accidentally. Later on you'll learn some instruction where data names can be used.

A data name can never be used in place of a register name. There are only eleven permissable register names, including M. There is no relationship between an address value and a register name. You may recall from frame 2 from this chapter that they're treated in completely different fashions by the assembler.

A data name can be used for an immediate operand if two bytes are needed. This means that the LXI instruction can use a data name; LXI is the only immediate instruction that permits a two-byte immediate operand. All the other immediate instructions are limited to a one-byte immediate operand.

The instruction LXI H,*label* is one of the handiest Assembly Language instructions. It loads the address of the memory area into H–L. Then you can access the area through M without knowing, or caring, what the actual address is.

Here's a short routine:

```
        LXI   H,STAR
        MOV   B,M
LOOP    CALL  OUTPUT
        JMP   LOOP
STAR    DB    '*'
```

This program points H–L at the data area named STAR. It then begins writing out that byte (a '*'), filling the screen until something from outside stops it.

(a) Which of the following take on address values?

______ a label on an Assembly Language instruction

______ a label on a DB or DS directive

(b) Can a symbolic address be used as a register operand? ______________

(c) Can a symbolic address be used as an address operand? ______________

(d) What kind of symbolic address should be used as the operand of a jump instruction? ______________

(e) Under what circumstances can a symbolic address be used as an immediate operand? ______________

(f) What is the only Assembly Language instruction that can use a symbolic address as an immediate operand? ______________

— — — — — — — — — — — — —

(a) both; (b) no; (c) yes; (d) a label on an Assembly Language instruction, not a DB or DS label; (e) if the operand requires two bytes; (f) LXI

25. Code a routine that reads one byte from the terminal, stores it in a memory area named ONEBYT, and halts.

— — — — — — — — — — — — —

Here's our solution:

```
        CALL INPUT
        LXI  H,ONEBYT
        MOV  M,B
PAUSE   JMP  PAUSE
ONEBYT  DS   1
```

26. Code a routine that reads a series of bytes from the terminal and stores them in a memory area named INTEXT. Reserve 80 bytes for INTEXT. Remember to increase the address in the H-L pair after storing each byte that comes in. Leave the program in a closed loop until the user stops it.

— — — — — — — — — — — — —

Here's our solution:

```
        LXI  INTEXT
INLOOP  CALL INPUT
        MOV  M,B
        INX  H
        JMP  INLOOP
INTEXT  DS   80
```

EQUATES

27. Let's move on now to another assembler directive. The EQU (equate) directive directly assigns a value to a label. *Any* value can be assigned. For example:

```
HIVAL   EQU   0FFH
LOVAL   EQU   0H
```

Now anywhere in the program that the label HIVAL is used as an operand, the assembler will substitute 0FFH. And 0H will be substituted for LOVAL.

Note the important difference between equates and symbolic addresses. In the above example, HIVAL and LOVAL are *not* symbolic address. They do not have address values; they have the value of their operands.

The EQU directive does not define a storage area. It is not translated into a machine instruction. It simply tells the assembler, "When I say *this*, I really mean *that*."

The format is:

label EQU *value* [;*comment*]

Notice that a label is required. Without a label, the instruction would make no sense.

(a) Code a directive to assign the value 10H to the label TTYPRT.

____

(b) Code directives to assign the value 0DH to the label CR and the value 0AH to the label LF.

____

____

- - - - - - - - - - - - -

(a) TTYPRT EQU 10H; (b) CR EQU 0DH; LF EQU 0AH

28. An EQU label can be used for any operand where its value makes sense. For example, suppose you had this set of equates:

```
HIVAL   EQU   0FFH
LOVAL   EQU   0H
REGA    EQU   A
MEM     EQU   M
MESAG   EQU   'HI'
```

For each of the following instructions, indicate which labels *could* be used. (Refer to Appendix C if you don't remember the formats of these instructions.)

(a) ADI ______________________

(b) ADD ______________________

(c) LXI H ______________________

(d) JMP ______________________

(e) TEXT DB ______________________

— — — — — — — — — — — — — —

(a) ADI takes a one-byte immediate operand—either HIVAL or LOVAL could be used; (b) ADD takes a register operand—either REGA or MEM could be used; (c) LXI takes a two-byte immediate operand—HIVAL would do because it will expand to two bytes with leading zeros, LOVAL will work for the same reason, and MESAG would work as it has a two-byte value; (d) JMP takes an address operand—HIVAL, LOVAL, and MESAG would all produce values in the proper range, 0H – 0FFFFH, but the addresses produced may have no meaning for this program; (e) HIVAL, LOVAL, and MESAG would all work.

29. Why do we use equates? Why not use the values themselves directly as operands? Because equates make it easier to revise a program. Suppose you need to change the address of an output port on your system from 110 to 115. If you have defined that address this way:

```
OUTPRT EQU  110
```

and then used OUTPRT in the instructions, you only have to make *one change*. If you didn't use the equate, you'll have to search the entire program for references to the 110 address.

A programmer spends about 25% of the time writing new programs and 75% of the time revising old programs—correcting, updating, expanding, adapting, and so forth. All new programs should be written with the thought in mind that they will be revised at least ten times before they have outlived their usefulness. Equates are one way to make the revision task easier later on.

(a) A really good program never needs to be changed.

True or false? ______________________

(b) How do equates make revisions easier? ______________________

____

— — — — — — — — — — — — — —

(a) false: the better a program is, the more likely it is to be borrowed and adapted, expanded, etc.; (b) by cutting down the number of instructions that have to be changed

30. Suppose you're writing a disk directory program, which formats and displays the directory of a floppy disk. Some of the values your program uses are:

- beginning address of the directory on the disk
- size of one directory entry
- maximum size of one disk in bytes
- maximum number of directory entries

(a) Which of these values might you equate instead of using directly?

____

____

(b) Why? ____

____

— — — — — — — — — — — — — —

(a) all of them; (b) they could all change, especially if you convert the program for another system.

31. Our system has a special equate instruction that looks like this:

label EQU $

This equate establishes the label as a symbolic address. The $ operand says "this address." Since the EQU instruction doesn't have its own address (it's not translated into machine language), the label becomes the address of the next Assembler instruction. Thus:

```
MIXER  EQU  $
       CALL INPUT
```

is the same as

```
MIXER  CALL INPUT
```

Why use the equate? To make future revisions easier. Suppose you find you need to add an instruction to the beginning of the MIXER routine. It's easier to make the revision if the symbolic address has its own line.

If you've never programmed in any assembler language before, this may seem like a relatively minor advantage. Believe us, it isn't. All experienced assembler programmers put their instruction names on separate lines. But it's just a convention, not a rule. We will observe it from here on in this book because we think it makes the program more readable.

The familiar echo routine is shown below. Revise it so the label is on a separate line.

```
ECHO   CALL INPUT
       CALL OUTPUT
       JMP  ECHO
```

____

____

____

____

- - - - - - - - - - - - -

```
ECHO    EQU   $
        CALL  INPUT
        CALL  OUTPUT
        JMP   ECHO
```

32. In the assembler listing in Figure 5.2, give the values of these labels.

(a) HIVALU: ______________

(b) ECHO: ______________

(c) MASK: ______________

(d) TEST: ______________

(e) STATBY: ______________

- - - - - - - - - - - - -

(a) 0FFH; (b) 0000; (c) 7FH; (d) 002C; (e) 1DH

THE ORG DIRECTIVE

33. The ORG (origin) directive specifies the current memory address to the assembler. The directive ORG 500H says, "No matter what memory address you're currently at, I want the next instruction to start at 500H." Subsequent instructions would follow, of course.

Suppose you assembled this program:

```
ORG   100H
MVI   A,1
ORG   105H
ADI   2
ORG   108H
HLT
```

The result when the program is loaded into memory is:

0000		//	0100	0101	0102	0103	0104	0105	0106	0107	0108	0109	010A
xx	xx	//	3E	01	xx	xx	xx	C6	02	xx	76	xx	xx

```
001C =          TERMIN EQU   1CH
001D =          STATBY EQU   1DH
007F =          MASK   EQU   7FH
0000 =          LOVALU EQU   0
00FF =          HIVALU EQU   0FFH
0000 =          ECHO   EQU   $
0000 CD0B00            CALL  INPUT
0003 CD1900            CALL  OUTPUT
0006 70                MOV   M,B
0007 23                INX   H
0008 C30000            JMP   ECHO
000B =          INPUT  EQU   $
000B F5                PUSH  A
000C =          STATUS EQU   $
000C CD2C00            CALL  TEST
000F CA0C00           JZ    STATUS
0012 DB1C             IN    TERMIN
0014 E67F             ANI   MASK
0016 47               MOV   B,A
0017 F1               POP   A
0018 C9               RET
0019 =          OUTPUT EQU   $
0019 F5                 PUSH A
001A =          STATOT EQU   $
001A 3E10              MVI   A,10H
001C D31D             OUT   STATBY
001E DB1D             IN    STATBY
0020 E60C             ANI   00001100B
0022 FE0C             CPI   00001100B
0024 C21A00           JNZ   STATOT
0027 78               MOV   A,B
0028 D31C             OUT   TERMIN
002A F1               POP   A
002B C9               RET
002C =          TEST   EQU   $
002C AF                XRA   A
002D D31D             OUT   STATBY
002F DB1D             IN    STATBY
0031 E601             ANI   1
0033 C8               RZ
0034 3EFF             MVI   A,HIVALU
0036 C9               RET
0037                  END
```

FIGURE 5.2. Assembler Listing

where xx is garbage. This program will bomb because the processor won't skip from location 100H to 105H. The processor will probably look for the first instruction in location 0H. Even if it gets to the MVI instruction at 100H, it will look for the next instruction at 102H. If it doesn't find an instruction there, it will quit its job.

The above program could be made to work by adding jump instructions.

```
        JMP   START
        ORG   100H
START   EQU   $
        MVI   A,1
        JMP   NEXT
        ORG   105H
NEXT    EQU   $
        ADI   2
        JMP   LAST
        ORG   108H
LAST    EQU   $
        HLT
```

But why would anyone want to do that? What is ORG good for? It's usually used when you don't want your program to begin at 0000. For example, our operating system uses addresses 0000—00FF for some of its code. We *must* start our programs at 100H. That's where our processor looks for the first instruction. So every one of our programs starts with ORG 100H.

Also, you can use ORG to create uninitialized data space if your assembler doesn't have a DS-type directive.

Suppose your assembler has no DS-type directive. Code an instruction (after the JMP instruction below) that will create three bytes of data space labeled INTEXT. (Assume the address of the JMP instruction is 200H and it takes three bytes.)

```
        JMP   START
```

____

- - - - - - - - - - - - - -

```
INTEXT ORG  206H
```

THE END DIRECTIVE

34. The END directive tells the assembler to stop assembling. It's used in cases where the assembler might not recognize the end of your Assembly Language instruction file.

If your instructions are stored on floppy disk as a file, the end will be obvious to the assembler. But other file types—paper tape, cards, magnetic tape—may or may not have clear cut terminations. At any rate, the END directive doesn't do any harm so we usually include it as the very last instruction. Its format is usually just the operation code END.

END is not an instruction and does not get translated. It does not halt processing. You must use HLT, a closed loop, or some other means to halt processing.

Where does the END instruction go?

_____ (a) After the HLT instruction or its equivalent.

_____ (b) After the main part of the program but before the called routines.

_____ (c) After everything else.

_____ (d) After every routine.

What does the END instruction do?

_____ (e) Halts your program.

_____ (f) Halts the assembler.

- - - - - - - - - - - - - -

(c), (f)

REVIEW

In this chapter, you have studied several assembler directives. Your assembler may have different directives, but they should include at least the functions shown here.

- The assembler program translates Assembly Language instructions into machine-language instructions. The operation code is translated into a numeric machine code. Register names are included in the machine code. Addresses are converted into binary and their bytes are reversed. Immediate data is converted into binary. Symbolic addresses are given numeric address values. Labels defined by equates are given their equated values. A linkage loader may be required to finalize the program before it can be executed.

- Assembler directives speak to the assembler program. They are not translated into machine language although their effect may be seen in the machine code that is produced.

- The DB directive defines and initializes memory bytes.
  Format: [*label*] DB *value*[,*value*...] [;*comments*]
  Each value defines one byte. However, ASCII text may be defined in one string instead of separate values for each byte. The label becomes the symbolic address for the beginning of that memory area; it can be used as a two-byte operand.

- The DS instruction defines uninitialized memory space.
  Format: [*label*] DS *size* [;*comments*]

Size gives the number of bytes to set aside. The bytes will contain garbage. The label becomes the symbolic address for that memory area; it can be used as a two-byte operand.

- The EQU instruction assigns a value to a label.
  Format: *label* EQU *value* [;*comments*]
  The assembler substitutes the value for the label wherever the label is used as an operand.
- *label* EQU $ is a special instruction that assigns a symbolic address to the current memory address.
- The ORG directive specified the current memory location to the assembler.
  Format: [*label*] ORG *addr* [;*comments*]
  ORG is used to skip over memory space, either because it's in use by other programs or to reserve data space without using the DS instruction.
- The END directive tells the assembler to stop assembling.
  Format: END

CHAPTER 5 SELF-TEST

1. Describe the function of the assembler.

   ____

2. Which of the following become part of the machine-language program?

   _____ a. labels

   _____ b. operation codes

   _____ c. operands

   _____ d. comments

3. Which of the following are replaced by the assembler with numeric values?

   _____ a. labels

   _____ b. operation codes

   _____ c. operands

   _____ d. comments

4. Which of the following are ignored by the assembler?

   _____ a. labels

_____ b. operation codes

_____ c. operands

_____ d. comments

5. Refer back to Figure 5.2 and answer the questions below.

   a. What is the address of the INX instruction? _____

   b. What is the value of the label STATOT? _____

   c. Look at the JZ instruction at address 000F. What value did the assembler substitute for the operand STATUS? _____

      Why? _____

   d. Look at the IN instruction at address 0012. What value did the assembler substitute for TERMIN? _____

      Why? _____

   e. Look at the ANI instruction at address 0020. What value did the assembler substitute for 00001100B? _____

      Why? _____

6. Match.

   _____ a. assembler directive

   _____ b. instruction

   1. translated into machine language; controls the microprocessor.
   2. not translated; controls the assembler program.

7. Code directives for each of the following functions.

   a. Define an uninitialized ten-byte data area named QUES7A.

      _____

   b. Define a data area named QUES7B initialized to 5BH.

      _____

   c. Define a string of initialized bytes containing the digits 0 through 9 in pure binary code, not ASCII. Name the area DIGITS.

      _____

d. Define a string of initialized bytes containing "SELF-TEST."

Name the area QUIZ. ______________________

e. Set the label ZEROS equal to zeros. ______________________

f. Set the label LIMIT equal to '**'. ______________________

g. Assign the label ANSWER to the first instruction of the routine below.

```
LXI  H,NOTEXT
MOV  B,M
CALL OUTPUT
```

h. Cause the routine below to be stored beginning at 100H.

```
LXI  H,NOTEXT
MOV  B,M
CALL OUTPUT
```

i. Cause the assembler to stop assembling after the lines below.

```
        HLT
DATA1   DB    0
DATA2   DB    0FH
SPACE   DS    80
```

Check your answers below.

Self-Test Answer Key

1. translates Assembly Language instructions into machine instructions

2. b, c

3. a

4. d

5. a. 0007

   b. 001A

   c. 0C00; this is the address of the instruction labeled STATUS (000C) with the bytes reversed

   d. 1C; TERMIN is assigned this value in an EQU directive

   e. 0C; this is the hex form of the value

6. a. 2

   b. 1

7. a. `QUES7A DS 10`

   b. `QUES7B DB 5BH`

   c. `DIGITS DB 0,1,2,3,4,5,6,7,8,9`

   d. `QUIZ DB 'SELF-TEST'`

   e. `ZEROS EQU 0`

   f. `LIMIT EQU '**'`

   g. `ANSWER EQU $`

   h. `ORG 100H`

   i. `END`

If you missed any of these, review the appropriate frames before going on the Manual Exercise.

MANUAL EXERCISE

Before continuing, you should find out what the assembler directives are for your assembler. Look them up in your manual under "directives" or "pseudo-operations." If that fails, try looking up EQU and ORG. Almost all assemblers use those two directives. Use your manual to find the answers to the questions below.

1. Show the format of the directive to define initialized space.

   ____

2. Show the format of the directive to define uninitialized space.

   ____

3. Show the format of an equate.

   ____

4. Show the format of the directive to specify an origin.

   ____

5. Show the format of the directive to stop the assembler.

   ____

6. What other directives are available to you?

____

____

____

____

Now go on to Chapter 6.

CHAPTER SIX

CONDITIONAL INSTRUCTIONS

In this chapter we're going to begin expanding on your basic set of instructions. You will learn how to use the conditional instructions, which test the values of the status flags and take appropriate action. (That is, they take action only if a certain *condition*—as indicated by the status flags—is true.) For example, you've learned how to use the JMP instruction to create a closed loop, but you can also tell the system to jump only if the zero flag is on (JZ) or jump if the carry flag is not on (JNC).

The conditional instructions are used to create open loops and alternate program paths. You'll learn how to code both of these types of program structures.

When you have finished this chapter, you will be able to:

- Code the following instructions:
  - JC (jump if carry)
  - JNC (jump if not carry)
  - JZ (jump if zero)
  - JNZ (jump if not zero)
  - JM (jump if minus)
  - JP (jump if plus)
  - CPI (compare immediate)
  - CMP (compare)
- Create the following types of program structures:
  - open loops
  - alternate paths

REVIEW OF THE FLAGS

The conditional instructions all use the status flags, so let's review those flags before we start on the instructions.

1. Five of the eight bits of the flag register are used as status flags. Normally, they reflect the status of the value in the A register. The five status flags are: sign, zero, parity, carry, and auxiliary carry. Of these, you'll probably only use the sign, zero, and carry flags so those are the ones we'll concentrate on in this book.

(a) How many status flags are there? ____________________

(b) Which ones will you normally use? ____________________

(c) What value is usually described by the status flags?

____

(d) If a flag is one bit, what are its two possible values?

____

— — — — — — — — — — — — —

(a) five; (b) sign, zero, carry; (c) the value in A register; (d) zero and one

2. The zero flag is turned on (set to 1) if the value in the A register becomes zero. Otherwise, it is turned off (set to 0). It is set (either on or off) as the result of any arithmetic operation on the accumulator. (You'll learn later that it is also set as a result of certain other instructions, such as "compare.")

Note that the zero flag and the other flags are not set by data movement instructions such as MOV or the jump instructions.

Below is a list of instructions you learned in Chapter 4. Select the instructions that affect the flags.

_____ (a) MOV

_____ (b) MVI

_____ (c) ADD

_____ (d) ADI

(e) SUB

(f) SUI

(g) JMP

— — — — — — — — — — — — —

(c), (d), (e), (f) (Remember that your reference summary in Appendix C shows the effect of each instruction on the status flags.)

3. Some people get confused by the setting of the zero flag when the accumulator reaches zero. A non-zero result turns the zero flag *off* (0) and a zero result turns it *on* (1).

In the following example, suppose that the instruction SUI 1 has just been executed.

(a) If the A register = 0, the zero flag = __________ .

(b) If the A register does not = 0, the zero flag = ___________.

— — — — — — — — — — — —

(a) 1; (b) 0

4. In each of the following examples, show whether the zero flag will be set on or off after the operation.

	zero flag	*accumulator*	*instruction*	*result on zero flag*
(a)	1	00000000	ADI 10H	——
(b)	1	00001010	MVI A,0	——
(c)	0	00001010	MVI A,0	——
(d)	0	00000010	SUI 00000010B	——
(e)	0	00000000	SUI 3	——

— — — — — — — — — — — —

(a) 0; (b) 1; (c) 0; (d) 1; (e) 0 (Notice that the status of the zero flag is not affected by the MVI instruction. It remains unchanged.)

5. The carry flag indicates whether the accumulator has overflowed. It is set after an arithmetic or logical operation. If the operation resulted in a one being carried from the most significant bit (the first bit) and potentially being lost, the carry flag is turned on. Otherwise, it is turned off.

Indicate the setting of the carry flag after each operation below.

	carry flag	*accumulator*	*instruction*	*result on carry flag*
(a)	0	00001111	ADI 01100011B	——
(b)	1	10000000	MVI 10110011B	——
(c)	0	10000000	MVI 11111111B	——
(d)	0	10100010	ADI 11000000B	——

— — — — — — — — — — — —

(a) 0; (b) 1; (c) 0; (d) 1

In the last problem:

```
                          10100010
this bit turns          + 11000000
on the - - - - - - →    101100010
carry flag
```

6. The carry flag also indicates whether borrowing took place by the most significant bit. If a digit was borrowed from outside the accumulator, then the result will be invalid, so the flag is turned on; otherwise, it is turned off.

Indicate the result on the carry flag for the following operations.

	carry flag	*accumulator*	*instruction*		*result on carry flag*
(a)	0	00110101	SUI	10000000B	———
(b)	0	11000000	SUI	00000001B	———

— — — — — — — — — — — — — —

(a) 1; (b) 0

The carry flag tells you whether the result of an arithmetic or logical operation has overflowed the accumulator. It's up to you to code your program to correctly handle overflow situations and keep the end result accurate. You'll learn how to handle the four basic arithmetic functions—addition, subtraction, multiplication, and division—in Chapter 11.

7. The sign flag reflects the value of the most significant bit (MSB) in the result field. If the MSB is on, the sign flag is on, and if the MSB is off, the sign flag is off. Why? Most programmers like to reserve the MSB as a sign bit, limiting the value in a byte to seven bits. If the sign bit is on, the value is negative. If the sign bit is off, the value is positive. The sign flag duplicates the information and can be tested by the conditional instructions.

You'll learn how to handle negative numbers in Chapter 11.

The sign flag is set as a result of arithmetic or logical operations but not moves or jumps.

Indicate the value of the sign flag after each operation below.

	sign flag	*accumulator*	*instruction*		*result on sign flag*
(a)	1	10001000	MVI	00H	———
(b)	1	00000000	ADI	00000011B	———
(c)	0	00001000	ADI	11000000B	———

(a) 1; (b) 0; (c) 1

You have reviewed the three major flags—zero, carry, and sign—and have seen that they are set as the result of arithmetic operations. Now let's go on to the instructions that use them. (We'll also briefly introduce the instructions that use the parity flag. There are no conditional instructions that use the auxiliary carry flag.)

CONDITIONAL JUMPS

8. You have already learned how to transfer control to another point in the program using the JMP instruction. JMP is called an *unconditional jump* because the jump always takes place when the instruction is executed.

A conditional jump only happens if the specified condition is true when the instruction is executed. Otherwise, control goes on to the instruction after the conditional jump. (We say that control "falls through" to the next instruction.)

Suppose your program contains this sequence of instructions:

```
MIXER   EQU   $
        CALL  INPUT
        MOV   A,B
        SUI   20H
        JZ    MIXER
        ADI   1
        ...
```

Figure 6.1 diagrams the logic of the routine. The diamond-shaped box is used to indicate the point at which a question is asked and a yes–no or true–false decision made. In this example, we get a value from the terminal and subtract 20H from it. We then ask the question: Does the result equal zero? (We don't really. We really ask if the zero flag is on. But the *effect* is the same.)

If the answer is yes, control is returned to the statement labeled MIXER and the loop is repeated. If the answer is no (the result is not zero; the zero flag is off), control falls through to the ADI instruction.

The overall function of the routine is to read characters from the terminal until a non-blank character is obtained. We add one to that character and what happens after that is not shown.

(a) Is JMP a conditional or unconditional instruction? ________________

(b) Is JZ a conditional or unconditional instruction? ________________

(c) In Figure 6.1, what happens if the user types a space? ________________

____

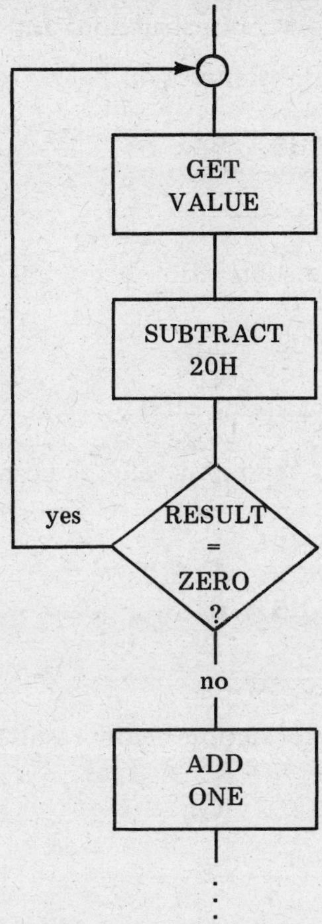

FIGURE 6.1. Sample Routine

(d) What happens if the user types a B? ____________________

(e) Is the MIXER loop closed or open? ____________________

— — — — — — — — — — — — —

(a) unconditional; (b) conditional; (c) control returns to the beginning of the loop; (d) control falls through; (e) open

9. These are the conditional jump instructions:

JC — Jump if Carry: jump if the carry flag is on
JNC — Jump if Not Carry: jump if the carry flag is off
JZ — Jump if Zero: jump if the zero flag is on
JNZ — Jump if Not Zero: jump if the zero flag is off
JM — Jump if Minus: jump if the sign flag is on
JP — Jump if Plus: jump if the sign flag is off
JPE — Jump if Parity is Even: jump if the parity flag is on
JPO — Jump if Parity if Odd: jump if the parity flag is off

Write the appropriate jump instructions for the following situations:

(a) Jump to ENDER if the subtraction below results in a zero.

```
SUB  B
```

____

(b) Jump to LOOP if the subtraction below results in a non-zero value.

```
SUI  1
```

____

(c) Jump to NEGVAL if the input value is negative.

```
CALL IN
MOV  A,B
SUB  0
```

____

(d) Jump to OK if the subtraction below results in a positive value.

```
SUB  C
```

____

(e) Jump to TOOBIG if the addition below results in overflow.

```
ADI  10H
```

____

(f) Jump to CYCLE if the addition below does not overflow.

```
ADI  B
```

____

— — — — — — — — — — — —

(a) JZ ENDER; (b) JNZ LOOP; (c) JM NEGVAL; (d) JP OK;
(e) JC TOOBIG; (f) JNC CYCLE

10. Figure 6.2 diagrams the general logic of an open loop. One or more instructions are executed in sequence. Then a question is asked. In a program, that means a condition is tested. If the condition is true, control is

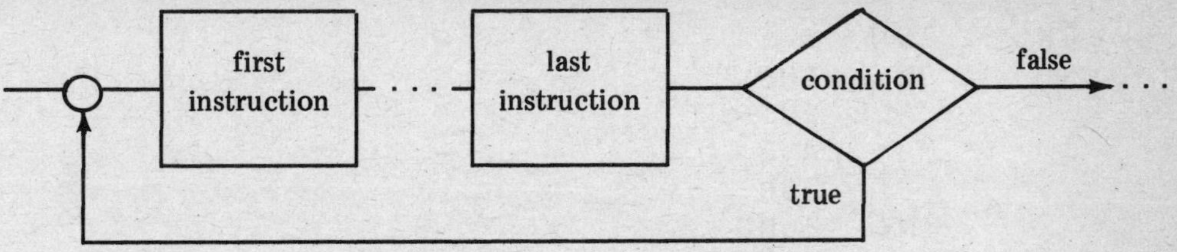

FIGURE 6.2. Open Loop

returned to the beginning of the loop. If the condition is false, control falls through the next statement.

Here is an example of an open loop in Assembly Language:

```
MIXER   EQU   $
        CALL  INPUT
        MOV   A,B
        ADI   1
        MOV   B,A
        CALL  OUTPUT
        SUI   31H
        JNZ   MIXER
```

This is our old MIXER routine with a difference. After writing the new value to the terminal, we subtract 31H from the A register. If the result does not equal binary zero, we loop back to MIXER. If the result does equal binary zero, control falls through to the next instruction. The total effect is to read characters from the terminal until an ASCII zero is found.

(a) What's the difference between a closed loop and an open loop?

____

____

(b) What type of jump is used to escape a loop, conditional or unconditional? ______________________________

(c) Code a routine to read and echo characters until the user types a carriage return. Then let control fall through to the next instruction.

____

____

____

____

- - - - - - - - - - - - -

(a) a closed loop has no natural exit while an open loop does;
(b) conditional;

(c)
```
ECHO    EQU  $
        CALL INPUT
        CALL OUTPUT
        MOV  A,B
        SUI  0DH
        JNZ  ECHO
```

11. We frequently want to execute a loop a specific number of times. Figure 6.3 shows the logic for executing a loop five times. First we set the accumulator equal to 5. Then we enter the loop. Each time the loop is executed, we subtract one from the accumulator. When the accumulator reaches zero, we know we have executed the loop five times so we allow control to fall through to the next instruction.

We can use the accumulator to count loops when the loop itself doesn't need to use the accumulator. Otherwise, we would need to keep a loop counter in another register.

The Assembly Language routine would look like this:

```
        MVI  A,5
LOOP    EQU  $
        first instruction
        ...
        last instruction
        SUI  1
        JNZ  LOOP
        ...
```

Code a routine that will write the letter 'X' on the terminal three times. Then stop processing.

____

____

____

____

____

____

____

- - - - - - - - - - - - -

```
        MVI  A,3
        MVI  B,'X'
XER     EQU  $
        CALL OUTPUT
        SUI  1
        JNZ  XER
        HLT
```

Your routine may not look exactly like ours but it should be close. Did you notice that you only need to put 'X' in the B register once? When you are coding loops, don't repeat instructions unnecessarily; they waste time.

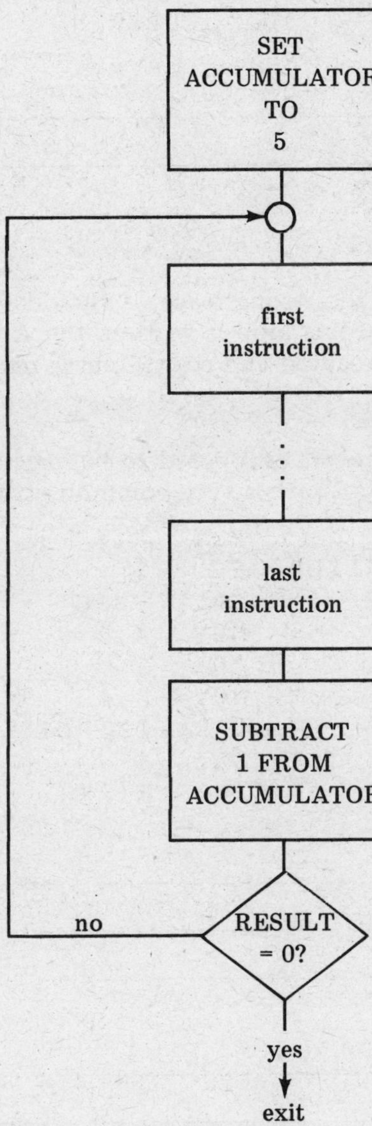

FIGURE 6.3. Counting Five Loops

12. The following routine was supposed to be executed ten times. But the programmer made a very common error and has created a closed loop instead.

```
CLEAR   EQU   $
        MVI   A,10
        first instruction
        ...
        last instruction
        SUI   1
        JNZ   CLEAR
        ...
```

What is the error? ______________________________

____

____

– – – – – – – – – – – –

The label, CLEAR, is in the wrong place. It should precede "first instruction," not MVI. The way this loop is written, the A register is reset to 10 every time the loop is executed and so will never reach zero.

13. The following routine was supposed to be executed three times. But the programmer has made another very common error.

```
        MVI   A,3
MIXER   EQU   $
        CALL  INPUT
        MOV   A,B
        ADI   1
        MOV   B,A
        CALL  OUTPUT
        SUI   1
        JNZ   MIXER
        ...
```

What is the error? ______________________________

____

____

Extra Thought Question:

How can it be corrected? ______________________________

____

____

– – – – – – – – – – – –

When the MOV A,B instruction is executed, the loop counting value is destroyed. Since this loop needs to use the A register, we must keep the loop counter somewhere else (in C, for example) and move it into a when we need it. A correct routine would be:

```
        MVI  C,3
MIXER   EQU  $
        CALL INPUT
        MOV  A,B
        ADI  1
        MOV  B,A
        CALL OUTPUT
        MOV  A,C
        SUI  1
        MOV  C,A
        JNZ  MIXER
```

14. See if you can write a loop that will display the numbers from 0 through 9 on the terminal, then halt.

Here's our loop. Yours may be somewhat different. We've numbered the lines so we can discuss them below.

```
10                MVI  B,'0'
20         WRINUM EQU  $
30                CALL OUTPUT
40                MOV  A,B
50                ADI  1
60                MOV  B,A
70                SUI  ':'
80                JNZ  WRINUM
90                HLT
```

Line 10 sets up the B register with the ASCII code for zero. Then we enter the loop. Line 30 writes out whatever value is in the B register. Line 40 copies the value into the A register, where we increment it (line 50). Thus, '0' becomes '1', '1' becomes '2', etc. Line 60 moves the new value into the B register from where it will be written out in the next loop. Lines 70 and 80 end the loop if '9' has already been written. Line 70 checks the value against ':'. ('9' + 1 = ':') Line 80 jumps if not zero; if zero, the value in B equals ':' and control falls through to the HLT instruction.

15. Write a loop that will accept a single digit from the terminal and print that number of X's on the terminal, then stop. Assume that the input digit is between '1' and '9'. Don't forget it will be in ASCII.

```
10                CALL  INPUT
20                MOV   A,B
30                SUI   30H
40                MVI   B,'X'
50         WRLOOP EQU   $
60                CALL  OUTPUT
70                SUI   1
80                JNZ   WRLOOP
90                HLT
```

Lines 10 and 20 get the digit from the terminal and move it into the A register. Line 30 converts the value from ASCII code to plain binary. (We say it strips out the most significant bits.) Line 40 sets up 'X' in the B register. Then we enter the loop, which is controlled by the value in the A register. Line 60 writes an 'X'. Line 70 decrements the A register, setting the zero flag on or off. Line 80 returns control to the top of the loop if the zero flag is off. If the flag is on, control falls through to line 90 and the program is halted.

SENDING MESSAGES

16. In this frame, we're going to show you how to write out a message from storage. Suppose we want to write the message "PLEASE TYPE YOUR NAME:" The program is shown in Figure 6.4.

```
              MVI   A,22
              LXI   H,MESSAG
       OUTLOO EQU   $
              MOV   B,M
              CALL  OUTPUT
              INX   H
              SUI   1
              JNZ   OUTLOO
              HLT
       MESSAG DB    'PLEASE TYPE YOUR NAME:'
```

FIGURE 6.4. Writing a Message

Line 10 moves decimal 22 into the A register. There are 22 characters in the message, so we'll write 22 characters. Another way to control the loop would be to check for the last byte in the message, ':'. But that would involve one more step in the loop—moving each byte from B to A. So the way we've chosen is faster; the loop counter stays in the A register.

Line 20 points the H-L pair at the data area named MESSAG.

Line 40 begins the loop by moving a byte from memory (pointed to by H-L) to the B register. Line 50 writes the byte. Line 60 increments the H-L pair, so it is now pointing to the next memory byte.

Lines 70 and 80 check for the end of the loop. Line 70 subtracts 1 from the loop counter in A. Line 80 jumps back to the head of the loop if the counter has not reached zero.

When the loop counter reaches zero, control falls through to the next instruction, HLT.

Line 100 defines a data storage area named MESSAG that contains the message we want to print.

Code a routine to write the message 'THANK YOU' on the terminal, then halt.

```
       MVI  A,9
       LXI  H,OUTMSG
WRITER EQU  $
       MOV  B,M
       CALL OUTPUT
       INX  H
       SUI  1
       JNZ  WRITER
       HLT
OUTMSG DB   'THANK YOU'
```

Be careful that control does not fall through to the DB instruction. The computer would try to execute 'THANK YOU' as an instruction, causing all kinds of strange errors.

17. Code a routine that reads a message from the terminal. Store the message, but do not echo it. When the user types a carriage return, write the following:

- carriage return and line feed
- the message
- a question mark

Programming Notes: Be careful the output message does not contain the carriage return typed by the user. Either don't store the CR or overlay it with the question mark.

Don't control the length of the message. But in defining your data area, assume that it will be 80 characters or less.

```
                MVI   C,0
                LXI   H,TEXT
        READIT  EQU   $
                CALL  INPUT
                MOV   M,B
                INX   H
                MOV   A,C
                ADI   1
                MOV   C,A
                MOV   A,B
                SUI   0DH
                JNZ   READIT
                DCX   H
                MVI   M,'?'
                LXI   H,ANSWER
                MOV   A,C
                ADI   2
        WRITIT  EQU   $
                MOV   B,M
                CALL  OUTPUT
                INX   H
                SUI   1
                JNZ   WRITIT
                HLT
        ANSWER  DB    0DH,0AH
        TEXT    DS    80
```

Notice how we set up the data storage area (lines 250 and 260) so that the address ANSWER refers to ASCII CR, which is followed by ASCII LF, which is followed by the area named TEXT where we store the input data.

Register C is used to count the number of input characters (lines 10 and 70 through 90). We add 2 to it to count the number of output loops (lines 170, 220, 230) since we're writing two more characters than we read.

Lines 30 through 120 are the input loop, reading characters and storing them in memory starting at TEXT.

Lines 130 and 140 replace the final character (ASCII CR) with '?'. Lines 150 through 170 set up the output loop by pointing H–L at ANSWER and setting up register A with the loop counter.

COMPARISONS

You've learned to use the conditional instructions and you've seen how open loops can be created. You've also seen that the status flags are set as the result of arithmetic operations. Now we're going to look at some instructions that set the flags without any arithmetic being performed.

18. Suppose we want to input values from the terminal until an asterisk is encountered. Here's one way:

```
RLOOP   EQU   $
        CALL  INPUT
        MOV   A,B
        SUI   '*'
        JZ    RLOOP
```

But we have destroyed the value in the register in order to find out if it was an asterisk. Here's another way:

```
RLOOP   EQU   $
        CALL  INPUT
        MOV   A,B
        CPI   '*'
        JZ    RLOOP
```

Notice the CPI instruction. It stands for "compare immediate." It compares the value in the A register with the immediate byte and sets the flags accordingly. How does it "compare" them? By pretending to subtract the immediate byte from the accumulator. The flags are set as if the subtraction had taken place. But the value in the A register is not altered.

(a) Write an instruction to compare the A register to an ASCII space—

20H. ______________________________

(b) Suppose the A register contains an ASCII zero—30H. What will be the effect of the above instruction (a) on the zero flag? ______________ The sign flag? ______________ The carry flag? ______________ The A register? ______________

(c) Suppose the A register contains an ASCII space. What will be the effect of the above instruction (a) on the zero flag? ______________ The sign flag? ______________ The carry flag? ______________ The A register? ______________

(d) Suppose you want to jump to PUTNEX if the value in the A register was an ASCII space. Otherwise, control should fall through. Write the jump instruction. ______________________________

— — — — — — — — — — — — — —

(a) CPI ' ' or CPI 20H; (b) set to zero, set to zero, set to zero, no change; (c) set to one, set to zero, set to zero, no change; (d) JZ PUTNEX

19. Here are some more problems using CPI.

(a) Write a set of instructions to compare the A register to 50H. If it does not equal 50H, jump to NEXONE. If it does equal 50H, let control fall through.

____

____

____

(b) Write a set of instructions to compare the A register to ASCII A. If it is equal to or greater than A, jump to LETTER. If it's less than A, let control fall through.

____

____

____

— — — — — — — — — — — — — —

(a)
```
CPI   50H
JNZ   NEXONE
```

(b)
```
CPI   'A'   or   CPI   41H
JNC   LETTER
```

Any value smaller than 41H will cause a borrow, thus turning on the carry flag. If the value is 41H or larger, the carry flag will be turned off.

20. You have learned the CPI instruction. There is also a CMP ("compare") instruction. It compares the value in a specified register, or M, with the A register. Here are the formats of both instructions.

[*label*] CPI *i* [;*comments*]
[*label*] CMP *r1* [;*comments*]

(a) Write an instruction to compare the A and B registers. ____________

(b) Write an instruction to compare the A and L registers. ____________

(c) Write a set of instructions to compare the E register with 10H.

____

____

____

(d) Write a set of instructions to compare the C and D registers.

____

____

____

(e) Write a set of instructions to read a value from the terminal. If it is equal to the value in the C register, jump to SAMVAL. Otherwise, let control fall through.

____

____

____

____

____

- - - - - - - - - - - - -

(a) CMP B
(b) CMP L
(c) Here are two ways to solve the problem:

```
MOV  A,E                    MVI  A,10H
CPI  10H                    CMP  E
```

They have different effects. In the first, 10H is "subtracted" from the value in E. In the second, the value in E is "subtracted" from 10H.

(d)
```
MOV  A,C
CMP  D
```

(e)
```
CALL INPUT
MOV  A,B
CMP  C
JZ   SAMVAL
```

ALTERNATE PATHS

21. You've learned how to code loops. Another extremely important program structure is illustrated by Figure 6.5. We call this alternate paths although there are many other names for the structure.

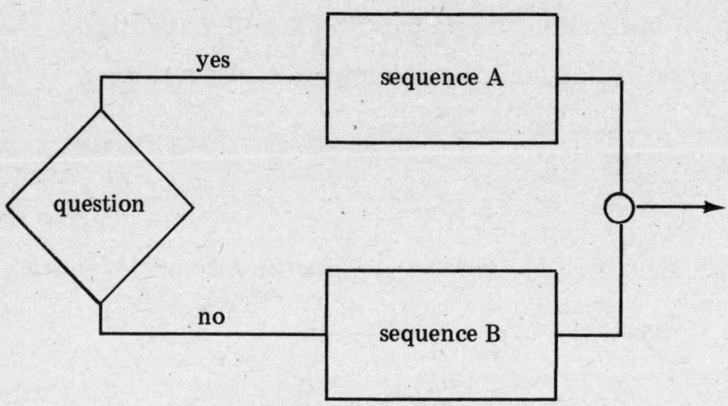

FIGURE 6.5. Alternate Paths

In this structure, a yes–no question is asked (or a true–false condition tested). If the answer is yes, one path is taken. If the answer is no, the other path is taken.

For example, suppose we want to read and edit the user's input. If the user types a digit between 0 and 9, we store the digit. If the user types any other character, we write an error message.

(a) In our example, what is the yes–no question? ____________________

____

(b) What is the "yes" path? ____________________

(c) What is the "no" path? ____________________

— — — — — — — — — — — —

There are two ways to answer these questions:
(a) Is the input value between 0 and 9? (b) store the digit;
(c) write error message

or

(a) Is the input value outside of the range of 0 to 9? (b) write error message; (c) store the digit

22. In Assembly Language, alternate paths are coded using comparisons and conditional jumps. Here's a simple example:

```
              CALL  INPUT
              MOV   A,B
              CPI   '5'
              JNZ   NOTFIV
       FIVE   EQU   $
              LXI   H,FIVMSG
              JMP   OUTMSG
       NOTFIV EQU   $
              LXI   H,NOTMSG
       OUTMSG EQU   $
              MVI   A,5
       LOOPER EQU   $
              MOV   B,M
              CALL  OUTPUT
              INX   H
              SUI   1
              JNZ   LOOPER
              HLT
       FIVMSG DB    'RIGHT'
       NOTMSG DB    'WRONG'
```

Which of the following diagrams correctly depicts what this routine does?

_____ (a)

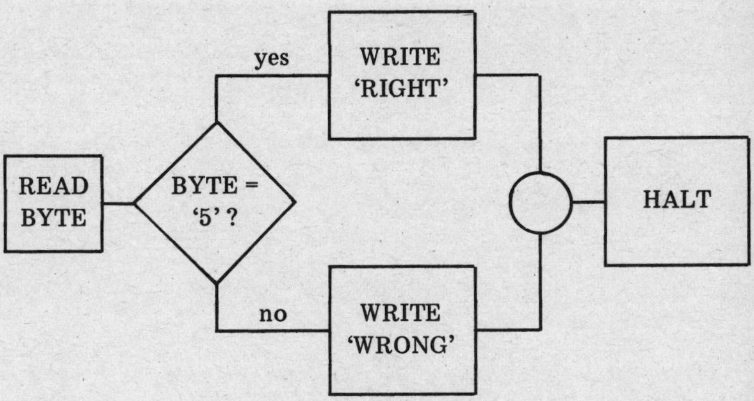

_____ (b)

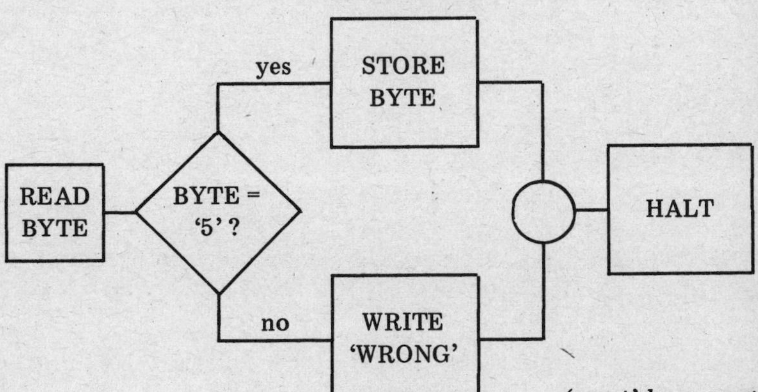

(cont'd on next page)

_____ (c)

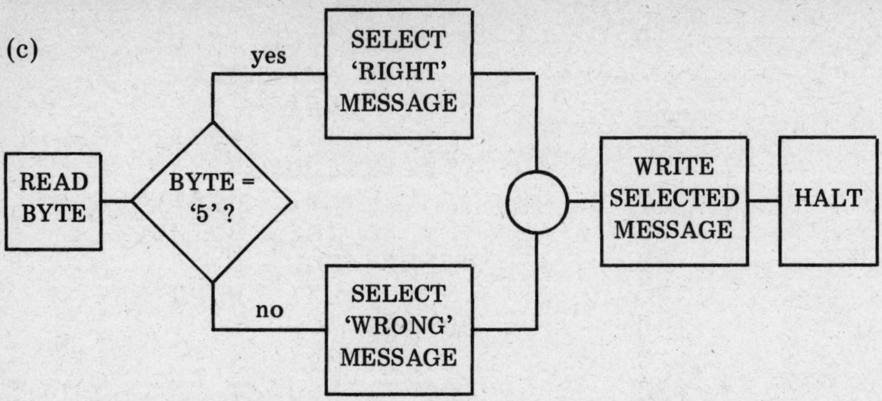

(c) is the most correct answer; (b) is close but not completely right

23. Now it's your turn. Write a routine to read and echo two characters from the terminal. If they're the same, write 'SAME'. If they're not the same, write 'DIFF'.

```
10              CALL INPUT
20              CALL OUTPUT
30              MOV  A,B
40              CALL INPUT
50              CALL OUTPUT
60              CMP  B
70              JNZ  DIFFER
80       SAME   EQU  $
90              LXI  H,SAMMSG
100             JMP  WRITER
110      DIFFER EQU  $
120             LXI  H,DIFMSG
130      WRITER EQU  $
140             MVI  A,4
150      LOOPIT EQU  $
160             MOV  B,M
170             CALL OUTPUT
180             INX  H
190             SUI  1
200             JNZ  LOOPIT
210             HLT
220      SAMMSG DB   'SAME'
230      DIFMSG DB   'DIFF'
```

Lines 10 through 50 read and echo the two characters. They are stored in the A and B registers. Line 60 compares them. Line 70 jumps control to DIFFER if they are not the same. We chose to jump if they're different so that our "good" case—they're the same—comes first. This makes the structure a little easier for someone else to follow.

Line 80 is not necessary. We coded it for human readers. If the two characters are the same, H–L is pointed at SAMMSG. Control is then jumped past the DIFFER routine to WRITER—a very important step. Be sure to always jump around your second path.

If the two characters are different, the H–L pair is pointed at DIFMSG.

The WRITER routine sets up 4 in the A register so output loops can be counted. Then LOOPIT puts out the message—whichever message is pointed to by the H–L pair.

24. Often an alternate path structure has an empty "yes" or "no" path. Figure 6.6 depicts the logic diagrams of such structures.

Suppose we want to read a byte and, if it's not a space, store it in memory and increment H-L. If it is a space, do nothing. Here's the code:

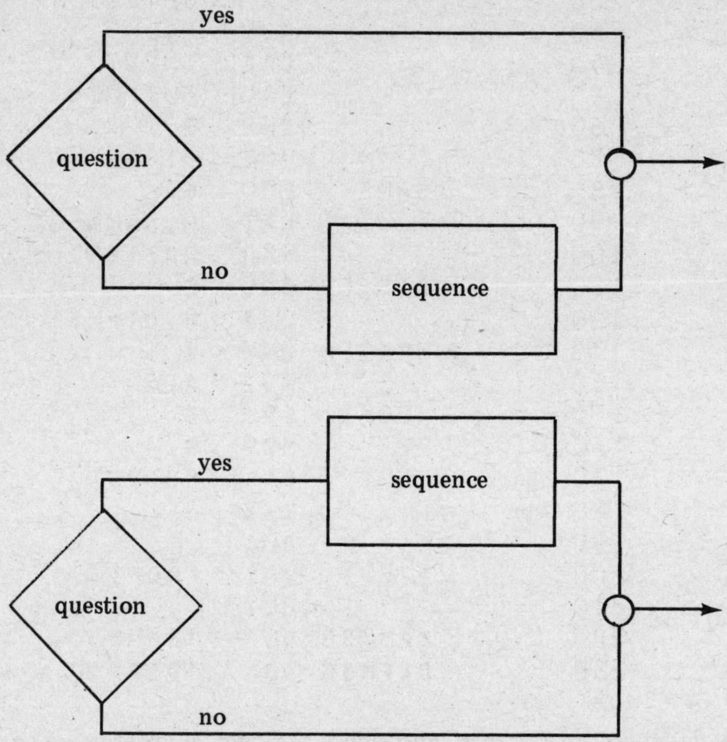

FIGURE 6.6. Empty Path Structures

```
        CALL INPUT
        MOV  A,B
        CMP  20H
        JZ   NEXTEP
NOTSPA  EQU  $
        MOV  M,B
        INX  H
NEXTEP  EQU  $
```

Whether it's the "yes" path or the "no" path that's empty is immaterial. The empty path jumps around the not-empty path, to the point where they rejoin.

Code a routine that will read and echo a byte. If it's a carriage return, also write a line feed. Then store the byte in memory.

```
- - - - - - - - - - - - - -
             CALL  INPUT
             CALL  OUTPUT
             MOV   A,B
             CPI   0DH       ; COMPARE TO CR
             JNZ   STORIT
             MVI   B,0AH     ; WRITE LF
             CALL  OUTPUT
     STORIT  EQU   $
             MOV   M,A
```

REVIEW

In this chapter, you have learned how to use the conditional instructions to handle loops and alternate path structures.

- The conditional instructions are based on the flags.
- The conditional jump instructions are:
  JC — Jump if Carry
  JNC — Jump if Not Carry
  JZ — Jump if Zero
  JNZ — Jump if Not Zero
  JM — Jump if Minus
  JP — Jump if Plus
  JPE — Jump if Parity is Even
  JPO — Jump if Parity is Odd
- The comparison instructions cause the status flags to be set without altering the value in the A register. They are:

  [*label*] CMP *r1* [;*comments*]
  [*label*] CPI *i* [;*comments*]

- An open loop is usually coded with a compare followed by a conditional jump. If the condition proves false, control falls through to the next instruction.
- In a counted loop, the count value is placed in the accumulator unless the accumulator is needed for other purposes in the loop. At the end of each loop, the loop counter is decremented. When it reaches zero, control falls out of the loop.
- An alternate path structure asks a yes–no question. One path is taken if the answer is yes and another is taken if the answer is no.

Either path may be empty. The structure is coded using conditional jumps. In Assembly Language, the structure looks like this:

```
        JNZ   NOPATH
YESPTH  EQU   $
        .
        .
        .
        JMP   REJOIN
NOPATH  EQU   $
        .
        .
        .
REJOIN  EQU   $
```

If there is an empty path, the structure looks like this:

```
        JZ    REJOIN
PATH    EQU   $
        .
        .
        .
REJOIN  EQU   $
```

CHAPTER 6 — SELF-TEST

Part I. Code instructions to solve the following problems.

1. Jump to START if the zero flag is off.

   ____

2. Jump to CARRY if the carry flag is on.

   ____

3. Jump to NEGIVE if the sign flag is on.

   ____

4. If the accumulator equals 20H, jump to SPACE. Otherwise, jump to NOTSPA.

   ____

   ____

   ____

5. If the accumulator is greater than the value in register B, jump to MORE.

____

____

____

Part II. In this exercise you will code a data compression program. Data compression is used when you have a lot of data to store and you want to conserve some space. It works this way: Repeated characters are removed from the data. For example (ƀ indicates a space):

JOHNƀJONESƀ[ƀƀƀƀ]21201ƀ[ƀƀƀ]180[000000]

The boxed characters would be removed. We have to tell the system that some characters have been removed. We do this by storing a warning flag followed by the count of the number characters that were removed. So the above data would be stored this way (0FFH is the warning flag):

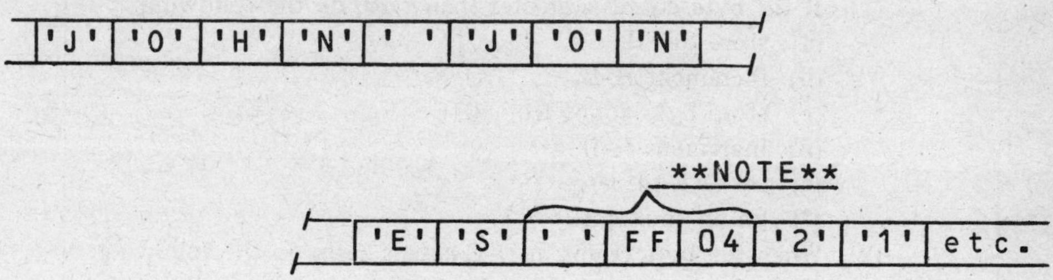

The three bytes—' 'FF04—tell the computer that 4 spaces were removed.

Your job is to write a program that will read a string of characters from the terminal and store them in compressed format. End the program when the user types a carriage return.

Figure 6.7 shows our program logic.

Programming Notes: Even though it's not completely efficient, compress any repeated character even if it's only repeated once.

Assume that the input string is less than 80 characters.

Strategy: In order to identify repeated characters, each character we read must be compared with the preceding character. We'll keep the preceding character in register C. When we find repeated characters, we must count them. We'll keep the count in register pair D-E (but assume that D will always contain zeros).

1. Initialization.
   a. Set register C to a value that *cannot* match the first input byte, such as 0FFH.
   b. Set register pair D-E to binary zero.
   c. Point register pair H-L at the beginning of the storage area.
2. Read and echo one character. Check for carriage return
3. If not a carriage return, compare new byte with last character stored in register C.
   a. If it's the same as the preceding byte, add one to the byte count in D-E and go back to step 2.
   b. If it's different from the preceding byte, check the byte count in D-E.
      (1) If the byte count is greater than zero, do the following:
         (a) store 0FFH
         (b) increment H-L
         (c) store byte count from D-E
         (d) increment H-L
         (e) set D-E to zero
         (f) go on to step (2)
      (2) When the byte count in D-E equals zero, do the following:
         (a) store the new byte in memory
         (b) increment H-L
         (c) move the new byte to register C
         (d) go back to step 2
4. If new byte is a carriage return, check the byte count in D-E.
   a. If the byte count is greater than zero, do the following:
      (1) store 0FFH
      (2) increment H-L
      (3) store the byte count from E
      (4) go on to b
   b. When there is no more data to be stored, stop.

FIGURE 6.7. Compression Program Logic

Self-Test Answer Key

Part I.

```
1.   JNZ   START

2.   JC    CARRY
```

```
3.  JM   NEGIVE

4.  CPI  20H
    JZ   SPACE
    JMP  NOTSPA (or JNZ  NOTSPA)
5.  CMP  B
    JNC  MORE
```

Part II.

```
; REGISTER C HOLDS PRECEDING BYTE
; REGISTER D-E COUNTS COMPRESSED BYTES
ZEROS  EQU  0
HIVAL  EQU  0FFH
CR     EQU  0DH
       MVI  C,HIVAL
       LXI  D,ZEROS
       LXI  H,STORAG
GETBYT EQU  $
       CALL INPUT
       CALL OUTPUT
       MOV  A,B
       CPI  CR
       JZ   ENDING
       CMP  C
       JNZ  DIFFER
SAME   EQU  $
       INX  D       ; INCREMENT BYTE COUNT
       JMP  GETBYT
DIFFER EQU  $
       MOV  A,E
       CPI  ZEROS
       JZ   STORE
       MVI  M,HIVAL
       INX  H
       MOV  M,E
       INX  H
       MVI  E,ZEROS
STORE  EQU  $
       MOV  M,B
       INX  H
       MOV  C,B     ; MOVE TO LAST BYTE
       JMP  GETBYT
ENDING EQU  $
       MOV  M,B
       HLT
STORAG DS   80
```

CHAPTER SEVEN

ADDITIONAL REGISTER INSTRUCTIONS

In Assembly Language, as you have already learned, the registers are extremely important. You have studied the most basic instructions for manipulating data in registers. In this chapter, you'll learn some more advanced register instructions.

When you have finished this chapter, you will be able to:

- Code the following Assembly Language instructions:
  - LDA (load A)
  - STA (store A)
  - LDAX (load A extended)
  - STAX (store A extended)
  - LHLD (load H–L direct)
  - SHLD (store H–L direct
  - XCHG (exchange)
  - INR (increment register)
  - DCR (decrement register)
  - DAD (double add)
- Indicate which flags are set by each of the above instructions.
- Code routines to solve the following types of problems:
  - Move data between the registers and memory without using the H–L pair for addressing.
  - Keep track of two memory addresses simultaneously.
  - Keep a tally in a register other than A.
  - Keep a loop counter in a register other than A.
  - Increase the address in the H–L pair by a variable amount.

THE LDA INSTRUCTION

1. The LDA instruction is used to move one byte of data from memory into the A register. LDA stands for "load A."

In computers, "load" always implies the movement and storage of data into something. Thus, we load a register when we move data into it. We load a program into memory in order to execute it. So, "load A" means to move data into the A register.

The format of the LDA instruction is:

[*label*] LDA *addr* [;*comments*]

The operand gives the memory address of the byte to be moved. It can be an actual address or the name of an address. This is the first instruction you've studied that accesses data in memory without using the H–L register pair.

(a) Write an instruction to load register A with the byte at memory address 025CH. ______

(b) Which of the following is equivalent to the above instruction?

```
__ MOV  H,A          __ LXI  H,025CH
   MOV  M,H             MOV  A,M
```

(c) Write an instruction to move one byte from the memory area named ERRFLG to register A. ______

– – – – – – – – – – – – – –

(a) LDA 025CH; (b) LXI H,025CH; MOV A,M; (c) LDA ERRFLG

2. When should you use LDA and when should you use LXI followed by MOV? When you're loading one byte, LDA is better, since it requires one fewer instruction. But if you're transferring more than one memory byte in a row, then LXI and MOV are better because you can use INX to increment the address in the H–L pair.

For each of the following functions, indicate which instructions would be better, LDA or LXI, MOV.

(a) Write the message "THANK YOU!" ______

(b) Move a loop counter named NUMTIM from memory into A. ______

– – – – – – – – – – – – – –

(a) LXI, MOV; (b) LDA

THE STA INSTRUCTION

3. The "opposite" of LDA is STA (store A), which stores the byte from register A in memory, at the location you specify. The format is:

[*label*] STA *addr* [;*comments*]

(a) Code an instruction to store the accumulator byte at the memory address named WHATX. ______________________________

(b) Code an instruction to store the accumulator byte at address 0100H.

____

(c) Code instructions to add 4 (decimal) to the value at the address named SAVIT. The result should be stored in SAVIT.

____

____

____

- - - - - - - - - - - - -

(a) STA WHATX; (b) STA 100H;

(c)
```
LDA   SAVIT
ADI   4
STA   SAVIT
```

4. Code a brief routine that reads and echos an input message 10 bytes long and stores it in memory starting at INTEXT. Decide whether to use addressing through H–L or LDA and STA instructions.

____

____

____

____

____

____

____

____

____

____

- - - - - - - - - - - - -

```
        LXI   H,INTEXT
        MVI   A,10   ; LOOP COUNTER
RLOOP   EQU   $
        CALL  INPUT
        CALL  OUTPUT
        MOV   M,B
        INX   H
```

(cont'd on facing page)

```
        SUI  1
        JNZ  RLOOP
        HLT
INTEXT  DS   10
```

(Addressing through H–L is better here because you are accessing more than one byte.)

5. Code a routine that will read and echo two digits between 0 and 4, add them, and put out a message in this format: THE SUM IS *n*.

```
        CALL INPUT
        CALL OUTPUT
        MOV  A,B
        CALL INPUT
        CALL OUTPUT
        ADD  B
        SUI  30H      ; ADJUST ASCII BITS
        STA  SUM
        MVI  A,12     ; LOOP COUNT
        LXI  H,ANSWER
OUTLOP  EQU  $
        MOV  B,M
        CALL OUTPUT
        INX  H
        SUI  1
        JNZ  OUTLOP
        HLT
ANSWER  DB   'THE SUM IS '
SUM     DS   1
```

(Since SUM immediately follows ANSWER in memory, it's written on the twelfth loop.)

THE LDAX AND STAX INSTRUCTIONS

6. Sometimes we want to use a register pair for memory addressing, but we don't want to use the H–L pair. Perhaps the H–L pair is busy holding another memory address that we don't want to lose track of.

The LDAX (load A extended) and STAX (store A extended) instructions load and store the accumulator at the memory address in the register pair that *you* specify, either B–C or D–E.

The formats are:

[*label*] LDAX *rp* [;*comments*]
[*label*] STAX *rp* [;*comments*]

For example, suppose we want to store the accumulator at SUM. We could do it this way:

```
LXI  B,SUM
STAX B
```

This will point the B–C pair at SUM, then store A at the address in B–C.

(a) Code an instruction to point the D–E pair at MESAG. ____________

(b) Code an instruction to increment the address in the D–E pair.

____

(c) Code an instruction to store the accumulator at the memory byte addressed by D–E. ____________

(d) Code an instruction to load the accumulator from the memory byte addressed by B–C. ____________

(e) Code an instruction to store the accumulator at the memory address in H–L. ____________

(f) Which of the following are legal instructions?

_____ LDAX H	_____ STAX B
_____ LDAX PSW	_____ LDAX A
_____ STAX PC	_____ STAX D

— — — — — — — — — — — —

(a) LXI D,MESAG; (b) INX D; (c) STAX D; (d) LDAX B;
(e) MOV M,A—hope we didn't catch you with this one; (f) STAX B and STAX D

7. Code a set of instructions to read and store an incoming ten-byte message at INTEXT. Don't use the H–L pair.

```
        LXI  D,INTEXT
        MVI  C,10      ; COUNT LOOPS
INLOOP  EQU  $
        CALL INPUT
        MOV  A,B       ; MUST STORE FROM A
        STAX D
        INX  D
        MOV  A,C       ; ADJUST LOOP COUNT
        SUI  1
        MOV  C,A
        JNZ  INLOOP
        HLT
INTEXT  DS   10
```

THE LHLD AND SHLD INSTRUCTIONS

8. Sometimes we want to store the address that is in the H–L pair in memory for a while, then retrieve it again. This can be done with the instructions you already know:

```
MOV   A,H
STA   ADDRES
MOV   A,L
STA   ADDRES+1
...
LDA   ADDRES
MOV   H,A
LDA   ADDRES+1
MOV   L,A
```

An easier way is to use the SHLD (store H-L direct) and LHLD (load H-L direct) instructions. Their formats are:

[*label*] SHLD *addr* [;*comments*]
[*label*] LHLD *addr* [;*comments*]

(a) Rewrite the above code using SHLD and LHLD.

(b) What register pairs can be stored and loaded using SHLD and LHLD?

_____ PSW

_____ B-C

_____ D-E

_____ H-L

_____ all of the above

— — — — — — — — — — — —

(a)
```
SHLD ADDRES
...
LHLD ADDRES
```

(b) H-L

9. SHLD and LHLD reverse the bytes in H-L as they're stored and loaded. Thus, it's always wise to use the two instructions as a pair. That way the value that's returned to H-L is the same as the one that was stored.

Suppose you have this situation:

H-L

00	01

memory (SUM points to address 0003)

3A	2B	1C	00	59
0000	0001	0002	0003	0004

(a) Show the effect of SHLD 0.

memory

0	1	2	3	4

(b) Show the effect of SHLD SUM.

memory

0	1	2	3	4

(a)

01	00	1C	00	59

; (b)

3A	2B	1C	01	00

10. The LXI instruction is preferable to LHLD for putting data in the H-L pair. When would you use LHLD and SHLD? When the value you want to store in H-L varies in the program.

Suppose you want to read a set of values from the terminal. Values less than 41H should be stored starting at NUMBERS. Values 41H or greater should be stored at LETTRS. Here's one way to accomplish the function:

```
              LXI   H,NUMBRS    ; POINT TO NUMBERS
              SHLD  NUMADR      ; STORE ADDRESS
              LXI   H,LETTRS    ; POINT TO LETTERS
              SHLD  LETADR      ; STORE ADDRESS
       RLOOP  EQU   $
              CALL  INPUT
              MOV   A,B         ; DECIDE LETTER OR NUMBER
              CPI   41H
              JNC   LETTER
              LHLD  NUMADR
              MOV   M,B
              INX   H
              SHLD  NUMADR
              JMP   RLOOP
       LETTER EQU   $
              LHLD  LETADR
```

(cont'd on next page)

```
170                MOV  M,B
180                INX  H
190                SHLD LETADR
200                JMP  RLOOP
210         LETTRS DS   10
220         NUMBRS DS   10
230         NUMADR DS   2               ; ADDRESS FOR NUMBERS
240         LETADR DS   2               ; ADDRESS FOR LETTERS
```

Line 10 points H–L at NUMBRS and line 20 stores that address (with reversed bytes) at NUMADR. Lines 30 and 40 do the same for LETTRS. Let's follow an input number through the loop. Lines 60 through 80 read the number and compare it with 41H. The comparison will cause the carry flag to be set since a number will be less than 41H. Therefore, control falls through to line 100. H–L is loaded with the data in NUMADR (with reversed bytes). So H–L is now pointing at NUMBRS. The input byte is stored there. That address is incremented then re-stored at NUMADR. The next input number will be stored at NUMBRS+1 and so forth. Then we restart the input loop. A letter is processed in exactly the same manner.

The following questions pertain to the above example.

(a) If the *second* input byte is a number, what address should it be stored at?

_____ NUMBRS

_____ NUMBRS+1

_____ It depends on whether the first byte was a letter or a number.

(b) Why don't we use LXI to load the address in H–L during RLOOP?

____

– – – – – – – – – – – – – –

(a) It depends on whether the first byte was a letter or a number.
(b) Because after the first loop we don't know where H–L should be pointing.

11. There's another way to code the problem in the previous frame. We could use two different register pairs to hold the two different addresses, then use STAX to do the storing. See if you can code the solution this way.

```
        LXI   H,NUMBRS   ; H-L WILL TRACK NUMS
        LXI   D,LETTRS   ; D-E WILL TRACK LETS
RLOOP   EQU   $
        CALL  INPUT
        MOV   A,B
        CPI   41H        ; DECIDE LETTER OR NUMBER
        JNC   LETTER
        MOV   M,B
        INX   H
        JMP   RLOOP
LETTER  EQU   $
        STAX  D
        INX   D
        JMP   RLOOP
LETTRS  DS    10
NUMBRS  DS    10
```

(This solution would be more readable if the two addresses were kept in B–C and D–E and STAX were used in both cases. But register B is needed for input, so we can't use it for addressing without a lot of bother. Thus, we used H–L, which requires a MOV instruction instead of STAX.)

THE XCHG INSTRUCTION

12. The XCHG instruction exchanges the values in the D–E pair with the values in the H–L pair. This can come in very handy if you are keeping track of more than one memory address at once but don't want to use LDAX and STAX to access memory.

The format is:

[*label*] XCHG [;*comments*]

(a) What registers are exchanged with XCHG? ______________________

(b) Revise the solution to the previous frame so that it uses XCHG.

(a) D–E and H–L

(b)

```
        LXI  H,NUMBRS
        LXI  D,LETTRS
RLOOP   EQU  $
        CALL INPUT
        MOV  A,B
        CPI  41H
        JNC  LETTER
        MOV  M,B
        INX  H
        JMP  RLOOP
LETTER  EQU  $
        XCHG           ; USE ADDRESS IN D-E
        MOV  M,B
        INX  H
        XCHG           ; PUT ADDRESS BACK IN D-E
        JMP  RLOOP
LETTRS  DS   10
NUMBRS  DS   10
```

13. So far in this chapter you have studied a new set of data movement instructions. Use them as you code instructions to meet the following specifications.

(a) Move the value from byte 2100H into register A. ____________

(b) Store register A at the address in the B–C pair. ____________

(c) Load the H–L pair with the data at address 500H, with bytes reversed.

____

(d) Swap the D–E pair with the H–L pair. ______________

(a) LDA 2100H; (b) STAX B; (c) LHLD 500H; (d) XCHG

Now let's go on and look at some other types of register operations.

THE INR AND DCR INSTRUCTIONS

14. You have already learned how to increment and decrement a register pair using INX and DCX. Other instructions can be used to increment and decrement single registers. The INR (increment register) instruction adds one to the indicated register and the DCR (decrement register) instruction subtracts one from the indicated register. The formats are:

[*label*] INR *r1* [;*comments*]
[*label*] DCR *r1* [;*comments*]

The following registers may be specified: A, B, C, D, E, H, L. M may also be specified.

(a) Code an instruction to increment the B register. ______________

(b) Code an instruction to decrement the L register. ______________

(c) Show two different ways to increment the A register. ______________

____

(d) Code a set of instructions to decrement the memory byte named COUNTER.

____

____

(a) INR B; (b) DCR L; (c) INR A and ADI 1;

(d)
```
LXI   H,COUNTER
DCR   M
```

15. INX and DCX do not affect the status flags but INR and DCR do.
This is the first instruction you've seen that sets the flags for a value that's not in the A register. But here's an important exception: The carry flag is not set.

(a) Which status flags are set by INR?

_____ carry

_____ auxiliary carry

_____ zero

_____ sign

_____ parity

_____ all of them

_____ none of them

(b) Which status flags are set by INX?

_____ carry

_____ auxiliary carry

_____ zero

_____ sign

_____ parity

_____ all of them

_____ none of them

- - - - - - - - - - - - - -

(a) auxiliary carry, zero, sign, and parity; (b) none of them

16. The INR instruction is usually used for tallying purposes. For example, suppose you want to keep track of the number of pages in a report. You know there won't be more than 0FFH (255D) pages.

Suppose the page counter is defined as:

```
PAGNUM DB  0
```

Code a routine that will increment the page counter in memory.

____

____

- - - - - - - - - - - - - -

```
LXI   H,PAGNUM
INR   M
```

17. Code a routine that will read, echo, and store an input message up to 80 bytes long. Keep track of the number of bytes that are entered. The end of the message is signalled by a carriage return. Do not echo, store, or

count the carriage return. When the carriage return is read, jump to a routine named PROCES (don't code the PROCES routine).

```
        MVI  D,0         ; D WILL COUNT INPUT BYTES
        LXI  H,INTEXT
INLOOP  EQU  $
        CALL INPUT
        MOV  A,B         ; TEST FOR CR
        CPI  0DH
        JZ   PROCES
        CALL OUTPUT      ; ECHO
        MOV  M,B         ; STORE BYTE
        INX  H
        INR  D           ; ADD 1 TO BYTE COUNTER
        JMP  INLOOP
INTEXT  DS   80
```

18. The DCR instruction sets all the status flags except for the carry flag.

(a) Which flags are set by DCX?

_____ carry

_____ auxiliary carry

_____ zero

_____ sign

_____ parity

_____ all of them

_____ none of them

(b) Which flags are set by DCR?

_____ carry

_____ auxiliary carry

_____ zero

_____ sign

_____ parity

_____ all of them

_____ none of them

— — — — — — — — — — — — —

(a) none of them; (b) auxiliary carry, zero, sign, and parity

19. The DCR instruction is primarily used to count loops. Do you remember learning to use the A register to hold a loop count? This is often inconvenient because the A register is needed in the loop.

Here's a routine we used in frame 7.

```
        LXI   D,INTEXT
        MVI   C,10        ; COUNT LOOPS
INLOOP  EQU   $
        CALL  INPUT
        MOV   A,B         ; MUST STORE FROM A
        STAX  D
        INX   D
        MOV   A,C         ; ADJUST LOOP COUNT
        SUI   1
        MOV   C,A
        JNZ   INLOOP
        HLT
INTEXT  DS    10
```

Simplify the routine by making the loop counting easier.

— — — — — — — — — — — — —

```
        LXI  D,INTEXT
        MVI  C,10        ; COUNT LOOPS
INLOOP  EQU  $
        CALL INPUT
        MOV  A,B         ; MUST STORE FROM A
        STAX D
        INX  D
        DCR  C           ; ADJUST LOOP COUNT
        JNZ  INLOOP
        HLT
INTEXT  DS   10
```

20. Because the A, H, and L registers are so busy, we usually want to do tallying and loop counting in B, C, D, or E.

(a) What instruction is best to add one to a tally in register C?

_____________________ .

(b) What instruction is best to subtract one from a loop count in register E?

____

– – – – – – – – – – – – – –

(a) INR C; (b) DCR E

THE DAD INSTRUCTION

21. The DAD (double add) instruction adds the value of another register pair to the H–L pair. The result remains in the H–L register. The format is:

[*label*] DAD *rp* [;*comments*]

The allowable values for *rp* are: B, D, H, and SP. The PSW–A pair can't be added to H–L.

(a) Code an instruction to add the value in the B–C pair to the H–L pair.

____

(b) Code an instruction to add the value in the D–E pair to the H–L pair.

____

(c) Code an instruction to double the value in the H–L pair.

____

(d) Which of the following instructions are legal?

_____ `DAD PC`

_____ `DAD SP`

_____ `DAD PSW`

— — — — — — — — — — — — —

(a) DAD B; (b) DAD D; (c) DAD H; (d) DAD SP

22. The DAD instruction sets the carry flag but no other flags.

(a) Code a set of instructions to add B–C to H–L. If the result overflows the H–L register pair, branch to a routine named OVERHL.

(b) What is the only flag set by DAD? ______________________________

— — — — — — — — — — — — —

(a)
```
DAD  B
JC   OVERHL
```

(b) carry

23. One disadvantage of INX is that the status flags aren't set. So if you're incrementing H–L, as in the routine shown below, you can't test to see if you have exceeded the highest memory address.

```
        MVI  D,100   ; COUNT LOOPS
        LXI  H,MESG
OUTER   EQU  $
        MOV  B,M
        CALL OUTPUT
        INX  H       ; <=== NOTE
        DCR  D
        JNZ  OUTER
```

Rewrite the above routine using DAD to increment H–L. If the result overflows, jump to TOOHI. (Don't code the TOOHI routine.)

```
        LXI  D,1     ; INCREMENT
        MVI  C,100
        LXI  H,MESG
OUTER   EQU  $
        MOV  B,M
        CALL OUTPUT
        DAD  D
        JC   TOOHI
        DCR  C
        JNZ  OUTER
```

24. Another advantage of DAD over INX is that it allows you to increment by amounts other than one.

(a) Code a routine to increment the H–L pair by two.

(b) Code a routine to increment the H–L pair by a variable amount, which is kept in a one-byte memory area called INCREM.

(a)
```
LXI  D,2 ; D-E HOLDS INCREMENT
DAD  D
```

(b) The major problem here is getting the value from INCREM into either the B–C pair or the D–E pair.

If you chose to load the value into A, then transfer it to the D–E pair, your solution will look something like this:

```
LDA  INCREM
MOV  E,A
MVI  D,0     ; YOU SHOULD CLEAR D
DAD  D
```

If you chose to load the value into H–L using LHLD, your solution will look something like this:

```
XCHG         ; PUT H-L IN D-E
LHLD INCREM  ; PUT INCREM IN L
MVI  H,0     ; CLEAR H
DAD  D
```

25. Were you surprised to find that your computer can only add up to

255 using ADD or ADI? Now you have an instruction, DAD, that will do 16-bit addition using H–L.

(a) What's the largest number that can result from DAD?

____

(b) Which flags are set by DAD? ______________________________

(c) DAD is often referred to as the double precision addition instruction. What do you think "double precision" means?

____

(d) Code a routine which will read, echo, and add a series of single digits. Use double precision arithmetic. If the sum overflows H–L, jump to TOOBIG. (Don't code the TOOBIG routine.)

(a) 1111111111111111B = 0FFFFH = 65,535; (b) carry only;
(c) it uses twice as many bits.
(d)

```
        LXI   D,0      ; CLEAR D-E
        LXI   H,0      ; CLEAR H-L
INLOOP  EQU   $
        CALL  INPUT
        CALL  OUTPUT
        MOV   A,B
        SUI   30H      ; ELIMINATE ASCII BITS
        MOV   E,A
        DAD   D
        JC    TOOBIG
        JMP   INLOOP
```

REVIEW

In this chapter, you have studied several more register instructions.

- The LDA (load A) instruction loads register A from the designated memory address.
  Format: [*label*] LDA *addr* [;*comments*]
- The STA (store A) instruction stores register A at the designated memory address.
  Format: [*label*] STA *addr* [;*comments*]
- LDA and STA are more efficient than LXI and MOV when only one byte is being moved.
- The LDAX (load A extended) instruction loads the A register from the memory location addressed by the designated register.
  Format: [*label*] LDAX *rp* [;*comments*]
- The STAX (store A extended) instruction stores the A register at the memory location addressed by the designated register.
  Format: [*label*] STAX *rp* [;*comments*]
- The LHLD (load H-L direct) instruction loads the H-L register pair with two bytes from the designated address. The bytes are reversed as they're loaded.
  Format: [*label*] LHLD *addr* [;*comments*]
- The SHLD (store H-L direct) instruction stores the H-L register pair at the designated address. The bytes are reversed as they're stored.
  Format: [*label*] SHLD *addr* [;*comments*]
- The XCHG (exchange) instruction exchanges the values in the D-E and H-L pairs.
  Format: [*label*] XCHG [;*comments*]
- The INR (increment register) instruction adds one to the designated register. PC, SP, and PSW may not be specified.
  Format: [*label*] INR *r1* [;*comments*]

  These flags are set: auxiliary carry, sign, parity, and zero. Note that carry is not set.
- The DCR (decrement register) instruction subtracts one from the designated register. PC, SP, and PSW may not be specified.
  Format: [*label*] DCR *r1* [;*comments*]

  These flags are set: auxiliary carry, sign, parity, zero.
- The DAD (double add) instruction adds the designated register pair to the H-L pair. It is known as a double precision add.
  Format: [*label*] DAD *rp* [;*comments*]

  Only the carry flag is set.

CHAPTER 7 SELF-TEST

1. Code instructions to meet the following specifications:

   a. Store the value in the A register at memory location 210H.

   ____

   b. Store the value in the A register at memory location SUM.

   ____

   c. Load the A register with the value in STAR.

   ____

   d. Load the A register with the value in memory location 400H.

   ____

   e. Load the A register from the memory location pointed at by the B–C pair.

   ____

   f. Store the A register at the memory location pointed at by the D–E pair.

   ____

   g. Load the H–L register pair from memory locations 0027 and 0026, respectively.

   ____

   h. Store the H–L pair at the memory location named TEMPHL, with bytes reversed.

   ____

   i. Swap the values in H–L and D–E.

   ____

   j. Increment the value in register E.

   ____

   k. Decrement the value in register H.

   ____

   l. Add the value in D–E to the value in H–L.

   ____

2. Indicate which flags are set by each instruction.

____________ a. LDA	C.	carry
____________ b. STA	A.	auxiliary carry
____________ c. LDAX	Z.	zero
____________ d. STAX	S.	sign
____________ e. LHLD	P.	parity
____________ f. SHLD		
____________ g. XCHG		
____________ h. INR		
____________ i. DCR		
____________ j. DAD		
____________ k. INX		
____________ l. DCX		

3. Code short routines to solve the following problems.
   a. Load D–E from memory locations 0142 and 0141. Load H–L from STOR. Then add the two and store the result in H–L.
   b. Place the value from location COUNT in register E. Decrease it by 1, then compare it to the value in the accumulator. If they are equal, jump to a ENDL routine.

Self-Test Answer Key

1. a. `STA 210H`
   b. `STA SUM`
   c. `LDA STAR`
   d. `LDA 400H`
   e. `LDAX B`
   f. `STAX D`
   g. `LHLD 26H`
   h. `SHLD TEMPHL`
   i. `XCHG`
   j. `INR E`
   k. `DCR H`
   l. `DAD D`

2. a. none
   b. none
   c. none
   d. none
   e. none
   f. none
   g. none
   h. A, Z, S, P
   i. A, Z. S, P
   j. C
   k. none
   l. none

3. a.
```
LHLD 0141H
XCHG
LHLD STOR
DAD  D
```
   b.
```
LXI  H,COUNT
MOV  E,M
DCR  E
CMP  E
JZ   ENDL
```

CHAPTER EIGHT

LOGICAL OPERATIONS

So far, you have learned data movement, arithmetic operations, comparisons, and jumps. In this chapter, you'll learn a set of instructions that are used for logical operations. These include the logical operations of AND, OR, and EXCLUSIVE OR, which will be defined, as well as bit rotation. You'll also learn how to force the carry flag on or off.

When you have finished this chapter, you'll be able to:

- Code the following instructions:
  - — ANA (AND with A)
  - — ANI (AND immediate)
  - — ORA (OR with A)
  - — ORI (OR immediate)
  - — XRA (EXCLUSIVE OR with A)
  - — XRI (EXCLUSIVE OR immediate)
  - — RAL (rotate A left)
  - — RLC (rotate left without carry)
  - — RAR (rotate A right)
  - — RRC (rotate right without carry)
  - — STC (set carry)
  - — CMC (complement carry)
- Solve the following types of problems:
  - — turn specified bits on or off in a value
  - — test specified bits against a mask
  - — clear the accumulator using a logical operation
  - — test the least significant or most significant bit of a value
  - — shift a value left or right
  - — set the carry flag

THE *AND* AND *OR* OPERATIONS

1. The logical operations, AND and OR, compare two bits and set a third bit to show the result of the comparison.

The AND operation says that if both bit A and bit B are on, turn the result bit on. Otherwise, turn it off.

If we use the symbol Λ to represent the AND operation, we can write the four AND facts this way:

$$\begin{array}{r} 0 \\ \wedge 0 \\ \hline 0 \end{array} \qquad \begin{array}{r} 0 \\ \wedge 1 \\ \hline 0 \end{array} \qquad \begin{array}{r} 1 \\ \wedge 0 \\ \hline 0 \end{array} \qquad \begin{array}{r} 1 \\ \wedge 1 \\ \hline 1 \end{array}$$

Notice that the result bit is on (1) only if both of the ANDed bits are on.

(a) If bit A is on and bit B is off, what is the result of A Λ B? ________

(b) If both A and B are off, what is the result of A Λ B? ________

(c) If bit A and B are both on, what is the result of A Λ B? ________

— — — — — — — — — — — — —

(a) 0; (b) 0; (c) 1

2. To AND multiple-bit values, do it one column at a time. Each column is independent. There are no carries or borrows to worry about.

$$\begin{array}{r} 1011001 \\ \wedge 0110101 \\ \hline 0010001 \end{array}$$

Show the results of the following AND operations.

(a) $\begin{array}{r} 11010001 \\ \wedge 10101000 \\ \hline \end{array}$ (b) $\begin{array}{r} 00001111 \\ \wedge 01010101 \\ \hline \end{array}$

— — — — — — — — — — — — —

(a) 10000000; (b) 00000101

3. The OR operation turns on the result bit if either A or B or both are on. If we use V to represent the OR operation, the OR facts are:

$$\begin{array}{r} 0 \\ \vee\ 0 \\ \hline 0 \end{array} \qquad \begin{array}{r} 0 \\ \vee\ 1 \\ \hline 1 \end{array} \qquad \begin{array}{r} 1 \\ \vee\ 0 \\ \hline 1 \end{array} \qquad \begin{array}{r} 1 \\ \vee\ 1 \\ \hline 1 \end{array}$$

Notice here that the result bit is off (0) only if both the ORed bits are off.

Show the results of the following operations.

(a) $\begin{array}{r} 10101111 \\ \vee\ 01000110 \\ \hline \end{array}$ (b) $\begin{array}{r} 01100110 \\ \vee\ 11010100 \\ \hline \end{array}$

— — — — — — — — — — — — —

(a) 11101111; (b) 11110110

4. The EXCLUSIVE OR operation is similar to OR, but if both bits are on, the result bit is turned off. Using the symbol $\veebar$ for EXCLUSIVE OR:

$$\begin{array}{r}0\\ \veebar 0\\ \hline 0\end{array}\qquad\begin{array}{r}0\\ \veebar 1\\ \hline 1\end{array}\qquad\begin{array}{r}1\\ \veebar 0\\ \hline 1\end{array}\qquad\begin{array}{r}1\\ \veebar 1\\ \hline 0\end{array}$$

The last fact, 1 $\veebar$ 1, is what makes EXCLUSIVE OR exclusive. If either of the ORed bits is on, the result bit is on. If both are on, the result is off.

Show the results of the following operations.

(a)
$$\begin{array}{r}10110101\\ \veebar 00001111\\ \hline\end{array}$$

(b)
$$\begin{array}{r}10001101\\ \veebar 01100110\\ \hline\end{array}$$

— — — — — — — — — — — — —

(a) 10111010; (b) 11101011

5. To summarize the logical facts, complete the three tables below.

Λ	0	1
0		
1		

AND

V	0	1
0		
1		

OR

⊻	0	1
0		
1		

EXCLUSIVE OR

— — — — — — — — — — — — —

Λ	0	1
0	0	0
1	0	1

AND

V	0	1
0	0	1
1	1	1

OR

⊻	0	1
0	0	1
1	1	0

EXCLUSIVE OR

THE *ANA* AND *ANI* INSTRUCTIONS

6. Assembler offers two AND instructions: ANA (AND with A) and ANI (AND immediate). Both instructions AND the specified value with the A register, leaving the result there. The former value in the A register is destroyed.

Their formats are:

[*label*] ANA *r1* [;*comments*]
[*label*] ANI *i* [;*comments*]

With ANA, the value in the specified register is ANDed with the value in A. With ANI, the one-byte immediate value is ANDed with A.

(a) Code an instruction to AND register B with register A. ____________

(b) Code an instruction to AND the value 01010000B with A. ________

(c) Show the effect of the instruction on the two registers.

```
        A                       C
    [11001011]              [00001111]

               ANA   C

        A                       C
    [        ]              [        ]
```

(a) ANA B; (b) ANI 01010000B;

(c) A [00001011]   C [00001111]

7. The ANA and ANI instructions set all the flags. The parity, sign, and zero flags are set according to the new value in A. Since AND operations never result in carries or borrows, the carry and auxiliary carry flags are always set to zero.

Suppose the A register contains 01001011. What effect will ANI 10001000B have . . .

(a) on the sign flag? ____________________

(b) on the carry flag? ____________________

(c) on the auxiliary carry flag? ____________________

(d) on the zero flag? ____________________

(e) What is the resulting value in A? ____________________

(a) turned off; (b) turned off; (c) turned on; (d) turned off;
(e) 00001000B

8. Here are some problems involving AND for you.

(a) The routine shown below moves a byte into the A register, then forces the various flags to be set for that value.

```
MOV   A,M
SUI   0
```

How can you accomplish the same function using an AND operation?

____

____

(b) Each of the instructions shown below clears the A register.

```
MVI  A,0

SUB  A
```

How can you do the same thing with an AND operation?

____

\- - - - - - - - - - - - -

(a)
```
MOV  A,M
ANA  A
```

ANDing a value with itself will always produce the same value as a result. So the value in A remains unchanged but the flags get set.

(b) ANI 0 would force all the result bits to zero.

9. Now that you can code an AND operation, let's talk about how we use them. AND operations are usually used when we want to turn off specific bits in a value.

Examine the instruction ANI 00001111B. This instruction would force the highest four bits in the A register to be turned off, regardless of what's currently in there. The lowest four bits retain their present value. Let's see why.

```
  00001111
∧ XXXXXXXX
  --------
  0000XXXX
```

Without knowing the value of X, we know that $0 \wedge X = 0$. If $X = 0$, $0 \wedge 0 = 0$. If $X = 1$, $0 \wedge 1 = 0$.

On the other hand, we know that $1 \wedge X = X$. If $X = 0$, $1 \wedge 0 = 0$. If $X = 1$, $1 \wedge 1 = 1$.

(a) AND operations are used to turn bits (on/off) ______________

(b) $0 \wedge X =$ ______________

(c) $1 \wedge X =$ ______________

(d) What value would you use in an ANI instruction to turn off the least significant bit in the A register and leave the rest alone?

____

\- - - - - - - - - - - - -

(a) off; (b) 0; (c) X; (d) 11111110B

10. In the instruction ANI 00001111B, the operand is called a *mask* be-

cause it is a pattern that blocks out (or affects) some bits but allows others through (or leaves them alone).

(a) In an AND mask, what value will turn off the corresponding bit in the accumulator? ____________

(b) What value will leave the corresponding bit in the accumulator alone?

____

(a) 0; (b) 1

11. Code ANI instructions to solve these problems. Masks are usually expressed in binary so you can see which bits are on and which are off.

(a) Turn off the most significant bit in the accumulator. Leave the other bits alone. ____________

(b) Turn off the third and fourth bits from the left. Leave the other bits alone. ____________

(a) ANI 01111111B; (b) ANI 11001111B

12. Here are some practical problems that involve turning bits off.

(a) Code a routine that reads an ASCII character from the terminal, strips out (or turns off) the ASCII zone bits (the first four bits), and stores the result in memory. (This means that '1', 'A', and 'a' would all be stored as 01H, whereas if stored normally, they'd be 31H, 41H, and 61H.)

____

____

____

____

____

(b) Code a routine that reads an input digit from the terminal. If the digit is even, jump to INEVEN. If the digit is odd, jump to INODD.

____

____

____

____

____

____

- - - - - - - - - - - - - -

(a)
```
CALL  INPUT
MOV   A,B
ANI   00001111B ; TURN OFF BITS 1-4
MOV   M,A
```

(b)
```
CALL  INPUT
MOV   A,B
ANI   00000001B ; TEST LSB
JZ    INEVEN
JMP   INODD
```

THE *ORA* AND *ORI* INSTRUCTIONS

13. Now let's consider the OR instructions. The two OR instructions are ORA (OR with A) and ORI (OR immediate). Both OR the operand with the A register and store the result there. Their formats are:

[*label*] ORA *r1* [;*comments*]
[*label*] ORI *i* [;*comments*]

The sign, parity, and zero flags are set according to the result in A. The carry and auxiliary carry flags are turned off.

(a) Code an instruction to OR the D register with the A register.

____

(b) Code an instruction to OR the value 10000000B with the A register.

____

- - - - - - - - - - - - - -

(a) ORA D; (b) ORI 10000000B

14. OR operations are used to turn bits on. A one in the mask will force the corresponding bit on, since 1 V X = 1. A zero in the mask will leave the corresponding bit alone since 0 V X = X.

(a) If X = 1, 1 V X = _____.

(b) If X = 0, 1 V X = _____.

(c) Therefore, 1 V X = _____.

(d) If X = 1, 0 V X = _____.

(e) If X = 0, 0 V X = ______.

(f) Therefore, 0 V X = ______.

(g) OR operations are used to turn bits (on/off) ______.

— — — — — — — — — — — — —

(a) 1; (b) 1; (c) 1; (d) 1; (e) 0; (f) X; (g) on

15. Code OR operations for the following problems.

(a) Turn all the bits in the accumulator on. __________________

(b) Don't change the value in the accumulator but set the flags.

____

(c) Turn on the high order bit in the accumulator. Leave the other bits alone. ____________________

— — — — — — — — — — — — —

(a) ORI 11111111B; (b) ORI 0; (c) ORI 10000000B

THE *XRA* AND *XRI* INSTRUCTIONS

16. The two EXCLUSIVE OR instructions are XRA (EXCLUSIVE OR with A) and XRI (EXCLUSIVE OR immediate). Their formats are comparable to ORA and ORI, and they set the same flags.

(a) Code an instruction to EXCLUSIVE OR register D with A. ________

(b) Code an instruction to EXCLUSIVE OR 10001000B with A.________

Label each of the following flags N for not affected, S for set, or 0 for set to zero.

(c) carry flag: ______

(d) sign flag: ______

(e) zero flag: ______

(f) auxiliary carry flag: ______

(g) parity flag: ______

— — — — — — — — — — — — —

(a) XRA D; (b) XRI 10001000B; (c) 0; (d) S; (e) S; (f) 0; (g) S

17. EXCLUSIVE ORs are usually used to *complement* bits. A bit is complemented when its value is reversed; a one becomes a zero and a zero becomes a one.

To complement a bit, the EXCLUSIVE OR mask should contain a one in the corresponding bit. To leave a bit alone, the mask bit should contain a zero.

(a) $1 \veebar 0 =$ _____

(b) $1 \veebar 1 =$ _____

(c) Therefore, $1 \veebar X =$ _____

(d) $0 \veebar 0 =$ _____

(e) $0 \veebar 1 =$ _____

(f) Therefore, $0 \veebar X =$ _____

(g) Code an instruction to complement (reverse) the least significant bit of the accumulator. ____________________

— — — — — — — — — — — — —

(a) 1; (b) 0; (c) the opposite of X; (d) 0; (e) 1; (f) X;
(g) XRI 00000001B

18. AND and EXCLUSIVE OR can both be used to zero the accumulator. Show both instructions.

(a) ____________________

(b) ____________________

— — — — — — — — — — — — —

(a) ANI 0; (b) XRA A will leave zero bits alone but complement all the one bits; it's more memory efficient since it's a one byte instruction.

19. You have now seen how to use the various AND and OR operations. The questions below will help you practice them.

(a) Turn off the high order bit. ____________________

(b) Turn on the high order bit. ____________________

(c) Complement the high order bit. ____________________

(d) Zero the accumulator. ____________________

(e) Set the accumulator to all ones. ____________________

(f) Convert a single digit in the accumulator between 0 and 9 to its ASCII code. Currently, the digit is in this form: 0000XXXXB. You want to change it to this form: 0011XXXXB.

(g) Convert a lower case ASCII letter in the accumulator to its upper case form. Currently, the value is in this form: 011XXXXXB. You want to change it to this form: 010XXXXXB.

- - - - - - - - - - - - - -

(a) ANI 01111111B; (b) ORI 10000000B; (c) XRI 10000000B; (d) ANI 0 or XRA A; (e) ORI 11111111B; (f) ORI 00110000B; (g) ANI 11011111B

REGISTER ROTATION

Assembly Language includes a set of instructions to rotate the value in the accumulator. The following frames discuss register rotation.

20. A value is rotated when all the bits are moved over one. A simple rotation to the left looks like this:

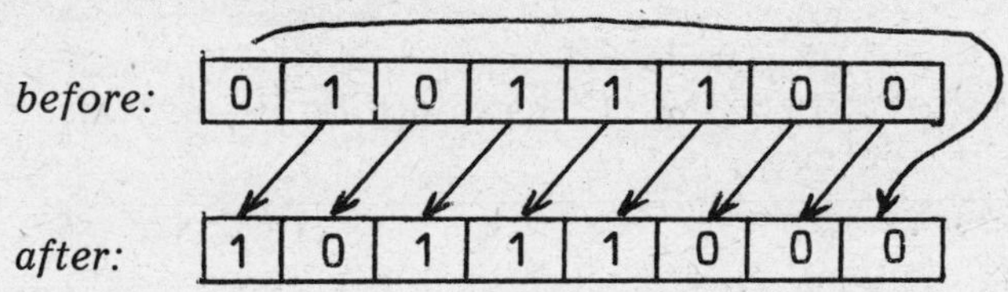

Notice that the most significant bit wraps all the way around and becomes the least significant bit.

(a) Show the results of a simple rotate to the right.

before:	1	0	1	1	1	0	1	1
after:								

(b) Show the results of a simple rotate to the left.

before:	1	1	0	0	0	1	1	0
after:								

- - - - - - - - - - - - - -

(a) 11011101; (b) 10001101

21. With simple rotates, only the carry flag is set. It reflects the bit that wrapped around. If a one bit wraps around, the carry flag is turned on. If a zero bit wraps around, the carry flag is turned off.

(a) Show the result of a simple rotate to the left on both the register and the carry flag.

	carry flag								
before:	1	0	0	0	0	1	1	1	1
after:									

(b) Show the result of a simple rotate to the right on both the register and the carry flag.

before:	0	0	0	0	0	1	1	1	1
after:									

(a)	0	0	0	0	1	1	1	1	0
(b)	1	1	0	0	0	0	1	1	1

22. You can also rotate through the carry flag. When you do this, nine bits are rotated, not eight. It looks like this:

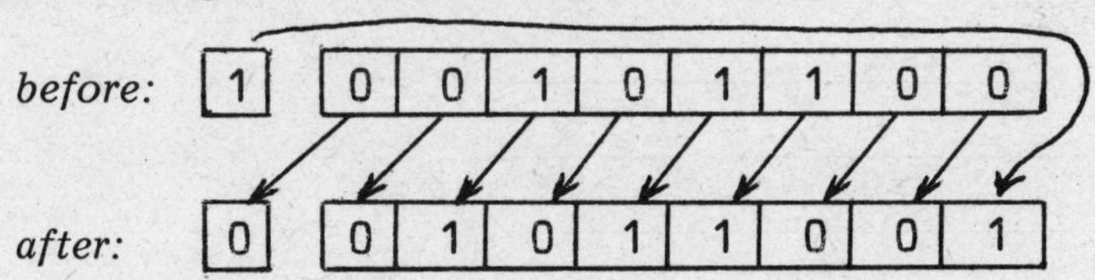

(a) Show the result of a right rotate through the carry flag.

before:	0	0	0	0	0	1	1	1	1
after:									

(b) Show the result of a left rotate through the carry flag.

before:	0	0	0	0	0	1	1	1	1
after:									

	Carry								
(a)	1		0	0	0	0	0	1	1	1
(b)	0		0	0	0	1	1	1	1	0

23. The four rotate instructions are:

RLC — rotate left without carry
RRC — rotate right without carry
RAL — rotate A left (through carry)
RAR — rotate A right (through carry)

Don't get mixed up on these four mnemonics. Read RLC as "rotate left *without* carry" and RRC as "rotate right *without* carry." RAL and RAR perform rotate operations *with* the carry flag.

These instructions have no operands.

(a) Code an instruction to rotate A left through the carry. ______________

(b) Code an instruction to rotate A right without the carry. ______________

(a) RAL; (b) RRC

24. Use rotate instructions to solve each of the following problems.

(a) Read a byte. If it's even, jump to INEVEN. If it's odd, jump to INODD.

____

____

____

____

____

(b) We *normalize* a value by shifting it left until the first bit is one. Write a routine that will normalize the value in A. Keep track of the number of shifts in B. (Assume that A contains a non-zero value. Remember that INR and DCR don't set the carry flag, so you can use them in your routine.)

____

____

____

____

____

____

____

____

____

(a)
```
CALL  INPUT
MOV   A,B
RAR
JC    INODD
JMP   INEVEN
```

(RRC would have done as well; in both cases the carry flag is turned on if the least significant bit was one and turned off if it was zero.)

(b)
```
         MVI   B,0
NORMAL   EQU   $
         RLC
         INR   B ; NOTE CARRY FLAG NOT AFFECTED
         JNC   NORMAL
; WHEN CONTROL FALLS THROUGH, A 1 HAS BEEN
; ROTATED.  IT NEEDS TO BE RESTORED.
         RRC
         DCR   B
```

(Note that you can't use the sign flag to identify when the value has been normalized because the rotate instructions don't set the sign flag.)

SETTING THE CARRY FLAG

26. You have already seen that sometimes we want to turn the carry flag on or off. Obviously, this can always be done with ADI or SUI instructions. But other flags may also be affected in a way we don't want.

A more direct means is to use STC (set carry) or CMC (complement carry). STC turns on the carry flag, regardless of its former value. CMC complements it. Neither instruction has any operands.

(a) Code an instruction to turn on the carry flag. ________________

(b) Code an instruction to complement the carry flag. ________________

(c) There is no instruction to directly turn off the carry flag. Code a set of instructions that will turn off the carry flag without affecting any other flags.

____

____

(a) STC; (b) CMC;

(c)
```
STC ; TURNS ON FLAG
CMC ; TURNS OFF FLAG
```

27. Code a routine to rotate the accumulator left through carry. Turn off the carry flag before rotating.

____

____

____

____

```
STC
CMC
RAL
```

REVIEW

In this chapter, you have learned several instructions that can be used to manipulate individual bits. They are called the logical instructions.

- The AND operation has these results:

$$\begin{array}{r}0\\ \wedge 0\\ \hline 0\end{array}\qquad\begin{array}{r}0\\ \wedge 1\\ \hline 0\end{array}\qquad\begin{array}{r}1\\ \wedge 0\\ \hline 0\end{array}\qquad\begin{array}{r}1\\ \wedge 1\\ \hline 1\end{array}$$

  The AND instructions are:

  [*label*] ANA *r1* [;*comments*]
  [*label*] ANI *i* [;*comments*]

  They operate on the accumulator, which is changed to show the result. The carry and auxiliary carry flags are always set to zero. Sign, parity, and zero flags are set as needed.

- We usually use AND to turn off individual bits. A zero in an AND mask forces the corresponding bit to be turned off. A one leaves the corresponding bit alone.

- The OR operation has these results:

$$\begin{array}{r}0\\ \vee\ 0\\ \hline 0\end{array}\qquad\begin{array}{r}0\\ \vee\ 0\\ \hline 1\end{array}\qquad\begin{array}{r}1\\ \vee\ 0\\ \hline 1\end{array}\qquad\begin{array}{r}1\\ \vee\ 1\\ \hline 1\end{array}$$

The OR instructions are:

[*label*] ORA *r1* [;*comments*]
[*label*] ORI *i* [;*comments*]

They operate on the accumulator, which is changed to show the result. The carry and auxiliary carry flags are turned off. The other flags are set as needed.

- We usually use OR to turn on bits. A one in the OR mask will turn the corresponding bit on. A zero will leave the corresponding bit alone.
- The EXCLUSIVE OR operation has these results:

$$\begin{array}{r}0\\ \veebar 0\\ \hline 0\end{array}\qquad\begin{array}{r}0\\ \veebar 1\\ \hline 1\end{array}\qquad\begin{array}{r}1\\ \veebar 0\\ \hline 1\end{array}\qquad\begin{array}{r}1\\ \veebar 1\\ \hline 0\end{array}$$

The EXCLUSIVE OR instructions are:

[*label*] XRA *r1* [;*comments*]
[*label*] XRI *i* [;*comments*]

They set the flags in the same way that the OR instructions do.

- We usually use EXCLUSIVE OR instructions to complement bits. A one in the mask causes the corresponding bit to be complemented. A zero leaves the corresponding bit alone.
- Bit rotation can be used for a variety of functions. Bits can be tested by rotating them into the carry flag position.
- Bits can be rotated left or right one position at a time. If rotating through the carry flag, the flag becomes the ninth bit in the rotation cycle standing in between the MSB and the LSB. If rotating without the carry flag, bits wrap around between the MSB and the LSB. The carry flag is set according to the wrap-around bit. No other flag is set.
- When counting rotations, INR and DCR are used because they *don't* affect the carry flag, thus leaving that flag free to hold the rotating bit. INR and DCR set all the other flags.
- The rotation instructions are:

[*label*] RAR [;*comments*]
[*label*] RRC [;*comments*]
[*label*] RAL [;*comments*]
[*label*] RLC [;*comments*]

RAL and RAR rotate through the carry. RRC and RLC rotate without the carry.

- STC turns on the carry flag and CMC complements it. Neither instruction affects any other flag. Their formats are:

  [*label*] STC [;*comments*]
  [*label*] CMC [;*comments*]

CHAPTER 8 SELF-TEST

Code instructions to solve the following problems:

1. Turn on the LSB in the accumulator. ____________________

2. Turn off the MSB in the accumulator. ____________________

3. Complement the third and fourth bits in the accumulator. __________

4. Use EXCLUSIVE OR to zero the accumulator. ____________________

5. Use AND to zero the accumulator. ____________________

6. Rotate the accumulator right through the carry flag. ______________

7. Rotate the accumulator right without the carry flag. ______________

8. Rotate the accumulator left through the carry flag. ______________

9. Rotate the accumulator left without the carry flag. ______________

10. Turn on the carry flag without disturbing the values of the other flags. ____________________

11. Reverse the value of the carry flag without disturbing the values of the other flags. ____________________

12. Turn off the carry flag without disturbing the values of the other flags. ____________________

    ____

13. Read a digit from the terminal. Remove the ASCII character bits leaving the binary value with at least four leading zeros. Then rotate the number to the left three times, effectively multiplying it by eight. Store the result in PRODCT.

14. Get the byte from the memory area named DECIDE. If the LSB is zero, jump to ROUTE1. Otherwise, jump to ROUTE2.

Check your answers below.

Self-Test Answer Key

1. `ORI 00000001B`

2. `ANI 01111111B`

3. `XRI 00110000B`

4. `XRA A`

5. `ANI 0`

6. `RAR`

7. `RRC`

8. `RAL`

9. `RLC`

10. `STC`

11. `CMC`

12.
```
STC
CMC
```

13.
```
CALL INPUT
MOV  A,B
ANI  00001111B (or 11001111B)
RLC
RLC
RLC
STA  PRODCT
```

14.
```
LDA  DECIDE
RAR
JC   ROUTE2
JMP  ROUTE1 (or JNC)
```
or
```
LDA  DECIDE
ANI  00000001B
JZ   ROUTE1
JMP  ROUTE2 (or JNZ)
```

CHAPTER NINE

THE STACK

The stack is used primarily for the temporary storage of data. This chapter reviews the concepts associated with the stack then introduces the instructions you can use to manipulate it.

When you have finished this chapter, you will be able to:

- Code the following instructions:
  - PUSH (push data into the stack)
  - POP (pop data out of the stack)
  - XTHL (exchange H–L with top of stack)
  - SPHL (move H–L to stack pointer)
- Code routines to accomplish the following functions:
  - Preserve the register values in the stack.
  - Reset the register from the stack.
  - Set the address in the stack pointer.
  - Use a stack to write a message.
- Given a beginning stack address, state what addresses the stack will occupy.
- Code data definitions for one or more stacks.

REVIEW OF CONCEPTS

1. The stack is a LIFO (last in, first out) storage area in memory. We use it for temporary storage. The stack pointer register points at the current stack entry.

Suppose there are five items in the stack, which we'll call A, B, C, D, and E. A was the first item stored and E the last.

(a) At what item is the stack pointer pointing? ____________

(b) If you remove an item from the stack, which item will you get?

____

(c) If you remove another item from the stack, which item will you get?

____

– – – – – – – – – – – – – –

(a) E; (b) E; (c) D

2. The stack is considered to have a top and a bottom. The bottom is the highest memory address and the top is the lowest memory address.

Suppose that a stack in memory looks like this:

0050	0051	0052	0053	0054	0055	0056	0057	0058	0059	005A	005B	005C	005D
XX	XX	XX	XX	XX	XX	XX	XX	XX	XX	XX	XX	XX	XX

(a) What address is the top of the stack? ____________________

(b) What address is the bottom of the stack? ____________________

(c) At what address would you expect the SP to be pointing? __________

(d) If you add two bytes to the stack, at what address would the stack start? ____________________

– – – – – – – – – – – – – –

(a) 0050H; (b) 005DH; (c) 0050H; (d) 004EH

3. We have been talking about the stack as if it always existed in memory. It doesn't. If your program wants to use a stack, you point the stack pointer and write the storage and retrieval instructions. There is no fixed size—if you push 100 items into the stack, it's 100 items long.

The CALL instruction also uses the stack so anytime your program contains a CALL, you're using the stack memory while that program is in control.

Which is the most accurate statement?

_____ (a) Every program must use a stack.

_____ (b) 100 bytes of memory are set aside for the stack, whether your program uses them or not.

_____ (c) A program may or may not have a stack; the stack may be any reasonable size.

– – – – – – – – – – – – – –

(c)

4. Your program is not limited to one stack. You can use two, three, or even more stacks. All you have to do is take care what address is loaded into the stack pointer. You will learn instructions to load an address into the stack pointer and to store an address from the stack pointer.

As an example, you might want to have one stack to save register values and another stack to save pertinent memory addresses. You could call the first stack REGSAV and the second stack MEMSAV. You would also define two two-byte fields: REGSP would hold the stack pointer for the REGSAV stack and MEMSP would hold the stack pointer for the MEMSAV stack.

At the beginning of the program you would initialize REGSP by storing in it the address of the bottom of the REGSAV stack. (You'll learn how in this chapter.) You'd do the same for MEMSP. Then when you want to access the REGSAV stack, you'd load the value from REGSP into the stack pointer. After the stack operation, the SP would have changed to show the new top of stack. You would store that address back in REGSP again.

Which of the following statements are true? (More than one are correct.)

______ (a) A program can use any number of stacks; the only limit is the amount of available memory space.

______ (b) Up to two stacks are permitted, but no more.

______ (c) Only one stack is permitted per program.

______ (d) The address in the SP is fixed and you cannot change it.

______ (e) You can load addresses into the stack pointer and store addresses from the stack pointer.

______ (f) The address in the SP is automatically incremented or decremented by a stack operation.

______ (g) The address in the SP is only incremented or decremented if you code an INX or DCX instruction.

– – – – – – – – – – – – – –

(a), (e), and (f) are true

5. A stack entry is two bytes, not one. When you push an item into the stack, two bytes are pushed. When you retrieve an item, two bytes are retrieved.

Which of the following do you think can be pushed or retrieved?

______ (a) A register such as A.

______ (b) A register pair such as H–L.

______ (c) A memory byte such as the value at address 0100H.

— — — — — — — — — — — — — —

(b)

6. When you add an item to a stack, here's what happens (Figure 1.2 in Chapter 1 might help you envision this):

- The SP is decremented by one.
- The 8 MSBs are stored (that's the first byte).
- The SP is decremented by one.
- The 8 LSBs are stored (that's the second byte).

Suppose you push the value 2345H into the stack. Before the operation, the SP is pointing at address 0155H.

(a) At what address will the first byte be stored? ______

(b) What is the value of that byte? ______

(c) At what address will the second byte be stored? ______

(d) What is the value of that byte? ______

(e) After the operation, where is the SP pointing? Give the address.

______

— — — — — — — — — — — — — —

(a) 0154H; (b) 23H; (c) 0153H; (d) 45H; (e) 0153H

7. When you retrieve an item from the stack, here's what happens:

- The first byte is retrieved; its value becomes the eight LSBs.
- The SP is incremented by one.
- The second byte is retrieved; its value becomes the eight MSBs.
- The SP is incremented by one.

Suppose the stack contains (from top to bottom): 04H, 05H, 73H, BBH. SP contains 0100H. Suppose you retrieve the top item into H–L.

(a) What value is put in H? ______

(b) What value is put in L? ______

(c) What does the SP contain after the operation? Give the address.

______

— — — — — — — — — — — — — —

(a) 05H; (b) 04H; (c) 0102H

8. Match.

_____ (a) add to stack

_____ (b) retrieve from stack

1. SP is incremented
2. SP is decremented
3. move toward lowest address
4. move toward highest address

- - - - - - - - - - - - -

(a) 2, 3; (b) 1, 4

9. Whenever you write a program that uses the stack either directly or indirectly (through CALL), you'll have to consider the initial value of the stack pointer. Many systems automatically initialize the stack pointer to some address. (Ours initializes it to 100H.) If you don't like the initial value, you can change it with LXI, as in:

```
               LXI   SP,RSTACK+10
               ...
               HLT
        RSTACK DS    10
```

We used RSTACK+10 to initialize the stack pointer *beyond* the bottom of the stack.

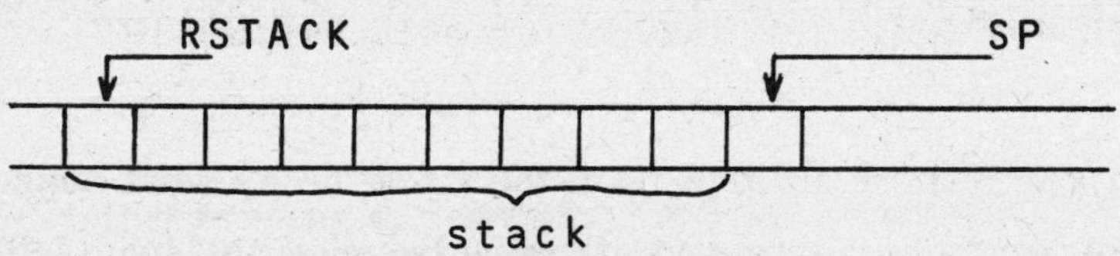

(a) Write instructions to reserve room for a stack of 20 items called REGSAV and initialize the stack pointer.

(b) Write instructions to reserve room for a stack of 100 items call TEMPER and initialize the stack pointer.

- - - - - - - - - - - - -

(a)

```
               LXI   SP,REGSAV+20
               ...
        REGSAV DS    20
```

(b)
```
         LXI  SP,TEMPER+100
         ...
TEMPER   DS   100
```

10. When you decide on the size of a stack, leave room for its maximum growth *and then some.* Every CALL instruction places an item in the stack; the item is removed by the time control returns from the called routine.

If your stack exceeds the size allotted to it, it will start to overlay other data or your machine language instructions.

Suppose your program will put up to 10 bytes into the stack, and it also contains some CALL instructions. How many bytes would you allot for the stack? ______________________

— — — — — — — — — — — — — —

We would allot 20.

11. Suppose you want to use two stacks, MEMSAV and REGSAV. You estimate that MEMSAV will take 100 bytes and REGSAV will take 10 bytes. Write the definition. Give each stack 10 extra bytes.

____

____

____

____

— — — — — — — — — — — — — —

```
MEMSAV DS   110
REGSAV DS   20
```

THE STACK INSTRUCTIONS

There are four new instructions you need to learn to use the stack: PUSH, POP, SPHL, and XTHL. You also need to review the functions of INX and DCX with relationship to the stack pointer.

12. An item is pushed into the stack by the PUSH instruction.

[*label*] PUSH *rp* [;*comments*]

The operand may be B, D, H, or PSW. If PSW is used, the A-flags pair is pushed into the stack. This and POP, taught next, are the only instructions that allow you to use A-flags as a pair. (That's why we said that they're occasionally a pair.) The flags are treated as the LSBs and the accumulator is treated as the MSBs.

Which of the following are legal PUSH instructions?

_____ (a) `PUSH B`

_____ (b) `PUSH L`

_____ (c) `PUSH PC`

_____ (d) `PUSH PSW`

_____ (e) `PUSH H`

_____ (f) `PUSH SP`

_____ (g) `PUSH INBYTE`

— — — — — — — — — — — — — —

(a), (d), (e)

(Some assemblers also allow you to use A as an operand. The effect is the same as using PSW.)

13. Code an instruction to save the contents of the D-E pair in the stack.

____

— — — — — — — — — — — — — —

PUSH D

14. Suppose you have this situation:

B-C: `2453H` SP: `0518H`

memory:	00	00	00	00	00	00
	0515	0516	0517	0518	0519	051A

Show the result of the instruction PUSH B. Use the diagrams at the top of the next page.

B–C: [ ] SP: [ ]

memory:						
	0515	0516	0517	0518	0519	051A

— — — — — — — — — — — — —

B–C: `2453H` SP: `0516H`

memory:	00	53	24	00	00	00
	0515	0516	0517	0518	0519	051A

15. The POP instruction retrieves an item from the stack into the designated register pair.

[*label*] POP *rp* [;*comments*]

The operand follows the same rules as the PUSH instruction.
Which of the following are legal POP instructions?

_____ (a) `POP C`

_____ (b) `POP PSW`

_____ (c) `POP D`

_____ (d) `POP M`

_____ (e) `POP PC`

_____ (f) `POP B`

— — — — — — — — — — — — —

(b), (c), (f)

16. Code instructions to meet the following specifications.

(a) Place the B–C pair into the stack. ______________________

(b) Retrieve the top stack item into the H–L pair. ______________

(c) Retrieve the top stack item into the PSW. _________________

— — — — — — — — — — — — —

(a) PUSH B; (b) POP H; (c) POP PSW

17. Suppose you have this situation:

B–C: [005AH] SP: [2300H]

memory:						
	19	52	68	7B	7F	33
	22FE	22FF	2300	2301	2302	2303

Show the effect of POP B.

B–C: [ ] SP: [ ]

memory:						
	22FE	22FF	2300	2301	2302	2303

B–C: [7B68H] SP: [2302H]

memory:						
	19	52	68	7B	7F	33
	22FE	22FF	2300	2301	2302	2303

18. Another means of accessing a stack is the XTHL (exchange top with H–L) instruction. XTHL swaps the top two bytes of the stack with the H–L register pair. The top byte is exchanged with L. The next byte is exchanged with H. Since an even exchange is made, the size of the stack does not change and the stack pointer is not modified.

The XTHL instruction has no operands.
Suppose you have this situation:

H–L: 2345H SP: 2305H

memory:	00	16	AA	BB	CC	DD
	2301	2302	2303	2304	2305	2306

Show the result of the instruction XTHL.

H–L: ______ SP: ______

memory:						
	2301	2302	2303	2304	2305	2306

H–L: 0DDCCH SP: 2305H

memory:	00	16	AA	BB	45	23
	2301	2302	2303	2304	2305	2306

19. Code instructions for the following specifications.

(a) Retrieve the top value from the stack into H–L. Decrease the stack size. ______

(b) Add the value in H–L to the stack. ______

(c) Exchange the value at the top of the stack with the value in H–L.

______

(a) POP H; (b) PUSH H; (c) XTHL

You've seen how we get values into and out of the stack. Now let's look at some instructions that control the stack pointer.

20. You already know how to set the stack pointer with LXI. Another way is the SPHL instruction, which has no operands. It moves an address from H–L into SP.

We use the SPHL facility when we want to manipulate the stack pointer address in some way. We can load the address into H–L, then adjust it using DAD, then move it into SP using SPHL. Thus, the stack pointer can be moved around as needed.

Code a set of instructions to load the address of REGSAV into H–L, add the value in B-C to it, and move the result to SP.

— — — — — — — — — — — —

```
LXI   H,REGSAV
DAD   B
SPHL
```

21. When using SPHL, observe some precautions:

- Make sure a legitimate address is moved into SP. Avoid allowing a stack to get out of its allotted area.
- Don't use SPHL in the middle of a called routine or you might cut off the return route for that routine.

(a) How should you use SPHL?

_____ It can be used freely.

_____ It should be used cautiously.

_____ It should never be used.

(b) Under what circumstance should you avoid SPHL?

_____ In the middle of a called routine.

_____ At the beginning of a program.

_____ When you're not sure of the value in H–L.

— — — — — — — — — — — —

(a) It should be used cautiously; (b) In the middle of a called routine; When you're not sure of the value in H–L.

22. The SP is incremented and decremented automatically as you push and pop items. If you leave it alone, it's always pointing to the top of the

stack. However, you should be aware that you can "manually" change the SP with INX and DCX.

(a) Code an instruction to add one to the SP. ____________

(b) Code a set of instructions to *overlay* the top item in the stack with the value in B–C.

____

____

____

(c) Code a set of instructions to move the top item into both B–C and PSW.

____

____

____

____

— — — — — — — — — — — —

(a)
```
INX  SP
```

(b)
```
INX  SP
INX  SP
PUSH B
```

(c)
```
POP  B        or     POP  B
DCX  SP              PUSH B
DCX  SP              POP  PSW
POP  PSW
```

(You can't POP B and then move the bytes into PSW because PSW can't be an operand of the MOV instruction.)

The operations shown in the preceding frame are seldom needed in a program. As much as possible, let the SP be handled automatically. But don't forget to initialize it before you PUSH the first item.

SOME STACK APPLICATIONS

In the following frames, we'll show you some of the common uses of stacks.

23. As you've seen, register A is very active. Sometimes we need to save one value while we use A for something else. Then we want to restore A to its former value. Naturally, we also want to save and restore the flags that match A.

Code a routine which will do the following:

- Save the values in the PSW.
- Subtract 35H from the value in B.
- Restore the former values of the PSW.

```
PUSH PSW
MOV  A,B
SUI  35H
MOV  B,A
POP  PSW
```

24. Sometimes we want to save the values of all the registers (A–L) before we execute a function.

Code a routine that does the following:

- Saves registers A–L.
- Calls a subroutine named XFER.
- Restores the registers.

Hint: Don't forget the LIFO nature of the stack. If the H–L pair is the last to be stored, it should be the first to be retrieved.

```
PUSH PSW
PUSH B
PUSH D
PUSH H
CALL XFER
POP  H
POP  D
POP  B
POP  PSW
```

You might have pushed them in a different order. Just make sure you retrieved them in reverse order.

25. Some programmers like to write messages from stacks. The automatic SP increments save some time. Also, since two bytes are handled at a time, you need half as many loops. Here's an example:

```
        MVI  C,5
        LXI  SP,MESAGE
OTLOOP  EQU  $
        POP  D
        MOV  B,E
        CALL OUTPUT
        MOV  B,D
        CALL OUTPUT
        DCR  C
        JNZ  OTLOOP
        HLT
        DS   10
MESAGE  DB   'THANK YOU!'
```

In this example, MESAGE is a ten-byte field that we use as a stack. But its contents are predefined. We initialize SP to the top of the stack, not the bottom, because we're only going to POP items from the stack; we won't add to it.

The first POP places 'HT' in D–E. We write them in reverse order. The next POP does the same with NA. And so forth.

Notice that we left 10 extra bytes preceding the message to hold other stacked items.

Code a routine to display the message 'PLEASE TYPE YOUR NAME:'. Use stack instructions.

— — — — — — — — — — — —

```
        LXI  SP,MESAGE
        MVI  C,11
WRITER  EQU  $
        POP  D
        MOV  B,E
        CALL OUTPUT
        MOV  B,D
        CALL OUTPUT
        DCR  C
        JNZ  WRITER
        HLT
        DS   10
MESAGE  DB   'PLEASE TYPE YOUR NAME:'
```

Each CALL instruction pushes an item into the top of the stack. This overlays any previous data there. After the first item from the message is popped, the SP has moved down to point to 'EA'. When CALL pushes an item, it overlays 'PL'. This continues to happen until the entire message is obliterated. So you can use this method of sending messages only if you send the message a single time.

REVIEW

In this chapter, you have learned how to set up and use one or more stacks.

- A stack is a LIFO storage area addressed by the SP (stack pointer) register. The top of the stack is the lowest address and the bottom is the highest. SP points to the top, where items are added or removed. Each stack item is two bytes. Bytes are reversed as they're stored and retrieved.
- You can define and use as many stacks as your program needs. It's up to you to load and store stack pointer values as necessary.
- The PUSH instruction adds an item to the top of the stack.
  Format: [*label*] PUSH *rp* [;*comments*]
  The operand may be B, D, H, or PSW. The stack pointer is decremented two by the operation.
- The POP instruction removes an item from the top of the stack.
  Format: [*label*] POP *rp* [;*comments*]
  The operand may be B, D, H, or PSW. The stack pointer is incremented by two.
- The XTHL instruction exchanges H–L with the top of the stack.
  Format: [*label*] XTHL [;*comments*]
- The stack pointer should be initialized before you use it. LXI can

be used to load the stack pointer. INX and DCX can be used to adjust it but such adjustments are not recommended.

- The SPHL instruction copies H–L into SP.
  Format: [*label*] SPHL [;*comments*]
- Stacks are used for such problems as temporarily saving register values and writing messages.

CHAPTER 9 SELF-TEST

Code instructions to solve the following problems.

1. Point the stack pointer at 500H. ______________________

2. For the above SP value, what addresses will be used for the first stack entry? ______________ For the second entry? __________

3. Point the stack pointer at STACK. ______________________

4. Point the stack pointer at REGSAV. Then save all the registers except SP and PC in that stack.

   ____

   ____

   ____

   ____

   ____

5. Restore the registers again.

   ____

   ____

   ____

   ____

6. Exchange the data in H–L with the top of the stack. __________

7. Exchange the data in D–E with the top of the stack. __________

8. Move the value in H–L to the stack pointer. ______________

9. Store the address of NEWDAT at the top of the stack.

10. Store two bytes of zeros in the stack.

11. After the HLT instruction below, define two stacks. The first will contain 30 bytes and should have a beginning address of STACK1. The second will contain 10 bytes and should have a beginning address of STACK2.

HLT

12. Using a stack, code a routine to write the message 'WRONG!'. Show the routine that writes the message as well as the stack definition.

Check your answers below.

Self-Test Answer Key

1. `LXI SP,500H`

2. 4FFH and 4FEH;

   4FDH and 4FCH

3. `LXI SP,STACK`

4.
```
LXI  SP,REGSAV
PUSH PSW
PUSH B
PUSH D
PUSH H
```

5.
```
POP  H
POP  D
POP  B
POP  PSW
```

   (Be sure you POPped the registers in exact reverse order to how you PUSHed them.)

6. `XTHL`

7.
```
XCHG  ; D-E TO H-L
XTHL  ; H-L TO STACK
XCHG  ; H-L TO D-E
```

8. `SPHL`

9.
```
LXI  H,NEWDAT
PUSH H
```

   (You could have used the B-C or D-E pair as easily as the H-L pair.)

10.
```
LXI  H,0
PUSH H
```

   (Again, you could have used B-C or D-E.)

11.
```
STACK1 DS   30
STACK2 DS   10
```

12.
```
        MVI  C,3      ; LOOP COUNT
        LXI  SP,BADMSG
WRITIT  EQU  $
        POP  D
        MOV  B,E
        CALL OUTPUT
        MOV  B,D
        CALL OUTPUT
        DCR  C
        JNZ  WRITIT
        HLT
        DS   10       ; STACK PADDING
BADMSG  DB   'WRONG!'
```

CHAPTER TEN

SUBROUTINES

One extremely important program structure is the subroutine. You have already learned how to call a subroutine and you have been calling INPUT and OUTPUT subroutines. In this chapter, you will learn how to code subroutines and how to conditionally call them. We'll also be taking a closer look at input/output (I/O) subroutines.

When you have finished this chapter, you will be able to:

- Code the following instructions:
  - CC (call if carry)
  - CNC (call if not carry)
  - CZ (call if zero)
  - CNZ (call if not zero)
  - CP (call if plus)
  - CM (call if minus)
  - RET (return)
  - RC (return if carry)
  - RNC (return if not carry)
  - RZ (return if zero)
  - RNZ (return if not zero)
  - RM (return if minus)
  - RP (return if plus)
- Given specifications, code a complete subroutine (including I/O subroutines).
- Given specifications for a complete program including one or more subroutines, code the complete program.

WHAT ARE SUBROUTINES?

1. Figure 10.1 shows a complete program that we will use as an example throughout this chapter. The program reads and adds two digits between

```
        ORG   100H
GETN1   EQU   $
        CALL  INPUT
        CALL  OUTPUT          ;ECHO
        CALL  NEWLIN
        MOV   A,B
        CALL  CHEKIT
        MOV   A,C
        CPI   0FFH
        JZ    SAVEN1
        CALL  ERROR
        JMP   GETN1
SAVEN1  EQU   $
        MOV   D,B
GETN2   EQU   $
        CALL  INPUT
        CALL  OUTPUT          ;ECHO
        CALL  NEWLIN
        MOV   A,B
        CALL  CHEKIT
        MOV   A,C
        CPI   0FFH
        JZ    ADDEM
        CALL  ERROR
        JMP   GETN2
ADDEM   EQU   $
        MOV   A,D
        ADD   B
        SUI   30H
        MOV   B,A
        CALL  OUTPUT
        CALL  NEWLIN
        JMP   GETN1
INPUT   EQU   $
        PUSH  PSW
STATUS  EQU   $
        CALL  TEST
        JZ    STATUS
        IN    1CH
        ANI   7FH
        MOV   B,A
        POP   PSW
        RET
OUTPUT  EQU   $
        PUSH  PSW
STATOT  EQU   $
        MVI   A,10H
        OUT   1DH
        IN    1DH
        ANI   00001100B
```

FIGURE 10.1. Sample Program *(cont'd next page)*

```
        CPI  00001100B
        JNZ  STATOT
        MOV  A,B
        OUT  1CH
        POP  PSW
        RET
TEST    EQU  $
        XRA  A
        OUT  1DH
        IN   1DH
        ANI  1
        RET
NEWLIN  EQU  $
        PUSH B
        MVI  B,0DH          ;CR
        CALL OUTPUT
        MVI  B,0AH          ;LF
        CALL OUTPUT
        POP  B
        RET
CHEKIT  EQU  $
        MVI  C,0FFH
        CPI  30H
        JNC  CHEKHI
        MVI  C,0
        RET
CHEKHI  EQU  $
        CPI  35H
        RC
        MVI  C,0
        RET
ERROR   EQU  $
        PUSH B
        PUSH D
        PUSH H
        LXI  H,NOMSG
        MVI  D,38           ;LOOP COUNT
OUTER   EQU  $
        MOV  B,M
        CALL OUTPUT
        INX  H
        DCR  D
        JNZ  OUTER
        CALL NEWLIN
        POP  H
        POP  D
        POP  B
        RET
NOMSG   DB   'YOU MUST ENTER A DIGIT BETWEEN 0 AND 4'
        END
```

FIGURE 10.1. Sample Program

0 and 4. It validates each input byte and writes an error message if a byte is invalid. Here's how it works:

- The GETN1 routine (lines 2 through 14) reads and validates the first input digit. It loops until a valid digit is obtained. SAVEN1 is part of GETN1.
- The GETN2 routine (lines 15 through 25) reads and validates the second input digit. It also loops until a valid digit is obtained.
- The ADDEM routine (lines 26 through 33) adds the two digits and writes the answer. Control is returned to GETN1 to start the next problem (creating a closed loop).
- The INPUT routine (lines 34 through 43) reads one byte from the terminal and places it in register B. STATUS is part of the INPUT routine.
- The OUTPUT routine (lines 44 through 56) writes one byte from B to the terminal. STATOT is part of the OUTPUT routine.
- The TEST routine (lines 57 through 62) tests the terminal to see if it's ready.
- The NEWLIN routine (lines 63 through 70) starts a new line on the terminal.
- The CHEKIT routine (lines 71 through 81) validates the byte in A. The byte is left in A and the result is put in C. If the input byte is between '0' and '4', C is set to 0FFH. If not, C is set to 0H. CHEKHI is part of the CHEKIT routine.
- The ERROR routine (lines 82 through 98) puts out a message if the input doesn't validate. OUTER is part of this routine.

What happens if the user types a 3?

_____ (a) It is accepted and the program continues normally.

_____ (b) The error message is written and the program loops back to get another digit.

_____ (c) The program terminates itself.

What happens if the user types a 7?

_____ (d) It is accepted and the program continues normally.

_____ (e) The error message is written and the program loops back to get another digit.

_____ (f) The program terminates itself.

— — — — — — — — — — — — —

(a) and (e) are correct

2 Most Assembly Language programs contain three major parts:

- The *main line* is the code that's logically between the start (at the top) and the stop (however that happens). If the main line contains more than one routine (as indicated by labeled statements), the routines receive control by fall-through or by jumps.
- The *subroutines* are sections of code that are not in the main line. They receive control only by calls. They are positioned and coded so that they never receive control by fall-through or jumps.
- The *data area definitions* reserve memory bytes to hold data. They are so positioned that they will never receive control.

Refer to the example in Figure 10.1.

(a) Which lines comprise the main line? ____________________

(b) Which lines comprise the subroutines? ____________________

(c) Which lines comprise the data area definitions? ____________________

— — — — — — — — — — — —

(a) 2 through 33; (b) 34 through 98; (c) 99

3. A subroutine is a routine that receives control only by a call. It usually performs one function (such as reading a byte from the terminal into register B). It releases control by a *return.* Control returns to the instruction following the CALL instruction.

(a) How does a subroutine receive control?

_____ by jumps

_____ by calls

_____ by fall-through

(b) How does a subroutine release control?

_____ by executing a return

_____ by reaching the last line

_____ by jumping

(c) How many functions do most subroutines accomplish? __________

— — — — — — — — — — — —

(a) by calls; (b) by executing a return; (c) one

4. Here's how a call works:

- The address in the PC register is pushed into the stack. Recall that the PC tells the system the address of the next instruction to be executed.

- The address in the calling instruction operand is loaded into the PC. Thus, that address becomes the next instruction address.

Here's how a return works:

- The top of the stack is popped into the PC. This should be the address that was pushed by the calling instruction.

Suppose you have this situation:

```
address                 instruction
0110                    CALL  GETIT
0112                    MOV   A,B
  .
  .
  .
0200            GETIT   EQU   $
0200                    MVI   M,0
  .
  .
  .
020A                    RET
```

(a) What address is pushed by the CALL instruction? ______

(b) What address is loaded into the PC by the CALL instruction? ______

(c) What is the next instruction to be executed after the CALL instruction? ______

(d) What address is popped from the stack into the PC by the RETurn instruction? ______

(e) What is the next instruction to be executed after the RET instruction? ______

(a) 0112H; (b) 0200H; (c) MVI M,0; (d) 0112H; (e) MOV A,B

5. Examine the program in Figure 10.1 again. Which of the following are subroutines?

______ (a) GETN1 ______ (f) OUTPUT ______ (k) CHEKHI

______ (b) GETN2 ______ (g) STATOT ______ (l) ERROR

______ (c) ADDEM ______ (h) TEST ______ (m) OUTER

______ (d) INPUT ______ (i) NEWLIN

______ (e) STATUS ______ (j) CHEKIT

(d), (f), (h), (i), (j), (l)
[(a) through (c) are part of the main line; (e) is part of INPUT since control falls through; (g) is part of OUTPUT since control falls through; (k) is part of CHEKIT since it is reached by a jump from CHEKHI; (m) is part of ERROR since control falls through]

CODING A SUBROUTINE

6. You must be careful when you code a subroutine. You want it to perform its function completely and accurately and have no unexpected side effects. And it must include at least one return instruction. It may have more than one return if alternate paths are established.

What are three characteristics of a good subroutine?

(a) ______________________________

(b) ______________________________

(c) ______________________________

(a) complete and accurate; (b) no side effects; (c) at least one return

PRESERVING ORIGINAL VALUES

7. A subroutine avoids side effects by returning memory, the registers, and the stack in exactly the same condition that it receives them. Of course, it may use these areas. But it also restores them to their original values.

The exception is any area that is supposed to be affected by the subroutine's function. For example, the INPUT subroutine reads a byte into register B. Register B comes out of the subroutine with its value changed. But all other registers, the stack, and memory should be unchanged.

The OUTPUT subroutine writes one character from register B to a terminal. What areas would you expect to have different values after the routine has returned control?

_____ (a) PSW

_____ (b) B

_____ (c) D–L

_____ (d) SP

_____ (e) the stack

_____ (f) memory

_____ (g) none of the above

— — — — — — — — — — — — — —

(g) is the correct answer. Register B still contains the byte that was written.

8. The CHEKIT subroutine (see Figure 10.1) analyzes a value in register A. It places its results in register C. If the value in A is between '0' and '4', 0FFH is placed in C. Otherwise, 0 is placed in C.

What areas would you expect to have different values after CHEKIT returns control?

_____ (a) A	_____ (d) D–E	_____ (g) the stack
_____ (b) B	_____ (e) H–L	_____ (h) memory
_____ (c) C	_____ (f) SP	_____ (i) none of them

— — — — — — — — — — — — — —

(c)

9. If your subroutine needs to use a register, you preserve the incoming contents of that register by pushing it into the stack. Then you pop it before returning control.

Suppose your subroutine uses registers A and D. Both should be returned to the calling routine in their original condition. Write the PUSH and POP instructions.

____

____

____

____

— — — — — — — — — — — — — —

```
PUSH PSW
PUSH D
 ...
POP  D
POP  PSW
```

(Be sure you popped them in reverse.)

10. It's critically important that your subroutine pops anything that it pushes. Remember that the return address is in the stack. If you leave the stack unbalanced, the remainder of the program won't work.

If your subroutine pushes register D and H, then what must it do before returning control? ______________________________

— — — — — — — — — — — — —

pop registers H and D

RETURN INSTRUCTIONS

11. A subroutine returns control via one of the return instructions. There are nine return instructions:

RET	(unconditional return)
RC	(return if the carry flag is on)
RNC	(return if the carry flag is not on)
RM	(return if the sign flag is on
RP	(return if the sign flag is not on)
RPE	(return if the parity flag is on)
RPO	(return if the parity flag is not on)
RZ	(return if the zero flag is on)
RNZ	(return is the zero flag is not on)

They have no operands.

Code instructions to meet the following specifications.

(a) Compare the value in A with 20H. Return if it is greater than or equal to 20H.

____

____

(b) Subtract 1 from the value in D. Return if the result equals zero.

____

____

(c) Restore the value of the PSW from the stack. Then return control to the calling routine.

____

____

— — — — — — — — — — — — —

(a)
```
CPI   20H
RNC
```

(b)
```
DCR   D
RZ
```

(c)
```
POP   PSW
RET
```

12. You should now be able to write subroutines. These next few frames will give you some practice.

Code a subroutine called ECHO that reads a byte into B, echoes it, and stores it in memory at whatever address is in H–L when the subroutine is called. Leave all the registers intact when you return control to the calling routine.

```
ECHO    EQU  $
        PUSH B
        CALL INPUT
        CALL OUTPUT
        MOV  M,B
        POP  B
        RET
```

13. Code a subroutine called STALL that writes out this message: PLEASE WAIT—I'M THINKING. (Don't forget to use two single quotes to store one single quote.)

```
-------------
STALL   EQU  $
        PUSH PSW
        PUSH H
        PUSH B
        PUSH D
        LXI  H,WAITMS
        MVI  D,27
PUTIT   EQU  $
        MOV  B,M
        CALL OUTPUT
        INX  H
        DCR  D
        JNZ  PUTIT
        POP  D
        POP  B
        POP  H
        POP  PSW
        RET
WAITMS  DB   'PLEASE WAIT -- I''M THINKING'
```

(You might have used different registers. Be sure you push the registers you use, and then pop them in reverse order.)

14. Code a subroutine that reads a byte from the terminal. If the input byte is less than 20H, return control. If the byte is 20H or more, move it to register D and then return control. Note that the contents of register D are intended to be changed by this subroutine and should not be preserved. Preserve all other registers as usual.

```
GEDATA EQU  $
       PUSH PSW
       PUSH B
       CALL INPUT
       MOV  A,B
       CPI  20H
       JC   ENDING
       MOV  D,B
ENDING EQU  $
       POP  B
       POP  PSW
       RET
```

15. Code a subroutine that adds 5 to the contents of register A. If the result overflows, reset the register to zero. Otherwise, just return control. It is not necessary to preserve the contents of any registers for this subroutine.

```
INC5   EQU  $
       ADI  5
       RNC
       MVI  A,0
       RET
```

(Note that it is possible to use the conditional return (RNC) here because we don't need to pop any registers before returning.)

CONDITIONAL CALLS

You have learned how to code a subroutine. There are also some new instructions for calling subroutines—the conditional calls. In the following frames, you will learn how to call subroutines.

16. You have already learned how to make an unconditional call using the CALL instruction. Here are the conditional calls:

CC (call if carry)
CNC (call if no carry)

CPE	(call if parity even)
CPO	(call if parity odd)
CM	(call if minus)
CP	(call if plus)
CZ	(call if zero)
CNZ	(call if not zero)

In each case, the operand is an address of the subroutine to be called.

Code calling instructions for each of the following situations.

(a) Subtract 1 from register A. If the result is zero, call a subroutine named ALLGON.

____

____

(b) Add registers D-E and H-L. If the result overflows, call a routine named OVERHL.

____

____

- - - - - - - - - - - - - -

(a)
```
SUI  1
CZ   ALLGON
```

(b)
```
DAD  D
CC   OVERHL
```

PASSING DATA

17. Many subroutines require data to be passed to them. For example, look at the CHEKIT routine in Figure 10.1. It operates on a value in register A. That value was placed in there by the calling routine. We call such values *passed data.*

Which of the following subroutines in Figure 10.1 requires data to be passed to it?

_____ (a) INPUT

_____ (b) OUTPUT

_____ (c) NEWLIN

- - - - - - - - - - - - - -

(b)

18. Data can be passed in the registers, the stack, or memory. Small amounts of data, one or two bytes, are usually passed in registers. Larger

amounts of data are usually passed in memory. The address of the passed data is placed in one of the register pairs.

Before you call a subroutine, be sure to place its required data where the subroutine expects to find it. For example, if the OUTPUT routine writes a byte in register B, don't place the intended byte in register A or C or some other place.

Suppose you are calling a subroutine that expects to write out an entire message. It expects to have the beginning address of the message passed to it in register H-L. Code a set of instructions to call this subroutine (named MESOUT) for the message starting at address HICARD.

```
LXI  H,HICARD
CALL MESOUT
```

I/O SUBROUTINES

In the preceding frames, you have learned how to code and call subroutines. Now we want to take a look specifically at input and output (I/O) subroutines. We can't show you exactly what subroutines you should use, but we can show you some common ones.

19. The major problem with I/O is that the microprocessor, which has no moving parts, can work so much faster than any I/O device. In fact, the average 8080/8085 microprocessor can read and store about 62,500 bytes per second. But a very fast CRT (cathode ray tube) terminal can only send about 960 bytes per second. The average typist can type about 4 bytes per second. The bytes can't be read any faster than they become available.

On the output side, again the microprocessor can write about 62,500 bytes per second (more if it's not retrieving them from memory), but a very fast line printer can only type about 120 bytes per second and 30 is a more common speed. A byte can't be written until the previous byte is completed.

(a) Suppose you're writing an input subroutine to read one byte. What condition would you wait for before issuing the IN (read) instruction?

____

(b) Suppose you're writing an output subroutine to write one byte. What condition would you wait for before issuing the OUT (write) instruction? ____________________

(c) What do you think an I/O subroutine spends *most* of its time doing?

____

- - - - - - - - - - - - - -

(a) when the input device has a byte available; (b) when the output device is ready for one; (c) stalling, pausing, waiting, spinning its wheels, slowing down the computer

20. The primary I/O device of a microcomputer is usually some kind of terminal. The input comes from a keyboard operated by a human being (we hope). The output goes to a printer device or a CRT screen.

There are several ways to coordinate the transfer of data with such a terminal. We'll describe the most common method in microcomputers.

There are two connections (called *ports*) between the terminal and the microprocessor. One port is for I/O data. The other port is for status information. The status information tells whether the terminal has an input byte ready to be read or is ready to receive an output byte.

(a) When you want to read a byte of data from the terminal, what port do you read from first, the data port or the status port?

____

(b) What does the status port tell you? ______________________

____

- - - - - - - - - - - - - -

(a) the status port; (b) whether the terminal is ready to send or receive data

21. Every port has a one-byte address. To read a byte from a port, we use the instruction:

[*label*] IN *port* [;*comments*]

The byte is placed in register A.

Suppose your terminal has its status byte at port 20H and its data byte at port 21H.

(a) Code an instruction to read the terminal status byte into register A.

____

(b) Code an instruction to read the terminal data byte into register A.

____

- - - - - - - - - - - - - -

(a) IN 20H; (b) IN 21H

22. The status byte contains flags to tell whether the terminal is ready to send or receive data. For example, it might work this way: If the LSB is on, the terminal has a byte to send; if the MSB is on, the terminal is ready to receive data. Other bits are ignored.

(a) If the status byte is 10001100, can we write a data byte? __________

Can we read a data byte? __________

(b) If the status byte is 01100001, can we write a data byte? __________

Can we read a data byte? __________

— — — — — — — — — — — — —

(a) yes, no; (b) no, yes

23. Code a loop that reads and tests a terminal status byte until it shows that the terminal is ready to receive data. Then control should fall through to the next statement.

Use these terminal specifications:

- data byte at port address 23H;
- status byte at port address 24H;
- MSB on indicates that terminal is ready to receive data.

— — — — — — — — — — — — —

```
OUTST  EQU  $
       IN   24H    ; GET STATUS BYTE IN A
       RLC         ; TEST MSB
       JNC  OUTST  ; LOOP IF OFF
```

(RAL would work the same as RLC in this loop. There are many other ways to test the MSB, also.)

24. Now code an input routine that tests a status byte until it shows that there is a data byte ready to be read. Then read the data byte.

Use these terminal specifications:

- status byte at port address 10H;
- data byte at port address 11H;
- the *two* LSBs must be on if there is a byte to be read (that is, XXXXXX11B).

```
INTEST EQU  $
       IN   10H       ; GET STATUS IN A
       ANI  00000011B ; TURN OFF UNNEEDED BITS
       CPI  00000011B ; TEST BITS
       JNZ  INTEST
; WHEN CONTROL FALLS THROUGH TO HERE, A
; BYTE IS READY TO BE READ
       IN   11H
```

25. Now convert your input routine from the preceding frame into a complete INPUT subroutine. Put the newly read byte in B before returning control. Preserve the original contents of any registers except B that are used.

```
INPUT  EQU  $
       PUSH PSW
INTEST EQU  $
       IN   10H       ; GET STATUS IN A
       ANI  00000011B ; TURN OFF UNNEEDED BITS
       CPI  00000011B ; TEST BITS
       JNZ  INTEST
; WHEN CONTROL FALLS THROUGH TO HERE, A
; BYTE IS READY TO BE READ
       IN   11H
       MOV  B,A
       POP  PSW
       RET
```

26. Some terminals have more than one status byte. You need to tell the terminal which status byte you want. You do this by sending a request code to the status port before reading the status byte.

For example, our CRT terminal has these specifications:

- Status port address—1DH
  - input status byte request code—0
  - output status byte request code—10H
  - bits indicating that an input byte is available—LSB is on (XXXXXXX1B)
  - bits indicating that the terminal is ready to receive a byte—5th and 6th bits are on (XXXX11XXB)
- Data port address—1CH

Here's a routine that tests our terminal status until a byte is ready for input.

```
INTEST EQU  $
       XRA  A       ; A = 0
       OUT  1DH     ; REQUEST INPUT STATUS
       IN   1DH     ; GET STATUS BYTE
       ANI  1       ; TEST LSB
       JZ   INTEST  ; LOOP IF LSB OFF
; CONTROL FALLS THROUGH WHEN A BYTE IS
; READY TO BE READ.
```

Code a routine that tests the output side of our terminal until it's ready to receive a byte.

```
OUTEST EQU  $
       MVI  A,10H
       OUT  1DH        ; REQUEST OUTPUT STATUS
       IN   1DH        ; READ STATUS BYTE
       ANI  00001100B  ; MASK OUT UNNEEDED BITS
       CPI  00001100B  ; ARE THEY BOTH ON?
       JNZ  OUTEST     ; LOOP IF NOT BOTH ON
```

27. Expand the routine you wrote for the preceding frame into a complete OUTPUT subroutine. The data byte to be written is stored in B. Preserve the original contents of all registers that are used.

```
OUTPUT  EQU   $
        PUSH  PSW
OUTEST  EQU   $
        MVI   A,10H
        OUT   1DH         ; REQUEST OUTPUT STATUS
        IN    1DH         ; READ STATUS BYTE
        ANI   00001100B   ; MASK OUT UNNEEDED BITS
        CPI   00001100B   ; ARE THEY BOTH ON?
        JNZ   OUTEST      ; LOOP IF NOT BOTH ON
        MOV   A,B
        OUT   1CH         ; WRITE TO THE DATA PORT
        POP   PSW
        RET
```

You have now seen how we write a complete input or output subroutine. Of course, they can be much fancier, especially if you want to do some error parity checking. Routines that access printers look much the same as these. Routines for devices such as disk, tape, and cards usually require a lot more control code and timing routines. We cannot cover them in this book.

As to how you access your own devices, you'll need to find out how they communicate with the microprocessor. What are their port addresses and how do they transmit status information? Your manuals or your technical representative may be able to help you.

PROGRAM DESIGN

How do you decide what to code as a subroutine and what to put in the main line? There's no hard and fast rule. But the following frames present some guidelines.

28. Subroutines make programs easier for people to read and write. At one extreme, your main line could consist entirely of subroutine calls. All the detail work would be done by the subroutines. The logic of a program written this way is usually very clear. But the overhead (extra computer time) is tremendous! A call instruction takes nearly twice as long to execute as a jump instruction. And all those PUSHes and POPs add to the time—and use up more memory space, too.

Of course, we're talking about time differences measured in *nanoseconds* (one-billionth of a second). For the average application program, the extra time and storage involved by using a lot of subroutines will never be noticed. But most system programs must make the best possible use of time and space.

(a) Subroutines use (more/less) _______ time and space than main line routines.

(b) Most application programs should use (many/few) _______ subroutines.

(c) Most system programs should use (many/few) _______ subroutines.

- - - - - - - - - - - - - -

(a) more; (b) many; (c) few

29. We do use subroutines in system programs, but we use them only where they're really needed. One situation where we usually create a subroutine is when the same routine is executed at several different places in the program. A subroutine saves us from having to write the code several times. Jumping doesn't work as well because there's no mechanism for returning to the previous place when the routine finishes.

Refer to Figure 10.1 to answer the following questions.

(a) How many different places call NEWLIN? _______________

(b) Why did we make NEWLIN a subroutine? _______________

____

- - - - - - - - - - - - - -

(a) 4; (b) because it's used in four different places in the program.

30. Another reason we use a subroutine in a system program is that it's the same routine that appears in many programs. For example, we almost always use the INPUT and OUTPUT subroutines even though a particular program may only call them once each. Why? They save us coding time and they've been thoroughly tested.

Suppose your system includes a CRT terminal. You want to code a routine that clears the screen and sends the cursor to the home position.

(a) Would you make it a subroutine? _______________

(b) Why or why not? _______________

____

- - - - - - - - - - - - - -

(a) we would; (b) because you'll use it over and over again in many different programs

31. Let's review what you've learned about program design with respect to subroutines.

(a) Which type of program can maximize the use of subroutines: system or application? ____________

(b) List two primary types of routines that you should consider making into subroutines. ____________

____

— — — — — — — — — — — — — —

(a) application; (b) ones that are used more than once in the same program and ones that are used in many different programs

REVIEW

In this chapter, you've learned how to code and call subroutines, especially I/O subroutines.

- A subroutine is a routine that is not in the main line of control. It receives control by being called and it returns control to the calling routine when it finishes.
- A good subroutine accomplishes one function completely and accurately, has no unexpected side effects, and contains at least one return instruction.
- Side effects are avoided by returning the stack, memory, and the registers in their original condition, except for those that are supposed to be affected. PUSH and POP instructions are used to preserve the registers and restore them. Be sure to POP all items, in reverse order, that have been pushed.
- The return instructions are:
  - — RET (return)
  - — RC (return if carry)
  - — RNC (return if not carry)
  - — RZ (return if zero)
  - — RNZ (return if not zero)
  - — RM (return if minus)
  - — RP (return if plus)
  - — RPO (return if parity is odd)
  - — RPE (return if parity is even)

  They have no operands. Don't use a conditional return if you need to POP registers.
- The call instructions are:
  - — CALL (call)
  - — CC (call if carry)

— CNC (call if not carry)
— CZ (call if zero)
— CNZ (call if not zero)
— CP (call if plus)
— CM (call if minus)
— CPO (call if parity is odd)
— CPE (call if parity is even)

The operand is the address of the first instruction of the subroutine.

- For many I/O subroutines for terminals and printers, it's necessary to read a status byte from a status port before reading or writing data. The status byte has one or more bits indicating whether the terminal is ready to send or receive data.
- Some terminals have multiple status bytes and it's necessary to send a request for the status byte you want.
- Application programs should make free use of subroutines because they make the program logic easier to understand. However, subroutines take more time and space and in general should be minimized in system programs. Routines that are good candidates for subroutines are those that are used several times in the same program and those that are used in many programs within a system.

CHAPTER 10 SELF-TEST

Part I. Code instructions according to the following specifications.

1. Call the subroutine named ERROR if the carry flag is on. __________
2. Call the subroutine named POSIV if the sign flag is not on. __________
3. Call the subroutine named AJUSTA if the zero flag is on. __________
4. Return control to the calling routine if the sign flag is on. __________
5. Return control to the calling routine if the zero flag is not on.

   ____
6. Return control to the calling routine if the carry flag is not on.

   ____
7. Return control unconditionally. ______________________________

Part II. Code the calling routines or subroutines specified below.

1. This subroutine writes out any message on the terminal. The beginning address of the message is passed in registers H–L. The length of the message is passed in register D. Call the OUTPUT routine to actually write each byte.

2. This subroutine reads, echos, and validates an incoming byte. A byte is valid if it is an upper case letter. If invalid, write the message WRONG—TRY AGAIN. Continue reading until a valid byte is obtained. Place the byte in D and return control.

   Use the INPUT and OUTPUT subroutines to read and write single bytes. Call the subroutine you wrote for question 1 to write the message.

3. This routine—not a subroutine—reads and stores an incoming message in memory. It should loop until the letter Z is read. That terminates the message. (Store the Z.)

   Each character of the incoming message should be read, echoed, and validated using the subroutine you wrote for question 2 above.

4. This subroutine writes one character from register B on a printer. Use these features:

   - Single status byte at port address 1FH.
   - MSB indicates output status; off for ready.
   - Data byte at port address 1EH.

5. This subroutine reads one character from a terminal. The terminal status byte is at port address 1CH. The first and second bits are on when a byte is ready to be read. The data byte is at address 1DH. Put the character in B.

6. This subroutine prints text on the printer by calling the print subroutine you wrote for question 4 above. After each character is printed, check for an input byte from the terminal described in question 5 above. If any byte is input, discontinue printing.

   The following data is passed to this subroutine: (a) The beginning memory address of the text is in H–L; (b) The length of the text is in D.

7. This routine causes the following message to be printed, preceded by line feed and carriage return:
   NOW IS THE TIME FOR ALL GOOD PEOPLE TO COME TO THE AID OF THEIR PARTY.

   Use the subroutine you wrote for question 6 above to print the text.

Part III. Code a complete program (except I/O subroutines) to meet these specifications.

This is a typing practice program. Write a random character on the terminal. The user then types that character. If it matches, write OK and go on to the next character. If it doesn't match, write NO and repeat the same character. Start a new line for each new character and each user's response, so that a set of messages looks like this.

```
program's message ---→  X
user's response   ---→  X OK  ←--- program's message
                        T
                        K NO
                        T
                        etc.
```

Our program logic is shown in Figure 10.2.

PROGRAMMING NOTES:

1. To select a character from the ASCII character set, we suggest arbitrarily selecting the first character and then add some variable to it to find the next character, adjusting the result to stay within the range of 21H-7EH. For example, you could always start with 'J'. For the second character, add the number of correct responses so far, plus 7, minus the number of incorrect responses so far to J. Adjust the result to be between 21H and 7EH.

2. There are several ways to adjust a value to be between 21H and 7EH.
   a. You could arbitrarily reset the value to 'J' or some other correct value whenever it gets out of range.
   b. You could add 21H to any value that's too low and subtract 7EH from any value that's too high.
   c. If a value is too low, you could turn on the third bit from the left, thus forcing the value to be at least 20H. If the result is 20H, make it 21H.
      If the value is too high, turn off the most significant bit, thus forcing the value below 80H. If the result is 7FH, make it 7EH. (This is the method we use in our answer.)

3. Some potential subroutines: read one character, write one character, start a new line, handle a correct response, handle an incorrect response, adjust result below 21H, adjust result above 7EH.

4. Don't bother coding the input and output subroutines unless you're actually going to test this program. In that case, code the appropriate routines for your system.

1. Initialize values
    a. set first character arbitrarily (we use 'J') in A
    b. set arbitrary increment (we use 7) in E
2. Test one character (repeat until user kills program)
    a. write out character from A
    b. start new line
    c. read and echo character
    d. if input is same as character in A
        (1) write OK message
        (2) adjust arbitrary increment (we add 1 to it)
        (3) increment character in A
            (a) add arbitrary increment
            (b) if sum below 21H, adjust up
            (c) if sum above 7EH, adjust down
        (4) go to step f
    e. if input is different from character in A
        (1) write NO message
        (2) adjust arbitrary increment (we subtract 1 from it)
        (3) don't change letter in A
        (4) go on to step f
    f. start new line

FIGURE 10.2. Program Logic for Self-Test

Self-Test Answer Key

Part I.

1. `CC ERROR`
2. `CP POSIV`
3. `CZ AJUSTA`
4. `RM`
5. `RNZ`
6. `RNC`
7. `RET`

Part II.

1.
```
TERMSG EQU  $
       PUSH PSW
       PUSH H
       PUSH B
       PUSH D
OTLOOP EQU  $
       MOV  B,M
       CALL OUTPUT
       INX  H
       DCR  D
       JNZ  OTLOOP
       POP  D
       POP  B
       POP  H
       POP  PSW
       RET
```

2.
```
GETLET EQU  $
       PUSH PSW
       PUSH B
       PUSH H
TRYONE EQU  $
       CALL INPUT
       CALL OUTPUT
       MOV  A,B
       CPI  41H
       JC   WRONG
       CPI  5BH
       JNC  WRONG
       MOV  D,A
       POP  H
       POP  B
       POP  PSW
       RET
WRONG  EQU  $
       LXI  H,MESSAG
       MVI  D,18
       CALL TERMSG
       JMP  TRYONE
MESSAG DB   'WRONG -- TRY AGAIN'
```

3.
```
GETMES EQU  $
       LXI  H,INTEXT
GETEXT EQU  $
       CALL GETLET
       MOV  M,D
```

```
        INX   H
        MOV   A,D
        CPI   'Z'
        JNZ   GETEXT
        HLT
INTEXT  DS    80
```

4.

```
PRINTR  EQU   $
        PUSH  PSW
READY   EQU   $
        IN    1FH
        RLC
        JC    READY
        MOV   A,B
        OUT   1EH
        POP   PSW
        RET
```

5.

```
TERMIN  EQU   $
        PUSH  PSW
INTEST  EQU   $
        IN    1CH
        ANI   11000000B
        CPI   11000000B
        JNZ   INTEST
        IN    1DH
        MOV   B,A
        POP   PSW
        RET
```

6.

```
MESOUT  EQU   $
        PUSH  H
        PUSH  D
        PUSH  PSW
        PUSH  B
PRTONE  EQU   $
        MOV   B,M          ; NEXT CHARACTER
        CALL  PRINTR
        IN    1CH          ; CHECK FOR INPUT
        ANI   11000000B
        CPI   11000000B
        JZ    ENDING       ; QUIT IF INPUT
        INX   H
        DCR   D
        JNZ   PRTONE
ENDING  EQU   $
        POP   B
        POP   PSW
```

```
        POP   D
        POP   H
        RET
```

7.
```
        LXI   H,NOWMSG
        MVI   D,72
        CALL  MESOUT
        HLT
NOWMSG  DB    0DH,0AH, 'NOW IS THE TIME FOR ALL GOOD
        DB    'PEOPLE TO COME TO THE AID OF THEIR PARTY.'
```

Sample Solution Part III

```
        ORG   100H
SPACE   EQU   20H
HIVAL   EQU   0FFH
; FOLLOWING IS THE MAIN CONTROL ROUTINE
; REGISTERS --
;       A - LAST CHARACTER DISPLAYED
;       E - ARBITRARY INCREMENT
        MVI   A,'J'       ;STARTING CHARACTER
        MVI   E,7
ROUND1  EQU   $
        MOV   B,A
        CALL  OUTPUT
        CALL  NEWLIN
        CALL  INPUT
        CALL  OUTPUT       ;ECHO
        CMP   B
        CZ    SAME
        CNZ   DIFFER
        MVI   B,SPACE
        CALL  OUTPUT
        MOV   B,M
        CALL  OUTPUT
        INX   H
        MOV   B,M
        CALL  OUTPUT
        CALL  NEWLIN
        JMP   ROUND1
; THE FOLLOWING ROUTINE STARTS A NEW LINE
NEWLIN  EQU   $
        PUSH  B
        MVI   B,0DH       ;CR
        CALL  OUTPUT
        MVI   B,0AH       ;LF
        CALL  OUTPUT
```

Sample Solution Part III *(cont'd)*

```
        POP  B
        RET
; THE FOLLOWING ROUTINE HANDLES A CORRECT ANSWER
SAME    EQU  $
        LXI  H,OKMESS
        INR  E
        ADD  E      ;GENERATE NEXT LETTER IN A
        CPI  21H
        CC   TOOLOW     ;A < 21H
        CPI  7FH
        CNC  TOOHI      ;A > OR = 7FH
        CMP  A          ;FORCES ZERO FLAG BACK ON
        RET
;THE FOLLOWING ROUTINE HANDLES AN INCORRECT ANSWER
DIFFER  EQU  $
        LXI  H,NOMESS
        DCR  E
        RET
;THE FOLLOWING ROUTINE ADJUSTS A CHARACTER < 21H
TOOLOW  EQU $
        ORI  00100000B  ;MAKES IT AT LEAST 20H
        CPI  21H
        RNC             ;VALUE > 20H
        ADI  1          ;MAKES IT 21H
        RET
;THE FOLLOWING ROUTINE ADJUSTS A CHARACTER > 7EH
TOOHI   EQU  $
        ANI  01111111B   ;MAKES IT < 80H
        CALL TOOLOW      ;KEEP IT ABOVE 20H
        CPI  7FH
        RC               ;VALUE IS < 7FH
        SUI  1           ;MAKES IT 7EH
        RET
OKMESS  DB   'OK'
NOMESS  DB   'NO'
;FOLLOWING ARE THE I/O ROUTINES FOR OUR TERMINAL
INPUT   EQU  $
        PUSH PSW
STATUS  EQU  $
        CALL TEST
        JZ   STATUS
        IN   1CH
        ANI  7FH
        MOV  B,A
        POP  PSW
        RET
```

Sample Solution Part III *(cont'd)*

```
OUTPUT EQU   $
       PUSH PSW
STATOT EQU $
       MVI  A,10H
       OUT  1DH
       IN   1DH
       ANI  00001100B
       CPI  00001100B
       JNZ  STATOT
       MOV  A,B
       OUT  1CH
       POP  PSW
       RET
TEST   EQU  $
       XRA  A
       OUT  1DH
       IN   1DH
       ANI  1
       RET
       END
```

CHAPTER ELEVEN

NUMERIC MANIPULATION

You have already learned how to add and subtract numbers up to 255D using one byte. And you can add numbers up to 65,535 using DAD. But many computer applications require much larger numbers than these. Multiplication and division are also necessary, as well as the ability to handle negative numbers.

In this chapter, we'll introduce you to some techniques for handling numbers with Assembly Language. There isn't room in this book to cover them all. But we will show you how to code a routine that will add numbers several bytes long. We'll show you how to handle basic multiplication and division. And finally, we'll show you how to use twos complement notation to handle negative numbers and subtraction.

When you have finished this chapter, you will be able to:

- Code the following instructions:
  - ADC (add with carry)
  - ACI (add with carry immediate)
  - SBB (subtract with borrow)
  - SBI (subtract with borrow immediate)
  - DAA (decimal adjust the accumulator)
  - CMA (complement the accumulator)
- Code routines to solve the following types of problems:
  - convert ASCII to binary coded decimal (BCD);
  - convert BCD to ASCII;
  - add multibyte BCD values;
  - multiply multibyte values;
  - divide single-byte values;
  - convert ASCII to twos complement notation;
  - convert twos complement notation to ASCII.

MULTIBYTE ADDITION

1. Multibyte arithmetic is done on values stored in memory. Each byte is moved into the accumulator as it is needed.

In multibyte arithmetic, we usually don't work with values that have been converted to pure binary form. We work instead with a data representation system called *binary coded decimal* (BCD). You'll also hear it referred to as *packed decimal.*

Here are some decimal values as they are represented in binary, hexadecimal, BCD, and the hexadecimal representation of BCD.

decimal value	*pure binary*	*(hex)*	*BCD*	*(BCD-hex)*
21D	00010101	(15H)	00100001	(21H)
18D	00010010	(12H)	00011000	(18H)
30D	00011110	(1EH)	00110000	(30H)

Notice the correlation between the decimal value and the BCD hex value.

Give the BCD values for these decimal numbers. Show your answers in hex.

(a) 05D = __________ (BCD)

(b) 19D = __________ (BCD)

(c) 54D = __________ (BCD)

— — — — — — — — — — — — —

(a) 05H; (b) 19H; (c) 54H

2. The BCD system simply splits the two halves of a byte apart and treats them as separate storage areas. Half a byte is called a nibble (that's someone's idea of a joke), and we'll speak of the least significant or lower nibble and the most significant or upper nibble.

In BCD, each nibble can hold a value from 0 to 9. Values between A and F are forbidden. The normal binary equivalents of 0 to 9 are used (see Figure 1.1).

Give the BCD equivalents of these decimal values. Write your answers in both binary and hex.

(a) 32D = __________B (BCD) = __________H (BCD)

(b) 10D = __________B (BCD) = __________H (BCD)

— — — — — — — — — — — — —

(a) 00110010B, 32H; (b) 00010000B, 10H (Be sure you translated each digit separately.)

3. Which of the following values are illegal in BCD?

_____ (a) 39H

_____ (b) 4BH

_____ (c) 20H

_____ (d) 0FFH

— — — — — — — — — — — — —

(b) and (d) are illegal because they contain digits above 9

4. Assume we have two one-byte BCD values in memory.

```
ADD1   05
ADD2   04
```

We want to add these together, with the result in ADD1. Write instructions to accomplish the following:

(a) Put the ADD2 value in the accumulator.

____

____

(b) Add the ADD1 value to it and put the result in ADD1.

____

____

(c) What is the hex form of the value in ADD1 now? _____________

(d) Is this a valid BCD value? _____________________________

(e) Suppose the original values were both 5. Would the result be a valid BCD value? _____________________________

— — — — — — — — — — — — —

(a)
```
LDA   ADD2
```

(b)
```
LXI   H,ADD1
ADD   M
MOV   M,A
```

(c) 09H; (d) yes; (e) no—A is not valid in BCD

5. The result in the accumulator may no longer be a BCD number because the computer uses binary/hexadecimal arithmetic. Here are some examples:

```
  03             06          27        39
+ 04           + 05          36      + 08
----           ----          --      ----
  07 (ok!)       0B          5D        41
```

To correct this problem, we need to use an instruction called DAA (decimal adjust the accumulator). This instruction, which has no operands, puts each digit in the accumulator back into decimal again.

When you're doing BCD arithmetic, every addition instruction should be followed by a ______ instruction.

— — — — — — — — — — — — — —

DAA

6. DAA works differently on the two halves of a byte. Here's how DAA works on the least significant nibble. (Remember that a nibble is half a byte.)

- If the nibble is 9 or less and the auxiliary carry flag is off, the nibble is left alone. The auxiliary carry flag would be on if overflow into the most significant nibble had occurred.
- If the nibble is above 9, or the auxiliary carry flag is on, the nibble is increased by 6. This may cause a carry into the upper nibble.

Apply these rules to the following problems. Give the value after DAA is executed.

ADD1	05H	06H	09H
ADD2	03H	09H	09H
sum:auxiliary carry	08H:0	0FH:0	12H:1
DAA	(a) ______	(b) ______	(c) ______

— — — — — — — — — — — — — —

(a) 08; (b) 15; (c) 18

(Inspect these answers and you'll see that they're the true decimal sums of 5 + 3, 6 + 9, and 9 + 9, respectively.)

7. Now let's see how DAA handles the most significant nibble.

- If the value is 9 or less and the carry flag is off, the value is left alone.
- If the value is greater than 9, or the carry flag is on, the value is incremented by six. If a carry results, the carry flag is turned on. Otherwise, it is left alone.

Apply these rules to the following problems. Give the byte value as well as the carry flag status.

ADD1	20H	70H	40H
ADD2	40H	90H	80H
carry:sum	0:60H	1:00H	0:C0H
DAA	(a) ___:___	(b) ___:___	(c) ___:___

(a) 0:60; (b) 1:60; (c) 1:20

It's not really necessary for you to remember exactly how DAA works. But you should be convinced now that DAA will convert a hex sum back into a BCD one.

8. Two BCD values in ADD1 and ADD2 can be added using these instructions:

```
LXI   H,ADD2
MOV   A,M
LXI   H,ADD1
ADD   M
MOV   M,A
```

(a) Code the instruction you would use to convert the result to BCD.

____

(b) Where would you insert that instruction in the routine above?

____

(a) DAA; (b) after ADD M

9. Now let's assume that we have two BCD values in memory, each two bytes long.

```
ADEND1
       |0X|XX|

ADEND2
       |0Y|YY|
```

We want to add these two values together, storing the sum in ADEND2. Notice that each of them has at least one leading zero. This will make sure the result will fit in ADEND2. First we'll add the rightmost bytes, using relative addressing.

Write a set of instructions that will move the least significant byte of ADEND1 into the accumulator, then add the least significant byte of ADEND2 to it. Leave the result in the accumulator.

Write your code on a separate piece of paper using pencil. You're going to add to and change this routine until you've built a complete addition program.

Programming Note: Right now we're working with only two bytes. But eventually you want to be able to add fields of any size. Don't use LDA to access these bytes. Use the H–L register pair for one addend and D–E for the other. Use XCHG to swap the addresses.

```
LXI   H,ADEND1+1   ; H-L ---> ADEND1
LXI   D,ADEND2+1   ; D-E ---> ADEND2
MOV   A,M          ; A = ADEND1
XCHG               ; H-L ---> ADEND2
ADD   M            ; ADEND2 + ADEND1
```

10. Add instructions to the routine you just wrote to correctly adjust the result in the accumulator. Then store the sum in the least significant byte of ADEND2.

You should have added these lines:

```
DAA
MOV   M,A   ; SUM STORED IN ADEND2
```

11. Now we're ready to handle the most significant byte. The only difference between this byte and the least significant byte is the possibility of a carry coming from the previous byte.

There is another set of arithmetic instructions that you'll need to use when doing multibyte arithmetic. They are:

ADC	(add with carry)
ACI	(add immediate data with carry)
SBB	(subtract with borrow)
SBI	(subtract immediate data with borrow)

Their formats are the same as those for ADD, ADI, SUB, SUI. In the case of the add instructions, they add the data *and the value of the carry flag* to A. In the case of the subtract instructions, they subtract the data and the value of the carry flag from A.

(a) Write an instruction that will add 5 to the accumulator and add in the value of the carry flag. __________

(b) Write an instruction that will subtract register B from register A and subtract the value of the carry flag. __________

(c) What is the difference between ADD and ADC? __________

____

— — — — — — — — — — — — — —

(a) ACI 5; (b) SBB B; (c) ADC also adds in the value of the carry flag while ADD doesn't

12. Suppose register A contains BCD 29, register B contains BCD 33, and the carry flag equals 0. What will be the effect of this set of instructions ...

```
ADC   B
DAA
```

(a) ... on register A? ___________

(b) ... on the carry flag? ___________

If the carry flag equals 1, what would the effect be ...

(c) ... on register A? ___________

(d) ... on the carry flag? ___________

— — — — — — — — — — — — — —

(a) changes to 62; (b) set to 0; (c) 63; (d) 0

13. Remember that when we added the least significant bytes of ADEND1 and ADEND2, we stored the sum in ADEND2. The carry flag was left intact. If there was a carry out of that first byte, the carry flag will be on. Otherwise, it will be off.

Now add a set of instructions to treat the most significant bytes. Write a routine that will:

(1) move the ADEND1 byte into the accumulator;

(2) add the ADEND2 byte to it, plus the value in the carry flag;

(3) decimal adjust the sum; and

(4) store it in the correct byte of ADEND2.

— — — — — — — — — — — — — —

Here is our whole routine so far:

```
ADDER   EQU   $
        LXI   H,ADEND1+1     ; H-L ---> ADEND1
        LXI   D,ADEND2+1     ; D-E ---> ADEND2
        MOV   A,M            ; ADEND1 INTO A
        XCHG                 ; H-L ---> ADEND2
        ADD   M              ; ADEND1 + ADEND2
        DAA
```

(cont'd next page)

```
MOV  M,A          ; SUM TO ADEND2
DCX  H            ; POINT TO THE FIRST BYTE OF ADEND2
XCHG
DCX  H            ; POINT TO THE FIRST BYTE OF ADEND1
MOV  A,M          ; (1)
XCHG
ADC  M            ; ADEND1 + ADEND2 + CARRY (2)
DAA               ; (3)
MOV  M,A          ; (4)
```

14. Notice that the routine so far adds two bytes, It contains two similar sets of instructions. Each set:

- — Points to bytes
- — Stores one byte in accumulator
- — Swaps addresses in H-L and D-E
- — Adds in other byte
- — Decimal adjusts
- — Stores result in memory

While the operations are accomplished a bit differently, we can create a loop that will add the two bytes for larger numbers.

The ADC instruction can be used instead of ADD—if you first make sure the carry flag is set to zero. You can do this by adding zero to register A.

Now adapt your addition routine so that it is one loop that adds two five-byte numbers and stores the sum.

Hints: Put the addresses in the register pairs before beginning the loop. The first loop adds the least significant bytes. Make sure the carry flag is set to 0 before entering the loop so you can use the ADC instruction.

— — — — — — — — — — — — —

```
ADDER   EQU  $
        LXI  D,ADEND2+4
        LXI  H,ADEND1+4
        MVI  C,5          ; C WILL COUNT 5 LOOPS
        ADI  0            ; TURN OFF CARRY
ADDBYT  EQU  $
        MOV  A,M          ; A = ADEND1
        XCHG
        ADC  M            ; ADEND1 + ADEND2 + CARRY
        DAA
        MOV  M,A
        DCX  H            ; DECREMENT ---> ADEND2
        XCHG
```

(cont'd next page)

```
DCX   H          ; DECREMENT ---> ADEND1
DCR   C          ; LOOP COUNTER
JNZ   ADDBYT
```

BCD CONVERSION

Now that you've seen how to add two BCD numbers, let's talk about where they came from in the first place. In the following set of frames, we'll show you how to expand the program you've already coded so that it reads a set of ASCII digits from a terminal and converts them to BCD.

15. Let's start by reading one digit from the terminal and converting it from ASCII to binary. All you have to do is turn off all the bits in the most significant nibble. Leave the result in the accumulator.

Write your code on a separate piece of paper so you can build an entire routine as before. Use CALLs for any I/O you need.

— — — — — — — — — — — — —

```
CALL INPUT
CALL OUTPUT
MOV  A,B
ANI  00001111B
```

16. In BCD, it's very important that only valid decimal digits are used. Convert the routine you coded in the previous frame into a complete subroutine that gets one *valid* digit:

(1) Read and echo one character.

(2) Validate range '0' to '9' (make sure the character is in the range).

(3) If the character is out of range, write an error message and try again.

(4) When a valid digit is obtained, convert it to binary and return control. Leave the new value in A.

— — — — — — — — — — — — —

```
GETDIG EQU  $
       PUSH B
       PUSH H
TRYONE EQU  $
       CALL INPUT
       CALL OUTPUT
```

(cont'd next page)

```
        MOV   A,B
        CPI   '0'     ; RANGE CHECK
        JC    ERROR
        CPI   ':'
        JNC   ERROR
        ANI   00001111B
        POP   H
        POP   B
        RET
ERROR   EQU   $
        MVI   C,26
        LXI   H,ERRMSG
MSGOUT  EQU   $
        MOV   B,M
        CALL  OUTPUT
        INX   H
        DCR   C
        JNZ   MSGOUT
        JMP   TRYONE
ERRMSG  DB    'INVALID DIGIT -- TRY AGAIN'
```

17. Now we have a subroutine that will put one valid binary digit in register A. How do we get from there to BCD? For correct BCD format, we have to work with two digits at a time. We combine them into one byte this way:

(1) Rotate the first digit into the upper nibble.

(2) Add in the second digit.

Code a routine that will get two valid decimal digits (by calling GETDIG) and create one BCD byte. Store the byte at ADEND1.

- - - - - - - - - - - - -

```
GETNUM EQU   $
       CALL  GETDIG   ; GET DIGIT (MOST SIGNIFICANT)
       RAL
       RAL
       RAL
       RAL
       MOV   B,A      ; SAVE UPPER NIBBLE
       CALL  GETDIG   ; GET DIGIT (LEAST SIGNIFICANT)
       ADD   B
       LXI   H,ADEND1 ; H-L ---> ADEND1
       MOV   M,A
```

18. Now complete your routine so that it gets and stores all of ADEND1 (ten digits = five bytes) and ADEND2 (also five bytes). For the user's benefit, start a new line on the display screen after each ten-digit number. You'll want to use a "nested loop." Have an inner loop that is executed five times for one ten-digit number. Have an outer loop that executes the inner loop twice for the two numbers.

— — — — — — — — — — — — —

Our complete routine looks like this:

```
GETADS EQU  $
       LXI  H,ADEND1
       MVI  D,2
ONEAD  EQU  $
       MVI  C,5
GETNUM EQU  $
       CALL GETDIG
       RAL
       RAL
       RAL
       RAL
       MOV  B,A
       CALL GETDIG
       ADD  B
       MOV  M,A
       INX  H
       DCR  C
       JNZ  GETNUM
       CALL NEWLIN
       DCR  D
       JNZ  ONEAD
       ...
ADEND1 DS   5
ADEND2 DS   5
```

(inner loop: GETNUM … JNZ GETNUM; outer loop: ONEAD … JNZ ONEAD)

19. You've seen how to get the BCD addends and how to add them. Now we need to convert the result (in ADEND2) back into ASCII. Code a routine that will:

(1) Get one byte from ADEND2.

(2) Split the two nibbles.

(3) Convert to ASCII.

(4) Write both digits.

(5) Repeat steps (1) through (4) until the entire sum is written out.

— — — — — — — — — — — — —

```
WRITIT EQU  $
       LXI  H,ADEND2
       MVI  C,5          ; COUNT 5 LOOPS
CONVRT EQU  $
       MOV  A,M
       ANI  11110000B    ; USE UPPER NIBBLE
       RAR
       RAR
       RAR
       RAR
       ORI  00110000B    ; CONVERT TO ASCII
       MOV  B,A
       CALL OUTPUT
       MOV  A,M
       ANI  00001111B    ; USE LOWER NIBBLE
       ORI  00110000B    ; CONVERT TO ASCII
       MOV  B,A
       CALL OUTPUT
       INX  H
       DCR  C
       JNZ  CONVRT
```

Figure 11.1 shows our entire program to read and add two ten-digit numbers. This program has certain awkward points. The user must type all ten digits, including leading zeros. Also, we haven't taken any steps to prevent overflow of the sum. The error message routine dumps the message in the middle of the user's number. To clean up these difficulties would require a lot of code that is not the subject of this chapter. But you would want to do so before actually using this program.

Subtraction routines may or may not be handled by the above techniques. With the 8080/8085 chips manufactured by Intel, the DAA instruction does not make a proper adjustment after subtraction. But with some 8080/8085 chips (NEC for example), it does.

```
        ORG  100H
GETADS  EQU  $
        LXI  H,ADEND1
        MVI  D,2
ONEAD   EQU  $
        MVI  C,5
GETNUM  EQU  $
        CALL GETDIG
        RAL
        RAL
        RAL
```

FIGURE 11.1. Multibyte Addition

(cont'd next page)

Figure 11.1 continued

```
        RAL
        MOV  B,A
        CALL GETDIG
        ADD B
        MOV  M,A
        INX  H
        DCR  C
        JNZ  GETNUM
        CALL NEWLIN
        DCR  D
        JNZ  ONEAD
ADDER   EQU  $
        LXI  H,ADEND2+4   ;H-L ---> ADEND2
        XCHG              ;D-E ---> ADEND2
        LXI  H,ADEND1+4   ;H-L ---> ADEND1
        MVI  C,5          ;C WILL COUNT 5 LOOPS
        ADI  0            ;TURN OFF CARRY
ADDBYT  EQU  $
        MOV  A,M          ;ADEND1 INTO A
        XCHG              ;H-L ---> ADEND2
        ADC  M            ;ADEND1 + ADEND2 + CARRY
        DAA
        MOV  M,A          ;SUM TO ADEND2
        DCX  H            ;DECREMENT ---> ADEND2
        XCHG
        DCX  H            ;DECREMENT ---> ADEND1
        DCR  C
        JNZ  ADDBYT
WRITIT  EQU  $
        LXI  H,ADEND2
        MVI  C,5          ;COUNT 5 LOOPS
CONVRT  EQU  $
        MOV  A,M
        ANI  11110000B    ;USE UPPER NIBBLE
        RAR
        RAR
        RAR
        RAR
        ORI  00110000B    ;CONVERT TO ASCII
        MOV  B,A
        CALL OUTPUT
        MOV  A,M
        ANI  00001111B    ;USE LOWER NIBBLE
        ORI  00110000B    ;CONVERT TO ASCII
```

(cont'd next page)

Figure 11.1 continued

```
        MOV  B,A
        CALL OUTPUT
        INX  H
        DCR  C
        JNZ  CONVRT
        JMP  0
INPUT   PUSH A
STATUS  CALL TEST
        JZ   STATUS
        IN   1CH
        ANI  7FH
        MOV  B,A
        POP  A
        RET
OUTPUT  PUSH A
STATOT  MVI  A,10H
        OUT  1DH
        IN   1DH
        ANI  00001100B
        CPI  00001100B
        JNZ  STATOT
         MOV  A,B
        OUT  1CH
        POP  A
        RET
TEST    XRA  A
        OUT  1DH
        IN   1DH
        ANI  1
        RET
GETDIG  EQU  $
        PUSH B
        PUSH H
TRYONE  EQU  $
        CALL INPUT
        CALL OUTPUT
        MOV  A,B
        CPI  '0'              ;RANGE CHECK
        JC   ERROR
        CPI  ':'
        JNC  ERROR
        ANI  00001111B
        POP  H
```

(cont'd next page)

Figure 11.1 continued

```
               POP   B
               RET
       ERROR   EQU   $
               MVI   C,26
               LXI   H,ERRMSG
       MSGOUT  EQU   $
               MOV   B,M
               CALL  OUTPUT
               INX   H
               DCR   C
               JNZ   MSGOUT
               JMP   TRYONE
       NEWLIN  EQU   $
               PUSH  B
               MVI   B,0DH
               CALL  OUTPUT
               MVI   B,0AH
               CALL  OUTPUT
               POP   B
               RET
       ADEND1  DS    5
       ADEND2  DS    5
       ERRMSG  DB    'INVALID DIGIT -- TRY AGAIN'
               END
```

MULTIPLICATION

Multiplication is really a process of repeated addition. In the frames that follow, we'll show you how to multiply numbers in Assembler. First you'll see how to do it in pure binary. Then we'll show you how to do it in BCD.

20. There are no multiply instructions. You have to multiply by successive additions.

Suppose you want to multiply the accumulator by two. Write an instruction that will do it. ______________________________

— — — — — — — — — — — — — —

ADD A

21. The first addition multiplies by two. The second doubles the first, or multiplies by four. The third doubles the second or multiplies by 8.

Using ADD, write a set of instructions to multiply by 16.

- - - - - - - - - - - - -

```
ADD  A   ;  TIMES 2
ADD  A   ;  TIMES 4
ADD  A   ;  TIMES 8
ADD  A   ;  TIMES 16
```

22. Write a set of instructions to read an ASCII byte, convert it to binary, multiply it by 8, and store it in memory.

- - - - - - - - - - - - -

```
CALL INPUT
CALL OUTPUT
MOV  A,B
ANI  00001111B   ; CONVERT TO BINARY
ADD  A           ; TIMES 2
ADD  A           ; TIMES 4
ADD  A           ; TIMES 8
MOV  M,A
```

23. You can also multiply by rotating left as long as you know that a 1 will not be wrapped around to the LSB.

(a) Could the problem in the preceding frame be solved by rotating left?

____

(b) If so, write the code.

(a) yes (because the four MSBs are 0);

(b)
```
        CALL INPUT
        CALL OUTPUT
        MOV  A,B
        ANI  00001111B
        RLC                 ; TIMES 2
        RLC                 ; TIMES 4
        RLC                 ; TIMES 8
        MOV  M,A
```

(In general, we prefer to use addition to multiply because we don't have to worry about wrap-around.)

24. Multiplying by a power of two is easy. But what about multiplying by a number that's not a power of two? We can accomplish any multiplicand by adding together the various powers of two. For example, to multiply by 5:

- put the original value (X) in register B as well as register A
- multiply the value in A by 2
- multiply again (this gives 4 times X)
- *add* X from register B (4X + X = 5X)

(a) Write a routine to multiply the value in the accumulator by 7.

(b) Write a routine to multiply the value in the accumulator by 10.

(a)
```
    MOV  B,A    ; SAVE X
    ADD  A      ; 2X
    MOV  C,A    ; SAVE 2X
    ADD  A      ; 4X
    ADD  B      ; 4X + X = 5X
    ADD  C      ; 5X + 2X = 7X
```

or
```
MOV  B,A   ; SAVE X
ADD  A     ; 2X
ADD  A,B   ; 2X + X = 3X
ADD  A     ; 6X
ADD  B     ; 6X + X = 7X
```

(b)
```
ADD  A     ; 2X
MOV  B,A   ; SAVE 2X
ADD  A     ; 4X
ADD  A     ; 8X
ADD  B     ; 8X + 2X = 10X
```

25. So far, you've been writing routines that operate on pure binary values. The same techniques also work on BCD values as long as you decimal adjust the accumulator after every operation.

In the preceding frame, you wrote a routine to multiply by 10. Convert that routine to work on a one-byte BCD value.

```
ADD  A    ; 2X
DAA
MOV  B,A  ; SAVE 2X
ADD  A    ; 4X
DAA
ADD  A    ; 8X
DAA
ADD  B    ; 10X
DAA
```

26. Now let's look at how we multiply a multibyte value.

MULTER ---→ | 0000XXXX | YYYYYYYY | ZZZZZZZZ |

Suppose we want to multiply the above three-byte value by six. (Notice that we've given it plenty of leading zeros.) You already know how to multiply it by two. All you have to do is add it to itself. Write a subroutine to do that. (Remember to do the three bytes in a loop. Use pure binary arithmetic.)

```
MULPLY EQU  $
       PUSH H
       PUSH B
       PUSH PSW
       LXI  H,MULTER+2
       MVI  B,3
       ADI  0           ; TURN OFF CARRY
TWOTIM EQU  $
       MOV  A,M
       ADC  A
       MOV  M,A
       DCX  H
       DCR  B
       JNZ  TWOTIM
       POP  PSW
       POP  B
       POP  H
       RET
```

27. Since we're multiplying by six, we need to save the partial product of 2 times MULTER. Code a routine to save this partial product somewhere else in memory.

Programming Note: You can't go from one memory byte to another directly. You'll have to use a register as a go-between.

```
        LXI  H,SAVTWO   ; H-L ---> SAVTWO
        LXI  D,MULTER   ; D-E ---> MULTER
        MVI  B,3        ; COUNT 3 LOOPS
MOVBYT  EQU  $
        LDAX D          ; A = MULTER
        MOV  M,A        ; SAVTWO = A
        INX  H          ; NEXT BYTE
        INX  D
        DCR  B          ; LOOP COUNTER
        JNZ  MOVBYT
        .
        .
SAVTWO  DS   3
```

28. Now let's complete our multibyte multiplication routine. Expand the routine you started in the previous frame so that it:

(1) multiplies by two

(2) saves the product

(3) multiplies by two again

(4) adds the saved product

```
        CALL MULPLY         ; 2X
        LXI  H,SAVTWO       ; H-L ---> SAVTWO
        LXI  D,MULTER       ; D-E ---> MULTER
        MVI  B,3            ; COUNT 3 LOOPS
MOVBYT  EQU  $
        LDAX D              ; A = MULTER
        MOV  M,A            ; SAVTWO = A
        INX  H              ; NEXT BYTE
        INX  D
        DCR  B              ; LOOP COUNTER
        JNZ  MOVBYT
        CALL MULPLY         ; 4X
        LXI  H,MULTER+2
        LXI  D,SAVTWO+2
        ADI  0
        MVI  B,3            ; LOOP COUNTER
SIXER   EQU  $
        LDAX D              ; SAVTWO TO A
        ADC  M              ; SAVTWO + MULTER + CARRY
        MOV  M,A            ; SUM TO MULTER
        DCX  D
        DCX  H
        DCR  B
        JNZ  SIXER
; NOW MULTER HAS BEEN MULTIPLIED BY SIX
```

29. How could you adapt the preceding routine to work on BCD values?

____

Insert DAA after every addition instruction.

You've seen how to multiply both binary and BCD values of any length. Let's turn our attention to division.

DIVISION

30. Division is a process of repeated subtraction. Before we start, review these terms.

```
          QUOTIENT
         __________
DIVISOR | DIVIDEND
          XXXXXXXX
          ________
          REMAINDER
```

Use this division problem to answer the questions below.

```
      2
  7 ) 15
      14
       1
```

(a) What is the dividend? ______

(b) What is the remainder? ______

(c) What is the divisor? ______

(d) What is the quotient? ______

— — — — — — — — — — — — —

(a) 15; (b) 1; (c) 7; (d) 2

31. Here's how we divide by two. Assume that the dividend is already in the accumulator, and it's between 2 and 255.

```
        MVI   B,0      ; CLEAR B
SUBIT   EQU   $
        SUI   2        ; SUBTRACT DIVISOR FROM A
        INR   B        ; COUNT THE SUBTRACTION
        CPI   2        ; CAN WE SUBTRACT ANOTHER?
        JNC   SUBIT
```

The quotient will end up in B and the remainder in A. What we do is count the number of times we can subtract the divisor (2) from the dividend.

(a) Code a routine to divide by 6. (Assume the dividend is already in A and is between 6 and 255.)

(b) Code a routine to divide by 10. (Assume the dividend is already in A and is between 10 and 255.)

(a)
```
        MVI  B,0    ; TO HOLD THE QUOTIENT
SUBIT   EQU  $
        SUI  6      ; A WILL HOLD THE REMAINDER
        INR  B
        CPI  6
        JNC  SUBIT
```

(b)
```
        MVI  B,0    ; TO HOLD THE QUOTIENT
SUBIT   EQU  $
        SUI  10     ; A WILL HOLD THE REMAINDER
        INR  B
        CPI  10
        JNC  SUBIT
```

(You could have stored the quotient in any register. A will always be left with the remainder.)

HANDLING NEGATIVE NUMBERS

So far in this book, we've been assuming that all values are positive. But the arithmetic routines should also be able to handle negative numbers. Negative numbers are stored using *twos complement* notation. In this section, we'll teach you how to use twos complement notation.

32. When we want to work with negative numbers, we usually use twos complement notation to represent negative numbers. When we're working with eight-bit numbers, twos complements are two numbers that add up to 100000000B. When we add complementary numbers in the accumulator, the result is zero with the carry flag on. For example, 10000001B and 01111111B are twos complements.

In binary, there's a very simple way to find the twos complement of any number. Complement (reverse the value of) each bit and add 1 to the result. For example:

```
01100011B  (value)
10011100B  (complemented bits)
      +1
10011101B  (twos complement)
```

Find the twos complements of the following numbers.

(a) 00001111B : __________

(b) 01101110B : __________

— — — — — — — — — — — — —

(a) 11110001B; (b) 1001001B

33. The twos complement of a number has a very interesting property: As long as you ignore the carry flag, it acts just like the negative of the original value. Thus, 11111111B acts just like —00000001B. And 00000001B acts just like —11111111B. For example, suppose we want to subtract 1 from 1011. There are two ways to do it:

```
   00001011B                00001011B
 - 00000001B      or      + 11111111B
   00001010B               (1)00001010B

               ignore
               carry
```

Which of the following looks like the easier way to handle negative numbers?

______ (a) Convert all negative numbers to twos complement notation as soon as they're entered. Then let all additions and subtractions proceed as if only positive numbers were in use, except ignore the carry flag.

______ (b) Store all numbers with either plus or minus signs. For each arithmetic operation, examine the signs of both operands and decide whether addition or subtraction is more appropriate. When subtracting two numbers, be sure to subtract the smaller from the larger absolute value.

— — — — — — — — — — — — —

(a) is much easier (and more efficient in terms of computer time and space)

34. In 8080/8085 Assembly Language, it's fairly easy to get the twos complement of a number. The CMA instruction complements each bit in the accumulator. Then you just add one.

The CMA instruction has no operands and does not affect the flags.

Code a set of instructions to find the twos complement of the value currently in the accumulator.

____

____

— — — — — — — — — — — — —

```
CMA
ADI  1
```

35. When we're using a twos complement system, we let the most significant bit act as the sign indicator. If it's on, the value is negative. If it's off, the value is positive. This means that we have to limit positive values to 01111111B per byte.

To convert to decimal, you examine the sign bit. If it's off, the number is positive. Just convert it directly. If it's on, find the twos complement of the number and put a minus sign in front of it.

In decimal, what are the equivalents of the following binary values?

(a) 00000000B = ____________

(b) 01111111B = ____________

(c) 10000000B = ____________

(d) 11111111B = ____________

— — — — — — — — — — — — —

(a) 0; (b) 127; (c) —128; (d) —1

36. In a twos complement system, what is the maximum positive value per byte? ____________

What is the most negative value that will fit in a byte? ____________

— — — — — — — — — — — — —

127; —128

37. Which flag will tell you whether the number you're working with is positive or negative when you're using twos complement notation?

____

— — — — — — — — — — — — —

the sign flag (remember the sign flag is set to match the MSB in the accumulator)

38. Now we'll start building a program that reads two single digits, adds them, and reports the sum. Either digit may be negative.

Let's start by coding a subroutine that gets one digit.

Read one byte. If it's '—', read another byte (a digit) and find the twos complement of that value. In either case, convert the value to binary and leave it in A. (Use separate paper, as you'll add to this routine in later frames.)

— — — — — — — — — — — — —

```
GETBYT  EQU   $
        PUSH  B
        CALL  INPUT
        CALL  OUTPUT
        MOV   A,B
        CPI   '-'
        JZ    NEGIVE
        ANI   00001111B
        JMP   ENDING
NEGIVE  EQU   $
        CALL  INPUT
        CALL  OUTPUT
        MOV   A,B
        ANI   00001111B
        CMA
        ADI   1
ENDING  EQU   $
        POP   B
        RET
```

39. Now code a routine that gets two bytes. Store the first byte in C. Leave the second byte in A. Add the two bytes and leave the sum in A. Call the subroutine you coded in the previous frame to get each byte.

— — — — — — — — — — — — —

```
ADDER   EQU   $
        CALL  GETBYT
        MOV   C,A
        CALL  GETBYT
        ADD   C
```

40. Now it's time to report the result. Assume the instruction JP SUMPOS follows the routine you just wrote. If the result is positive and under ten, we want to convert it to ASCII and write it out.

Code a routine (SUMPOS) to check the size of the result. If it's under ten, convert the value in A into ASCII and write it out. If the value is ten or more, branch to a routine named TWODIG (don't code TWODIG yet.)

— — — — — — — — — — — — —

```
SUMPOS  EQU   $
        CPI   10
        JNC   TWODIG
        ORI   00110000B
        MOV   B,A
        CALL  OUTPUT
```

41. Now code the TWODIG routine. If the sum is positive and larger than nine, you must convert it to two decimal digits. Since you haven't been using BCD arithmetic, here's what you have to do.

(1) Divide the value in A by ten.

(2) The quotient is the most significant digit. Convert it to ASCII and write it out.

(3) The remainder is the least significant digit. Convert it to ASCII and write it out.

```
TWODIG EQU  $
       MVI  C,0          ; C WILL HOLD QUOTIENT
DIVIDE EQU  $
       SUI  10
       INR  C
       CPI  10           ; ARE THERE ANY 10'S LEFT?
       JNC  DIVIDE
       MOV  D,A          ; TEMP HOLD REMAINDER
       MOV  A,C          ; A = QUOTIENT
       ORI  00110000B
       MOV  B,A
       CALL OUTPUT
       MOV  A,D
       ORI  00110000B
       MOV  B,A
       CALL OUTPUT
```

42. Now let's deal with a negative result. All you have to do is write a '—', find the twos complement of the value in the accumulator, then follow the same routine as SUMPOS. Write the code and fit it between JP SUMPOS and the SUMPOS routine in the program.

```
        JP   SUMPOS
        MVI  B,'-'
        CALL OUTPUT
        CMA
        ADI  1
 SUMPOS EQU  $
        etc.
```

(Our entire program is shown in Figure 11.2.)

```
        ORG   100H
ADDER   EQU   $
        CALL  GETBYT
        MOV   C,A
        CALL  GETBYT
        ADD   C
        JP    SUMPOS
        MVI   B,'-'
        CALL  OUTPUT
        CMA
        ADI   1
SUMPOS  EQU   $
        CPI   10
        JNC   TWODIG
        ORI   00110000B
        MOV   B,A
        CALL  OUTPUT
        JMP   0
TWODIG  EQU   $
        MVI   C,0          ;C WILL HOLD QUOTIENT
DIVIDE  EQU   $
        SUI   10
        INR   C
        CPI   10           ;ARE THERE ANY 10'S LEFT?
        JNC   DIVIDE
        MOV   D,A          ;TEMP HOLD REMAINDER
        MOV   A,C
        ORI   00110000B
        MOV   B,A
        CALL  OUTPUT
        MOV   A,D
        ORI   00110000B
        MOV   B,A
        CALL  OUTPUT
        JMP   0
GETBYT  EQU   $
        PUSH   B
        CALL  INPUT
        CALL  OUTPUT
        MOV   A,B
        CPI   '-'
        JZ    NEGIVE
        ANI   00001111B
        JMP   ENDING
NEGIVE  EQU   $
        CALL  INPUT
        CALL  OUTPUT
```

FIGURE 11.2. Adding Positive and Negative Digits *(cont'd next page)*

```
        MOV  A,B
        ANI  00001111B
        CMA
        ADI  1
ENDING  EQU  $
        POP  B
        RET
INPUT   PUSH A
STATUS  CALL TEST
        JZ   STATUS
        IN   1CH
        ANI  7FH
        MOV  B,A
        POP  A
        RET
OUTPUT  PUSH A
STATOT  MVI  A,10H
        OUT  1DH
        IN   1DH
        ANI  00001100B
        CPI  00001100B
        JNZ  STATOT
        MOV  A,B
        OUT  1CH
        POP  A
        RET
TEST    XRA  A
        OUT  1DH
        IN   1DH
        ANI  1
        RET
        END
```

REVIEW

In this chapter, we have introduced the subject of numeric manipulation.

- Multibyte addition is usually done in binary coded decimal (BCD) notation because it's easier to work with. In BCD, each nibble (half-byte) represents a decimal digit from 0 to 9. To convert ASCII input to BCD, the first digit is converted to binary then rotated to the upper nibble. The second digit is converted to binary then added to the lower nibble.

- To account for carries from one byte to the next, perform addition with one of these instructions:

  [*label*] ADC *r1* [;*comments*]
  [*label*] ACI *i* [;*comments*]

If using BCD notation, follow each addition instruction immediately with a DAA instruction, which adjusts the sum into BCD format.

- To convert from BCD to ASCII, you'll need two copies of the same byte. For the upper nibble (the first digit), eliminate the lower nibble, rotate the upper nibble into the lower nibble, and convert to ASCII. For the lower nibble, eliminate the upper nibble and convert to ASCII.
- We use BCD because the conversion procedures between ASCII and pure binary are so complex.
- Multiplication is a process of repeated addition — a value is added to itself. Each addition multiplies the value by a power of two. To multiply by a factor that is not a power of two, save the needed partial products, such as 1X and 2X, and add them in.
- On most 8080/8085 chips the DAA instruction does not cover subtraction. You'll have to use pure binary numbers or twos complement notation for subtraction unless you have a chip that DAA works on. For multibyte subtraction, use these instructions:

  [*label*] SBB *r1* [;*comments*]
  [*label*] SBI *i* [;*comments*]

- Division is done by repeated subtraction. The divisor is subtracted from the dividend until the remainder of the dividend is smaller than the divisor. Each subtraction is tallied in another register. The tally becomes the quotient and the amount left over in the accumulator is the remainder.
- Negative values are usually handled by twos complement notation. To convert a binary value in the accumulator to twos complement notation, use the CMA instruction, which complements all the digits; then add 1 to the result. When working with twos complement notation, limit all positive values to seven bits (127D). Negative values range from 11111111B (—1D) to 10000000B (—128D). There is no —0.

You have only begun to solve the problems of numeric manipulation. We'll have to leave the rest up to you. Here are some areas you may want to explore: multibyte division, multiplication and division of negative numbers, fractional quantities, and finding roots. There are no additional 8080/8085 instructions that you'll need. It's simply a matter of how you combine the ones you already know.

CHAPTER 11 SELF-TEST

Part I. Code the instructions described below.

1. Add register B to the accumulator, with carry. ____________

2. Subtract 5 from the accumulator, with borrow. ____________

3. Subtract register E from the accumulator, with borrow. ____________

4. Add 1 to the accumulator, with carry. ____________

5. Complement all the bits in the accumulator. ____________

6. Convert the binary value in the accumulator to BCD. ____________

Part II. Code routines to accomplish the following functions.

1. Registers A and B contain two ASCII digits. Convert them to one BCD byte and leave it in A. The most significant digit is in B and the least significant digit is in A. They have been validated to be between '0' and '9'.

2. Register A contains a positive BCD value. Convert it to ASCII and write it out.

3. These two fields have been defined and are currently holding BCD values. Add them, leaving the sum in X.

X	0X	XX	XX		Y	0Y	YY	YY

4. Multiply X (from question 3 above) by 9.

5. Register A is holding a positive, pure binary value between 20 and 255. Divide it by 20. Leave the quotient in B and the remainder in A.

6. Register A is holding an ASCII value between 0 and 127. Convert it to twos complement notation.

7. Register A is holding a negative value between —1 and —9 in twos complement notation. Convert it to ASCII.

Self-Test Answer Key

Part I.

1. `ADC B`
2. `SBI 5`
3. `SBB E`
4. `ACI 1`
5. `CMA`
6. `DAA`

PART II.

1.
```
ANI   00001111B   ; CONVERT TO BINARY
MOV   C,A         ; SAVE LSB IN C
MOV   A,B
ANI   00001111B
RAL
RAL
RAL
RAL
ADD   C
```

2.
```
MOV   C,A         ; SAVE A COPY OF VALUE
ANI   11110000B   ; MASK OUT LOWER NIBBLE
RAR
RAR
RAR
RAR
ORI   00110000B   ; CONVERT TO ASCII
MOV   B,A
CALL  OUTPUT      ; WRITE FIRST DIGIT
MOV   A,C         ; GET COPY
ANI   00001111B   ; MASK OUT UPPER NIBBLE
ORI   00110000B   ; CONVERT TO ASCII
MOV   B,A
CALL  OUTPUT
```

3.
```
        MVI   B,3      ; LOOP COUNTER
        LXI   H,X+2    ; POINT H AT X
        LXI   D,Y+2    ; POINT D AT Y
        ADI
LOOP    EQU   $
        MOV   A,M
        XCHG           ; SWITCH H AND D
        ADC   M        ; ADD BYTES
        DAA            ; VERY IMPORTANT
        XCHG
        MOV   M,A
        DCX   H
        DCX   D
        DCR   B
        JNZ   LOOP
```

4.
```
; FIRST WE HAVE TO SAVE A COPY OF X.  WE'LL
; SAVE IT AT Z.
        LXI  H,X
        LXI  D,Z
        MVI  B,3     ; LOOP COUNTER
LOOP    EQU  $
        MOV  A,M     ; GET BYTE FROM X
        XCHG
        MOV  M,A     ; STORE IT IN Z
        XCHG
        INX  H
        INX  D
        DCR  B
        JNZ  LOOP
; NOW WE CAN MULTIPLY X BY 8.
        MVI  C,3     ; COUNT NUMBER OF MULTIPLIES
MUL1    EQU  $
        LXI  H,X+2
        MVI  B,3     ; COUNT BYTES
        ADI  0       ; TURN OFF CARRY FLAG
ONEBYT EQU  $
        MOV  A,M     ; GET BYTE
        ADC  A       ; DOUBLE IT
        DAA          ; ADJUST IT
        MOV  M,A     ; STORE IT
        DCX  H       ; POINT TO PRECEDING BYTE
        DCR  B       ; COUNT ONE BYTE
        JNZ  ONEBYT
; WHEN CONTROL REACHES HERE, X HAS BEEN DOUBLED
        DCR  C       ;
        JNZ  MUL1
; X HAS BEEN DOUBLED 3 TIMES
        LXI  H,X+2
        LXI  D,Z+2
        MVI  C,3
        ADI
ADDIT   EQU  $
        MOV  A,M
        XCHG
        ADC  M
        XCHG
        DCX  H
        MOV  M,A
        DCX  D
        DCR  C
        JNZ  ADDIT
```

5.
```
        MVI  B,0
DIVIDE  EQU  $
        SUI  20
        INR  B
        CPI  20
        JNC  DIVIDE
```

6.
```
ANI  00001111B
CMA
ADI  1
```

7.
```
CMA
ADI  1
ORI  00110000B
```

CHAPTER TWELVE

ADDITIONAL INSTRUCTIONS

You have learned to code the most heavily used Assembly Language instructions. In this final chapter, we'll briefly introduce some instructions that are less frequently used. Some day you might be trying to solve a problem that requires one of these instructions and you'll remember that it's available. These instructions are presented out of the context of programs because the programs that use most of them would be quite complex. You'll just learn what the instructions are and how they function.

When you have finished this chapter, you will be able to code the following instructions.

- NOP (no operation)
- EI (enable interrupts)
- DI (disable interrupts)
- RIM (read interrupt mask)
- SIM (send interrupt mask)
- RST (restart)
- PCHL (H–L to PC)

THE *NOP* INSTRUCTION

1. NOP (no operation) does absolutely nothing active. It takes up one byte of memory space and uses up a little bit of time.

With very primitive systems, NOPs were important. The programmer inserted several NOPs between all the instructions to leave room for insertions later. This isn't necessary for systems with an editor and a terminal because it's fairly east to insert instructions.

What instruction causes nothing active to happen? ______________

– – – – – – – – – – – – –

NOP

2. Many microcomputers can receive a signal from the outside to interrupt it and get the processor's attention. Such a signal is called an *interrupt* request because it asks the microcomputer to interrupt whatever it is doing and service some more urgent need. The computer receives the interrupt request, finishes the instruction it is processing, then acknowledges the request, and services it by running a special program. It then continues the interrupted program where it left off. The interrupt system is dependent on the hardware. On some systems, I/O operations are handled this way. The instructions you'll read about below are all concerned with programming that uses interrupt I/O.

An interrupt occurs when one program is interrupted, an interrupt service program is executed, then the first is picked up where it left off.

You can only interrupt if you have an external device capable of sending an "interrupt request." If your system has a monitoring device attached, for example, its input might be processed on an interrupt basis rather than a normal read basis. The external monitor would send an interrupt request when it senses a situation that needs immediate processing.

(a) Which of the following best describes an interrupt?

_____ Pausing in program A to execute program B, then resuming program A at the same point.

_____ Discontinuing program A to run program B.

_____ Stopping program A to run program B, then restarting program A from the beginning.

(b) How do you cause an interrupt?

_____ By typing any key when the program isn't expecting input.

_____ By hitting the "break" key on any device.

_____ By causing an I/O device to send an interrupt request.

_____ By pulling the plug.

— — — — — — — — — — — —

(a) pausing in program A to execute program B, then resuming program A at the same point; (b) by causing an I/O device to send an interrupt request (the means is device specific)

EI AND *DI* INSTRUCTIONS

3. The 8080/8085 microprocessor will only respond to an interrupt request if interrupts are enabled. You must enable interrupts for each program that you want to be interruptable by using the EI instruction. EI uses only the operation code; it has no operands.

Shown below is the beginning of a routine we used in Chapter 11. Add an instruction to make the routine interruptable.

```
GETADS EQU  $
       LXI  H,ADEND1
       MVI  D,2
ONEAD  EQU  $
       MVI  C,5
GETNUM EQU  $
```

— — — — — — — — — — — — —

```
GETADS EQU  $
       EI
       LXI  H,ADEND1
       .
       .
       .
```

4. You may have certain routines that you don't want to be interrupted. For example, if you've written a timing loop to count off exactly 2.3 microseconds, an interrupt would destroy the timing. If so, you might want to disable interrupts when you enter the loop and enable them again when the loop is over. You disable interrupts with the DI instruction. Like EI, DI has no operands.

(a) What instruction enables interrupts? __________

(b) What instruction disables interrupts? __________

— — — — — — — — — — — — —

(a) EI; (b) DI

5. Interrupt processing itself automatically disables interrupts. That is, when the microprocessor interrupts program A and gives control to program B, it automatically issues a DI instruction. This is to prevent the interrupt service program (program B) from being interrupted.

If you want the interrupt program to be interruptable, you include an EI instruction at the beginning of it. If not, then you code an EI at the end before returning control to the interrupted program. That will make the interrupted program continue to be interruptable.

(a) How does the microprocessor prevent interrupt routines from being interrupted? __________

(b) Why should an interrupt program contain at least one EI instruction?

____

— — — — — — — — — — — — —

(a) by disabling interrupts when it transfers control to the interrupt program; (b) to re-enable interrupts before returning control to the interrupted program

Some terminals and line printers communicate on an interrupt basis rather than the status byte basis you learned in Chapter 10. When they're ready to send or receive a byte of data, they send an interrupt request. This system allows the microprocessor to work on other programs while it's waiting for the I/O device to be ready. If your system doesn't use interrupts, you may want to skip ahead to the PCHL instruction.

THE *RIM* AND *SIM* INSTRUCTIONS

6. In a basic interrupt system, there's only one device that can interrupt and it only interrupts for one reason. There only needs to be one program that services interrupts and it can be permanently stored in a low address portion of memory. Any time there's an interrupt, control is automatically branched to the first instruction of that program.

But many systems are more complex than that. There may be several devices that can send an interrupt request and one device may interrupt for more than one reason. In such systems, there needs to be some mechanisms for communicating to the microprocessor which type of interrupt is being requested. There must also be some way of handling simultaneous interrupts of more than one type.

One means of dealing with a complex interrupt system is by interrupt masks, similar to those for logical instructions. An input mask can be used to indicate the type and priority of an interrupt being requested. It can also be used to find out which interrupts are currently enabled. An output mask can be used to enable or disable individual interrupt programs as well as enabling or disabling the entire facility.

The RIM instruction receives an interrupt mask from an external device and stores it in the accumulator. The SIM instruction sends an interrupt mask to the device from the accumulator. These instructions are not available for the 8080, just the 8085.

(a) What is the function of an input interrupt mask? (Choose one.)

_____ To pass data from the interrupted program to the interrupt program.

_____ To pass data from the I/O device to the interrupt program.

_____ To indicate the type or types of interrupts being requested.

(b) What instruction reads an interrupt mask? __________

(c) What is the function of an output interrupt mask? (Choose one.)

_____ To transmit data to the output device to be printed or displayed.

_____ To enable/disable individual interrupt programs.

_____ To request specific interrupt information from the interrupting device(s).

(d) What instruction writes an output interrupt mask? _____

(e) With what microprocessor are RIM and SIM available: 8080, 8085, or both? _____

— — — — — — — — — — — — —

(a) To indicate the type or types of interrupts being requested;
(b) RIM; (c) To enable/disable individual interrupt programs;
(d) SIM; (e) 8085

THE *RST* INSTRUCTION

7. The RST (restart) instruction is a special type of calling instruction. It functions just like a CALL but it can only call certain areas of memory.

RST 0 calls a program starting at 0000H.

RST 1 calls a program starting at 0008H.

RST 2 calls a program starting at 0010H.

RST 3 calls a program starting at 0018H.

RST 4 calls a program starting at 0020H.

RST 5 calls a program starting at 0028H.

RST 6 calls a program starting at 0030H.

RST 7 calls a program starting at 0038H.

These instructions are used in interrupt processing. They may appear in an Assembly Language program or be transmitted by the interrupting device. RST is used to call one of the interrupt servicing programs; they are permanently stored in memory at the addresses indicated above.

Most interrupt service programs are longer than the few bytes allocated. All that is stored at the permanent address is a JMP instruction to the real service program.

(a) Code an instruction to call the program at address 0000H. _____

(b) How is RST intended to be used?

_____ To process multiple interrupts.

_____ As an alternative to CALL in normal application programs.

_____ To power up the system in the morning.

— — — — — — — — — — — — —

(a) RST 0; (b) to process multiple interrupts.

The previous frames have just brushed on the area of interrupt processing so you'll know it exists. How, where, and when you use the interrupt instructions to build a coordinated interrupt system are topics beyond the scope of this book.

THE *PCHL* INSTRUCTION

8. The final instruction we'll present in this book is PCHL. The PCHL (H–L to PC) instruction moves the value in the H–L pair into the PC register. The effect is to jump to whatever address is in H–L.

PCHL can always be replaced by a JMP instruction. PCHL does allow you to manipulate the address in H–L through INX, DCX, and DAD before you jump to it. But such sophistications are usually the result of overly complex program logic. There is always a simpler way to accomplish the same function.

PCHL is dangerous because of the possibility of transferring control to some part of memory not belonging to this program's sequence of instructions. You may thus invalidate data this program was working on or damage portions of your operating system, and so forth.

(a) What instruction will cause a jump to the address contained in the H–L pair? ________________

(b) What instruction is always preferable to the above instruction?

____

— — — — — — — — — — — — —

(a) PCHL; (b) JMP

REVIEW

In this chapter, we have briefly introduced some instructions that are useful in some situations.

- NOP causes nothing to happen.
- Several instructions are designed for use in interrupt processing:
  - EI enables interrupts.
  - DI disables interrupts.
  - RIM reads an interrupt mask to determine what type of interrupt is being requested (8085 only).
  - SIM sends an interrupt mask to enable/disable various interrupt programs (8085 only).
  - RST *n* causes a call to a permanently specified memory

address which contains the first instruction of the interrupt processing program.

— PCHL moves the value in H–L to the PC register, causing a jump to an address of that value. It is considered a dangerous and unnecessary instruction.

You have now learned, or at least been introduced to, all the 8080/8085 Assembly Language instructions. After you complete the following Self-Test, you'll be done with this book. You'll be able to use the documentation for your system as you modify or create Assembly Language programs.

CHAPTER 12 SELF-TEST

1. Code an instruction to receive an interrupt mask. ________________

2. Code an instruction to call the interrupt service program at location 0008. ________________

3. Code an instruction to do nothing. ________________

4. Code an instruction to send a mask to enable some interrupt processing but disable others. ________________

5. Code an instruction to disable all interrupt processing. ________________

6. Code an instruction to enable all interrupt processing. ________________

7. Code an instruction to jump to FINAL, which is the address in H–L.

____

Self-Test Answer Key

1. `RIM`

2. `RST 1`

3. `NOP`

4. `SIM`

5. `DI`

6. `EI`

7. `PCHL` or `JMP FINAL`

APPENDIX A

HEXADECIMAL ADDITION-SUBTRACTION TABLE

0	1	2	3	4	5	6	7	8	9	A	B	C	D	E	F
0	1	2	3	4	5	6	7	8	9	A	B	C	D	E	F
1	2	3	4	5	6	7	8	9	A	B	C	D	E	F	10
2	3	4	5	6	7	8	9	A	B	C	D	E	F	10	11
3	4	5	6	7	8	9	A	B	C	D	E	F	10	11	12
4	5	6	7	8	9	A	B	C	D	E	F	10	11	12	13
5	6	7	8	9	A	B	C	D	E	F	10	11	12	13	14
6	7	8	9	A	B	C	D	E	F	10	11	12	13	14	15
7	8	9	A	B	C	D	E	F	10	11	12	13	14	15	16
8	9	A	B	C	D	E	F	10	11	12	13	14	15	16	17
9	A	B	C	D	E	F	10	11	12	13	14	15	16	17	18
A	B	C	D	E	F	10	11	12	13	14	15	16	17	18	19
B	C	D	E	F	10	11	12	13	14	15	16	17	18	19	1A
C	D	E	F	10	11	12	13	14	15	16	17	18	19	1A	1B
D	E	F	10	11	12	13	14	15	16	17	18	19	1A	1B	1C
E	F	10	11	12	13	14	15	16	17	18	19	1A	1B	1C	1D
F	10	11	12	13	14	15	16	17	18	19	1A	1B	1C	1D	1E

APPENDIX B

ASCII CODE

second hex digit	first hex digit (8-F not used): 0	1	2	3	4	5	6	7
0	NUL	DLE	space	0	@	P		p
1	SOH	DC1	!	1	A	Q	a	q
2	STX	DC2	"	2	B	R	b	r
3	ETX	DC3	#	3	C	S	c	s
4	EOT	DC4	$	4	D	T	d	t
5	ENQ	NAK	%	5	E	U	e	u
6	ACK	SYN	&	6	F	V	f	v
7	BEL	ETB	'	7	G	W	g	w
8	BS	CAN	(	8	H	X	h	x
9	HT	EM	)	9	I	Y	i	y
A	LF	SUB	*	:	J	Z	j	z
B	VT	ESC	+	;	K	[	k	{
C	FF	FS	,	<	L	\	l	|
D	CR	GS	-	=	M	]	m	}
E	SO	RS	.	>	N	^	n	~
F	SI	US	/	?	O	_	o	DEL

EXPLANATION OF CONTROL CHARACTERS

NUL—null character; eight zero bits

The following are used in data communications (transmitting data via phone lines):

SOH — start of heading
STX — start of text
ETX — end of text
EOT — end of transmission
ENQ — enquire ("Are you there?")

ACK — acknowledge ("Yes")
DLE — data link escape
NAK — negative acknowledgement ("No")
SYN — synchronous idle
ETB — end of transmission

BEL — bell; rings the terminal alarm
BS — backspace
HT — horizontal tab; tab across to next tab stop
LF — line feed; move down one line
VT — vertical tab; tab down to next vertical tab stop
FF — form feed; go to top of next page
CR — carriage return; go to beginning of line
SO — shift out; shift out of ASCII code
SI — shift in; shift back into ASCII code
DC1
DC2 — device controls 1 to 4; the meaning of these
DC3 — four codes depends on the terminal equipment
DC4
CAN — cancel
EM — end of medium
SUB — substitute
ESC — escape; used like a shift key to extend ASCII code
FS — file separator
GS — group separator
RS — record separator
US — unit separator
DEL — delete

APPENDIX C

INSTRUCTION REFERENCE

GENERAL INSTRUCTION FORMAT:

[*label*] *operation* [*operands*] [;*comments*]

COMMON ASSEMBLER DIRECTIVES

instruction	*explanation*	*comments*
label EQU *value*	assign value to label	$ = "this address"
DB *value* [,*value*...]	puts value in memory	ASCII strings in quotes
DS *n*	reserve *n* bytes in memory	
ORG *addr*	store the next instruction at *addr*	
END	end of program; stop assembling	

THE ARITHMETIC INSTRUCTIONS

instruction	*explanation*	*flags* *C*	*A*	*Z*	*S*	*P*	*comments*
ACI *i*	add with carry immediate data to A	X	X	X	X	X	result in A
ADC *r*	add with carry *r* to A	X	X	X	X	X	result in A
ADD *r*	add *r* to A	X	X	X	X	X	result in A
ADI *i*	add immediate data to A	X	X	X	X	X	result in A
CMP *r*	compare *r* to A	X	X	X	X	X	"subtract" *r* from A
CPI *i*	compare *i* to A	X	X	X	X	X	"subtract" *i* from A
DAA	decimal adjust the accumulator	X	X	X	X	X	for BCD addition
DAD *rp*	double precision add *rp* to H–L	X					
DCR *r*	decrement register		X	X	X	X	
DCX *rp*	decrement register pair						
INR *r*	increment register		X	X	X	X	
INX *rp*	increment register pair						

THE ARITHMETIC INSTRUCTIONS *(cont'd)*

Instruction	Description	*C*	*A*	*Z*	*S*	*P*	Notes
SBB *r*	subtract with borrow *r* from A	X	X	X	X	X	result in A
SBI *i*	subtract with borrow *i* from A	X	X	X	X	X	result in A
SUB *r*	subtract register from A	X	X	X	X	X	result in A
SUI *i*	subtract immediate data from A	X	X	X	X	X	result in A

THE LOGICAL INSTRUCTIONS

Instruction	Description	*C*	*A*	*Z*	*S*	*P*	Notes
ANA *r*	AND *r* with A	0	0	X	X	X	result in A
ANI *i*	AND immediate byte with A	0	0	X	X	X	result in A
CMA	complement the accumulator						result in A
CMC	complement the carry flag	X					
STC	set the carry flag to one	1					
ORA *r*	OR *r* with A	X	X	X	X	X	result in A
ORI *i*	OR immediate byte with A	X	X	X	X	X	result in A
RAL	rotate accumulator left thru carry	X					
RAR	rotate accumulator right thru carry	X					
RLC	rotate accumulator left without carry	X					
RRC	rotate accumulator right without carry	X					
XRA *r*	EXCLUSIVE OR register with A	X	X	X	X	X	result in A
XRI *i*	EXCLUSIVE OR immediate data with A	X	X	X	X	X	result in A

THE DATA MOVEMENT INSTRUCTIONS

Instruction	Description	*C*	*A*	*Z*	*S*	*P*	Notes
LDA *addr*	load A from memory at *addr*						
LDAX *rp*	load A from memory at address in *rp*						B or D only
LHLD *addr*	load H–L from memory at *addr*						bytes reversed
LXI *rp,i*	load *rp* with immediate data						*i* two bytes
STA *addr*	store A in memory at *addr*						
STAX *rp*	store A in memory at address in *rp*						B or D only
SHLD *addr*	store H–L in memory at *addr*						bytes reversed
MOV *r1,r2*	copy byte from *r2* to *r1*						
MVI *r,i*	move immediate data to *r*						
XCHG	exchange D-E and H–L						

THE BRANCHING INSTRUCTIONS

Instruction	Description	*C*	*A*	*Z*	*S*	*P*	Notes
CALL *addr*	call subroutine at *addr*						return pushed into stack
CC *addr*	call if carry flag is on						
CNC *addr*	call if carry flag is off						
CZ *addr*	call if zero flag is on						
CNZ *addr*	call if zero flag is off						
CM *addr*	call if sign flag is on						

THE BRANCHING INSTRUCTIONS *(cont'd)*

CP *addr*	call if sign flag is off						
CPE *addr*	call if parity is even						
CPO *addr*	call if parity is odd						
JMP *addr*	jump unconditionally to *addr*						
JC *addr*	jump if carry flag is on						
JNC *addr*	jump if carry flag is off						
JM *addr*	jump if sign flag is on						
JP *addr*	jump if sign flag is off						
JZ *addr*	jump if zero flag is on						
JNZ *addr*	jump if zero flag is off						
JPE *addr*	jump if parity is even						
JPO *addr*	jump if parity is odd						
RET	return unconditionally						return address popped
RC	return if carry flag is on						
RNC	return if carry flag is off						
RM	return if sign flag is on						
RP	return if sign flag is off						
RZ	return if zero flag is on						
RNZ	return if zero flag is off						
RPE	return if parity is even						
RPO	return if parity is odd						
PCHL	jump to address is H–L						

THE STACK INSTRUCTIONS

PUSH *rp*	place data from *rp* at top of stack						SP–2
POP *rp*	place data from top of stack in *rp*						SP+2
SPHL	copy address from H–L to SP						
XTHL	exchange top of stack and H–L						SP not changed

THE INTERRUPT INSTRUCTIONS

DI	disable interrupts						
EI	enable interrupts						
RIM	read interrupt mask into A						
SIM	send interrupt mask from A						
RST *n*	call subroutine at address 8 x *n*						

MISCELLANEOUS INSTRUCTIONS

IN *port*	read data from *port*						
OUT *port*	write data to *port*						
NOP	no operation						
HLT	halt						

APPENDIX D

TYPING, ASSEMBLING, AND TESTING PROGRAMS

This appendix will give you some idea of how you can type, assemble, and test programs if your operating system is CP/M®. We can't tell you exactly how to do this for your system because each assembler is different. You'll have to check the manual for your system for details. You can learn the details of CP/M® programs from *Using CP/M®*, another Wiley Self-Teaching Guide.

TYPING PROGRAMS

Your assembler should either include or be accompanied by some type of editor. The editor usually allows you to name a file, enter text into it, save the file on a storage device (tape or disk), and make revisions to the file. You use the editor at your terminal.

With CP/M, the editor is called ED. Following is a printout of an editing session with ED in which we create a file named ECHO. Our input is in lower case and CP/M's output is in upper case.

```
A>ed echo.asm

NEW FILE
*vi
     1:             call input
     2:             call output
     3:             jmp  0
     4:   input     equ  $
     5:             push psw
     6:   status    equ  $
     7:             call test
     8:             jz   status
     9:             in   1ch
    10:             ani  7fh
    11:             mov  b,a
```

```
                pop   psw
                ret
        output  equ   $
                push  psw
        statot  equ   $
                mvi   a,10h
                out   1dh
                in    1dh
                ani   00001100b
                cpi   00001100b
                jnz   statot
                mov   a,b
                out   1ch
                pop   psw
                ret
        test    equ   $
                xra   a
                out   1dh
                in    1dh
                ani   1
                ret
                end
  1: *q

Q-(Y/N)?y
```

ASSEMBLING PROGRAMS

You assemble a program by running the assembler program with your Assembly Language code as the source file. The assembler program translates the code into machine language and produces an object program. It usually stores the object program on a storage device.

Other output from your assembler may include a listing of error messages and a listing of the object program such as the one you saw in Figures 5.1 and 5.2.

Any error messages must be dealt with before going on with the process. You'll have to figure out what mistake caused the error, go back and correct the source code, then rerun the assembler. This process is repeated until the program assembles with no errors.

In CP/M, we run the assembler by issuing the command ASM followed by the file name of the program we want to assemble, as in ASM ECHO. Error messages are displayed on our terminal, but the listing file is stored on disk. We can display it or print it if we want to, or erase it if we don't need it.

LOADING PROGRAMS

If your system also requires a linkage loader, you must run the loader program using the object program produced by the assembler as the input file.

For CP/M, we run the loader by issuing the command LOAD followed by the file name, as in LOAD ECHO. The loader turns our program into a .COM file, ready to be executed, and stores it on disk. Any error messages are displayed on the terminal.

TESTING THE PROGRAM

After your program has been assembled and loaded, it is ready to run. You test the program by executing it. If input data is required, you use data with known results, so you can make sure the output is correct. You also test the full range of possible input values to make sure the program handles them correctly.

Of course, as program errors are identified, you must go back and correct the source program using the editor; then reassemble, reload, and retest.

CP/M has a special program called DDT, the Dynamic Debugging Tool. DDT allows us to test programs interactively and make temporary changes to them as we go. For example, we can tell DDT to execute the next five instructions then stop and display the contents of all the registers. If you have an interactive debugging program such as DDT, you use it to track down program errors that you can't figure out from just looking at the output.

INDEX

Bold numbers indicate pages where topic is introduced or explained.

NOTES